FORTUNE FAVORS THE BOLD

A British LRRP with the 101st

James W. Walker

D031138C

IVY BOOKS • NEW YORK

An Ivy Book
Published by The Ballantine Publishing Group
Copyright © 1998 by James William Walker

All rights reserved under International and Pan-American Copyright Conventions. Published in the United States by The Ballantine Publishing Group, a division of Random House, Inc., New York, and simultaneously in Canada by Random House of Canada Limited, Toronto.

http://www.randomhouse.com

Library of Congress Catalog Card Number: 97-95365

ISBN 0-8041-1600-8

Manufactured in the United States of America

First Edition: May 1998

10 9 8 7 6 5 4 3 2 1

We finally heard the distinct thumping sound of a Huey drawing near. As the noise grew louder, we prepared to run for the LZ. My heart was already pounding. I was praying that the NVA had gone back into hiding during daylight hours. The chopper made its approach as we began to sprint for the clearing. The aircraft came in fast and settled into the grass. We dove aboard so fast that I couldn't detect a change in the rotor pitch. We were all aboard and screaming for the pilot to go. The peter pilot turned around, smiled, and gave us a thumbs-up. We forgave the young warrant officer's theatrics. He was just playing a role. But I could have kissed his smiling face anyhow.

As we pulled away from the LZ, I looked back to see clouds of smoke rising from where we had been just seconds ago. I looked over at Lieutenant McIsaac with a look of bewilderment on my face. Grinning, he said, "The fucking dinks are a day late and a dollar short with that mortar fire. . . ."

THIS BOOK IS DEDICATED TO:

David Allen Dixon
KIA 5/15/67, Duc Pho, RVN

John Lester Hines
KIA 9/15/67, Chu Lai, RVN

George Buster Sullens Jr.
KIA 11/1/67, Chu Lai, RVN

Ernest Gregory Winston
KIA 6/6/68, A Shau Valley, RVN

Lloyd "Top" Smith
RIP 2/5/95
A Soldier's Soldier

Bryan Douglas Linderer
RIP 1/27/95
My Little Buddy

In moments of peril,
the brave shall heed the call.

ACKNOWLEDGMENTS

To Owen Lock, my publisher, for allowing me to tell my story.

To Gary Linderer, my copy editor, for his advice and expertise. If it was not for him, this book would consist of one continuous paragraph.

To the men of the 1/101st Airborne LRRP, with whom I served, for their continual support and input.

To my wife, Linda, for her love and her loyalty, and for her many hours in front of the computer. Without her, I would still be hunting and pecking.

To my children, Randy, Richele, and Rachele, for not giving up on me when things got tough.

INTRODUCTION

Having spent a number of years as an enlisted man and having also commanded two other very good units in combat, I take great pride and pleasure in the honor of being asked to write an introduction to Limey's book. Limey, James W. Walker, was an Englishman fighting an American war because, as he put it, "it needed to be done, and it was fun!" Our unit was both unique and elite. As the commander of the 1st Brigade Long Range Reconnaissance Patrol Detachment of the 101st Airborne Division (Separate), I was able to serve with some of the best and most skilled men I have ever known in situations that ranged from small six-man recon and hunter-killer teams that operated independently deep behind enemy lines, to large raiding teams that landed in the middle of enemy encampments, struck with lightning speed, and shot their way out, gathering prisoners, weapons, and documents. It was not rare for the Lurp/Ranger detachment to have more kills in a given week than any other unit in the brigade. The nature of our business was to bring the fight to the VC and the NVA, and we did that with a vengeance! We were known as the Foul Dudes, and we turned the table on the enemy. We were the hunters, and they were the prey!

Some thought we were crazy to do what we did. They were right in a way; we were crazy as foxes. We understood the truth behind the saying "Stay a Lurp, stay alive." The Lurp/Rangers understood that their skills were their best weapon. We trusted each other with our very lives each day without a moment's hesitation! We might have died where we stood, but we never left a brother behind, dead or alive.

Sometimes I think that we may have caused as many problems for the REMFs as we did for Charlie. The brigade's Lurps were young men who knew how to live, and their postmission parties were legendary. When you got the Lurp/Rangers together, watch out! Many a lifer REMF rued the day we came in. (On a personal note, I should add that after too many ass-chewings, I took a real interest in keeping Limey in the field.)

The most telling thing that I can say about us is that we are still friends to this day! At a reunion three years ago, one of us got in trouble (surprise!), and he was asked to leave the hotel. One out all out, was the response. In thirty minutes over one hundred Lurp/Rangers and their family members were in a new hotel. To this day we meet with our young Lurp/Ranger counterparts and provide them with support and brotherhood.

Dan McIsaac,
Detachment Commander,
1/101st Abn. LRRP, 1967

FORTUNE
FAVORS
THE BOLD

Operations, 1st Brigade, 101st Airborne Division 1965–1968

1. Cam-ranh Bay (arrival, 29 July 1965)
2. Nha-trang (Operation BARRACUDA, 12–20 August 1965)
3. An Khe (Operation HIGHLAND, 26 August–1 October 1965)
4. Qui-nhon (LRRP Detachment formed, 15 October 1965; Operation SAYONARA, 1 October–11 November 1965)
5. Phan-rang (22 November–10 December 1965)
6. Bien-hoa
7. Ben Cat, Lai Khe (Operation CHECKER BOARD, 10–19 December 1965)
8. Song Mao (13–17 January 1966)
9. Tuy-hoa (Operation VAN BUREN, 15 January–21 February; Operation HARRISON, 22 February–15 April)
10. Phan-thiet (Operation FILLMORE, 16–23 April 1966)
11. Nhon Co (Operation AUSTIN VI, 25 April–19 May 1966)
12. Cheo Reo (brigade split 20–26 May 1966)
13. Pleiku (brigade split, 20–29 May 1966)
14. Dak-to (Operation HAWTHORNE, 29 May–22 June 1966; Operation BEAUREGARD, 24 June–15 July)
15. Tuy-hoa (Operation JOHN PAUL JONES, SEWARD, and GERONIMO, 15 July–1 December 1966)
16. Kontum (Operation PICKETT, 2 December 1966–23 January 1967)
17. Phan-rang (Operation FARRAGUT, 24–29 January 1967)
18. Bao-loc (Operations GATALING I and II, 1–15 February 1967)
19. Phan-thiet (Operations GATALING I and II, 16 February–1 March 1967)
20. Di Linh (Operations GATALING I and II, 1–12 March 1967)
21. Song Mao (Operations GATALING I and II, 12–24 March 1967)
22. Tuy-hoa (brigade separated, 1–24 March 1967)
23. Phan-rang (brigade reorganized and refitted, 24–28 March 1967)
24. Khanh Duong (Operation SUMMERALL, 30 March–29 April 1967)
25. Duc Pho (Operation MALHEUR I, 30 April–7 June 1967; Operation MALHEUR II, 8 June–1 August 1967; Operation HOOD RIVER, 2–13 August 1967)
26. Chu Lai (Operation BENTON, 13–29 August 1967)
27. Duc Pho (Operation COOK, 1–10 September 1967)
28. Chu Lai (Operation WHEELER, 11 September–23 November 1967)
29. Phan-rang (reorganization and refitting, 26 November–3 December 1967)
30. Phan-thiet (Operation KLAMATH FALLS, 4–12 December 1967)
31. Bao-loc (Operation KLAMATH FALLS, 13 December 1967–13 January 1968)
32. Song Be (Operation SAN ANGELO, LRRP Detachment 1/101st disbanded, 14 January–5 February 1968)

VIETNAM

PROLOGUE

The year was 1991, and the Vietnam War was little more than a memory. A memory that I must admit had both its good side and its bad side. For over twenty-four years, I had wondered what had happened to my comrades. I often found myself trying to conjure up images of their faces, with little or no luck. Even their names began to fade from my memory. These efforts usually left me frustrated and depressed. I longed to see them again, if for no other reason than to ask them if I had done my job well while serving with them. That was a validation that I desperately needed.

I was with my wife, Linda, in a bookstore when the title of a book on the shelf got my immediate attention. It was called *The Eyes of the Eagle*, the motto of my old unit, the 1/101st LRRP. I put the book back in its place when I read on the cover that it was a book about F Company 58th LRP of the 101st Airborne. I walked away, only to return a few minutes later and pick it up again. Then I set it down once more and walked away.

Cash was short at the time, and we were only window shopping. I had no intention of spending five dollars on a book. But Linda had seen me put the book back the second time. Without a word, she took it off the shelf, went to the front desk, and purchased it. That simple act changed my life forever.

I took the book home and placed it on the kitchen counter as I went to my bedroom to change. As was typical for me, I was running late for work, so I hurriedly kissed my wife as I grabbed my lunch from the kitchen counter and left.

After I got to work, I noticed that Linda had packed my new

1

book along with the sandwiches she had made. I worked at a major chemical plant at the time, and my job allowed me a generous amount of free time. After my first round through my area of responsibility, I opened the book and began to read. The epilogue mentioned my old unit, and my interest was immediately aroused. I opened the book to where the pictures were and immediately recognized Rey Martinez posing with a team called "Terrible Team 10." My interest was piqued. I managed to read half the book between rounds at the plant. I knew then that I had committed myself to finishing the book before going to sleep.

Getting home from work, I curled up in my chair to finish the mission that I had started at work. The book filled in some of the blanks that I had often wondered about. The 1/101st LRRP had become F/58th LRP after the rest of the 101st Division arrived in Vietnam. F/58th LRP had later become L/75th (Ranger). To me the most important thing in the book was the KIA roster in the back that showed that none of the Foul Dudes from the 1/101st LRRP whom I had served with had been killed after I had left. I was ecstatic!

Two weeks after finishing the book, I decided to see if I could locate the author. In the author's profile in the back of the book, it stated that the author, Gary A. Linderer, lived in Festus, Missouri, so I had a starting point. I called information and was amazed to discover that he had a listed phone number. I called the number, and when it began to ring, I almost hung up the phone. Did I really want to find my old teammates? What if they didn't remember me, or what if they slammed the phone down after hearing who was calling? Was I ready for the rejection?

The voice at the other end came over loud and clear with a "Hello." I waited for a second or two, and then blurted out, "Hi, you don't know me, but I served with the brigade Lurps in Vietnam."

"Another Old Foul Dude!" was his immediate response.

The ice was broken. Over the next hour, we shot the breeze, and every now and then, Gary would give me a name and a number. By the time we finished, I had a piece of paper filled with names and telephone numbers of men I had served with. I had a long day ahead of me.

The next five hours were spent talking to old comrades and reminiscing. By the time I had finished talking with the guys who were on the list I had gotten from Gary Linderer, I was exhausted. Spread out across the carpet, I was just beginning to doze when the phone rang. It was Gary, who wanted to know how things were going. What an overwhelming sequence of events this was for me.

The 75th Ranger Regiment Association had scheduled a reunion for June 1991, and I felt that it was my duty to get as many of the Old Foul Dudes to come as was possible. Over the next three months, I begged and even threatened suicide to get people to attend.

My efforts were rewarded. With my son, Randy, I arrived early to get to my room, and then made it to the airport in time to pick up Rey Martinez and Kenn Miller. Just before I left for the airport, Al "Lurch" Cornett and Danny Williams walked into the motel. All I could say was "Hi, catch ya later. I gotta pick up Rey."

By the time I got back to the motel with Rey, Dan McIsaac and Peppy Wenglarz had arrived. Kenn Miller's plane had been late, and we would pick him up later. By day's end, Top Smith and Lester "Super Spade" Hite had also arrived.

The next four days were spent reminiscing. At times the experience was so overwhelming that I had to go back to my room to be alone so I could regain my composure. It would take a few more years before I would be really comfortable with my past.

After that first reunion I halfheartedly decided to write a book about my own experiences. I had read a number of books on Vietnam, but only a few, in my opinion, told the full story. I wanted to write about the good as well as the bad—after all, that's the way it was.

I wrote a half dozen chapters and sent them to Gary Linderer—he was the only author I knew well at the time. I was surprised when he edited some of them and sent them back with a note reading, "Keep on working on them. Except for your lousy grammar, you're not too bad." With those words of encouragement, I went after it with gusto. What follows this prologue is the result of that push from Gary.

As with all personal works, the contents of this book are the product of my memory. I have talked with many of the men I served with, and where there was a minor discrepancy, I went with my own perceptions. If there was a major discrepancy, I omitted the story from the manuscript. I have tried to be fair and as accurate as possible, but the reader should realize that this book is primarily a product of many memories recalled more than thirty years after the event.

I apologize for omitting any of my comrades I should have included. It was not because you are not dear to my heart. The language in the text gets pretty rough at times. But we were young back then, and the times were tough. That's the way it was, and for that I do not apologize. Our attitude kept us alive!

Derby Jones, a 1/101st LRRP team leader and wise beyond his years, told me at a recent reunion, "Screw it, Limey! If the guys don't like what you said about them in your book, they can go write their own." Thanks, Derby.

All the names in this book are real with the exception of Lieutenant Shields, Jacobs, Brown, and Richards.

CHAPTER 1

For the people of Great Britain, 1945 was a memorable year. The Second World War was drawing to a close. England, though much violated and in a state of great disrepair, had survived the greatest challenge to its existence since the Spanish Armada. Her empire in shambles, countless thousands of her sons dead on foreign soil, she would never again be the colonial power of years gone by. But she was still Majestic England, and for her citizens, that was more than enough.

For the Walker family residing at 28 Marshall Street in Kingston Upon Hull, 1945 meant even more than peace and a return to normalcy. It also meant the birth of their first child, a son, delivered by a midwife. His arrival resulted in an immediate argument over the selection of his birth name. I don't remember the details for I was very young at the time; it was my name that they were arguing over.

My father, James Mackenzie Walker, wanted me to carry our Scottish family name, Mackenzie, but my mother, Marguerite Patricia Walker, would have no part of it. She felt it wiser to christen me with a more conventional middle name like William, after Wilberforce and Shakespeare. A strong-willed woman, my mother had the last say. I became James William Walker long before I ever realized that it was my name.

My father was a full-fledged, card-carrying Scot-Englishman, which was rather boring when compared to my mother's hot-blooded pedigree—French Canadian and MicMac Indian. My father was an officer in the merchant navy, and during a port of call in Canada, his libido had shifted into maximum overdrive when he first spotted the dark-haired beauty who was

5

Marguerite Patricia Chiasson. Before God and the queen, he swore to his shipmates that he would marry that fair lass before he left port. A man of his word, when his ship docked in England, he had a new bride—straight off the reservation.

During the war years, my father remained at sea, transporting war materials from U.S. and Canadian ports to destinations in the British Isles. During the North African campaigns, his ship was torpedoed. He would never tell me the details, but I soon grew to realize that life at sea during a world war was even more hazardous than normal.

While my father was at sea, my mother decided to do her part for the war effort and enlisted in the British Army. She was stationed at Hull and assigned to man an antiaircraft gun. At the time, it was not uncommon for women in the British Isles to take up the slack for their men who were away fighting the Germans and Italians.

It was common knowledge in Britain—and also in Germany—that Hull was a major manufacturing center. It was also within range of German bombers operating from northern France and paid a heavy price as a result. My mother was pregnant with me and still on active duty when the Germans decided to make one final raid on Hull. After bombing the nearby docks, the Luftwaffe made a strafing run on their way back to the fatherland. My mother was on the floor, under a table, giving birth to me when numerous large-caliber bullets ripped through our house, pockmarking the plaster walls and damaging a painting of Gainsborough's *Blue Boy*. The painting survived the attack and was never removed from its honored spot on the wall, nor were the bullet holes in the wall ever repaired. It was my family's badge of honor, and we wore it with pride.

During this period, Aunt Ida had joined the Canadian Army and been stationed in Aldershot, England. She visited my mother at every opportunity, helping her prepare for my arrival. After I was born, she seemed to spend every free moment she had visiting with us. I was told that she fawned over me something terrible, spoiling me. She even taught me a few things that would help me get by later in life, such as how to get attention when I needed it. Evidently, I felt the need for attention when I was eating. If I had a bowl of food in front of me, and no one was paying attention to me, I would unceremoniously overturn the bowl on my head. Most of the time, the bowl would be full of porridge, and my mother soon became expert at cleaning it up.

My parents had a turbulent marriage, at least until I was born, when things seemed to settle down a little. I believe that my father's long absences at sea had much to do with it. My sister was born in 1947 but died shortly after birth. This seemed to open old wounds, and before long the marriage was back on the rocks. This time the differences were irreconcilable, and my parents divorced in 1949. Calling her a witch, my father blamed everything on my mother; she accused him of being a tyrant and claimed that no woman should live "this way." Of course, I didn't know any of this at the time they split up but heard it later when they thought I was old enough for their excuses.

For only two episodes in my life do I actually remember my parents' being together. One was when I used to blow a party whistle, which scared the dickens out of me. I would blow it, drop it, then run, only to return a little later to repeat the process all over again. This seemed to bring a great amount of joy to my parents. The other was at Paddington railroad station when my parents said good-bye to each other forever. My mother had brought along a Rupert book and a box of chocolates for me, which at the time I believed was a farewell present. She was talking to me when an argument broke out between the two of them. I didn't care about the chocolates, but I really wanted the Rupert book. Suddenly, my father grabbed the book and threw it across the station floor as a parting gesture to my mother. It wasn't until much later that I discovered that my mother also had my passport and visa with her. She had intended on taking me to the United States with her, but my father had torn them up just before the episode with the Rupert book. As we were leaving the station, I remember asking my father to get the Rupert book for me. He shook his head and told me not to worry about it, he would get me another one.

I remember that it was the first time I had ever been lied to and the first time I had ever gotten really mad. I was only four years old at the time, and was naive enough to believe what an adult told me. But I never got that Rupert book.

My father went back to sea and left me to be raised by my grandmother and my aunt Marlene. Aunt Marlene was a beautiful, caring lady, but my grandmother proved to be a real Scottish battle-ax. I loved her dearly, and I'm sure she loved me just as much, but I'll never forget how strict she was. The problem with Grandmother Mackenzie was that she believed that the "spoken word," when she uttered it, was to be attested to by everyone in the neighborhood. In addition, I firmly believed that she thought she was the heavyweight champion of the United Kingdom! She wouldn't hesitate to knock the stuffing out of me for the slightest infraction.

I vividly recall life at 28 Marshall Street. The school across the street, and the neighborhood, were full of kids, and I never lacked someone to play with. The Lewis and Clark of Yorkshire, Jerry Woodard and I would often go off together to explore our neighborhood and its surroundings. We never did anything illegal, unless one might call "scrumping" illegal. Scrumping was a lot like shoplifting, but it didn't sound quite as evil. We took great pride in being able to scrump more apples and pears than anyone else in our neighborhood.

When it came to Guy Fawkes Day, we were always the ones who pulled the successful raids on the other neighborhood bonfire woodpiles. Our single major vice was playing in the bombed-out buildings that dotted the area. The bigger the "danger" signs they posted, the bigger the adventure therein. Today, I realize how foolish we were at the time because we had both watched demolition disposal teams defusing unexploded German bombs among the ruins. Most of the bombs had already been located and disposed of, but occasionally one would surface that had been missed by the demo people.

Naturally, when we were kept after school for some infraction, real or imagined, my grandmother blamed Jerry, and Jerry's parents blamed me. Through all the arguments and fights our guardians had over us, Jerry and I remained steadfast friends.

It seemed to us that fighting and arguing were the favorite pastimes of most of the adults living on Marshall Street. The most humorous of these were over shit. That's right, *shit!* During the days after the war and well into the 1950s, milk was delivered twice a week by horse-drawn cart. Jerry and I used to sit on the front stoop and watch for the horse to take a healthy crap. It was then that, shovels held high, adults would pour out of the houses and converge on the horse apples. The victors would then shuffle off to the gardens at the rear of their houses to deposit the spoils of battle. It was hilarious!

Once the gardeners called a truce and came to a mutual agreement. They decided that whenever the horse decided to make a deposit for the neighborhood fertilizer bank, the droppings would belong to the house closest to the "dump site." This arrangement worked until everyone realized that the horse crapped in front of the same house all of the time. Neighbors began to accuse each other of "dump-site fixing" and various other fecal misconduct. Jerry and I spent a lot of time on the front stoop enjoying the battles, often eating our lunch there.

The pleasure of sharing my adventures with Jerry will always be close to my heart. However, I must admit that I had another friend just as close as Jerry. Her name was Peggy, the prettiest thing I had yet to set eyes on. The only problem was that Peggy couldn't speak a lick of English. But she walked me to school in the morning and was there when I got out to walk me home again. It didn't matter if it rained or snowed or if I was held after school for punishment. She was still there waiting when I got out. She was my most trusted friend and one of the prettiest Dalmatians in the world.

Peggy was not only my buddy, but she was also my bodyguard. The word soon spread that anyone who messed with the Walker kid ran the risk of losing a fist-size chunk of ass. My grandmother had not been very happy when Aunt Marlene bought me Peggy, and her unhappiness turned to pure, unabashed hatred when she realized that it had become plain old-fashioned unhealthy to admonish me in front of Peggy. Peggy would not tolerate her buddy being screamed at or walloped. My grandmother had always believed that "spare the rod and spoil the child" was the gospel of the Lord, but Peggy had her own version of that old adage—"Hurt the child, and I'll tear your damn kneecap off." My aunt Marlene took great pleasure watching my grandmother tiptoeing around the house trying to avoid the dog. Peggy had become a heroine in our eyes.

But one day I got out of school, and Peggy was not there to meet me. I was panic-stricken, worrying about all of the evil things that could have befallen her. Kraut spies must have taken her, I thought, or even worse—a Frenchman. When I arrived home, I was met at the door by my grandmother, who triumphantly admitted that she had gotten rid of my dog. The reason she gave was that Peggy kept getting under her feet. I knew that this was a lie because Peggy wouldn't go anywhere near her except to defend me. That was the last time I spoke to my grandmother unless I was ordered to. I may have over-reacted a bit, but as far as I was concerned my grandmother had committed the unpardonable sin. Grandmother was the first person I ever sent to Coventry, and I was only six years old.

Peggy's loss hurt me deeply, but I still had Jerry. I envisioned Jerry and me growing old, even dying, together. Isn't that what good friends were for? And we were best friends.

Since my grandmother refused to go to the seashore, I usually went with Jerry's family. I eagerly looked forward to each summer when we would take the train ride to Witherinsea. The train ride was as much an adventure as the time at the seashore, where most of our time was spent at the arcades or playing in the sand; the frigid North Sea was not the most pleasant water in which to take a dip. Those were happy days, playing with my best friend and his family.

It was during this period that Jerry and I got our first *Eye Spy* books. I recall that the very first one was about trains. It wasn't long before we defied our elders to sneak away from the neighborhood and travel for miles to distant railroad stations and crossings to "eye" a train like the one the book described.

All the many trains that then crisscrossed England were listed in that precious little book, and we spent days trying to locate each one. The days ran into months, and before long we had spent an entire summer attempting to find the elusive trains and record their serial numbers.

When not at a rail line or a train station, we would take our homemade fishing poles to the nearby river to catch minnows. On one particular day, we caught over a hundred and brought them home. I took our metal bathtub down from its storage area and filled it with water. The minnows were still enjoying their new pond when my grandmother came home. Since I no longer had Peggy to protect me, I got a bum-burning to end all bum-burnings. Until the next week when I filled it with tadpoles.

The tadpole operation was much better planned than the minnow escapade. This time, I waited until the day after bath day to plan our little expedition to the river. There were tadpoles everywhere, and Jerry and I were not satisfied until we had a couple of hundred pollywogs. When we got back to the neighborhood, we hid the tub behind an outbuilding and released our newfound friends into their new home. We checked them every day and watched as they transformed from tadpoles to frogs. On about the third day, my grandmother asked me if I had seen the bathtub. Not wanting to risk losing my amphibian friends or to absorb another beating, I did the first thing that came to mind—I lied. The lie was bad enough, but my overactive imagination prompted me to deflect her inquiries in a new direction. "Grandmother, maybe a spy has stolen it!" It sounded damned good to me, but Grandmother saw it for what it was, a lame attempt at a cover-up.

In a near panic, I sprinted three doors down the street to Jerry's house. Returning to the scene of the crime, we sneaked through the alley to the back of my house to retrieve our frogs and to empty the bathtub. But when we turned the corner, my grandmother was waiting next to the tub with a switch in her hand. I recall her demonic cackle as she vowed how this was going to hurt me worse than it hurt her. She tore my bottom up for the second time in two weeks. I swore a silent oath never to bring another critter or put anything in Granny's bathtub but my own scarred backside.

My grandmother died when I was seven years old. For some reason unknown to me, I cried at the funeral. I think I did it because it was expected of me. Everyone else was doing it, so I joined in to avoid standing out in the crowd.

It was a sad day when I had to leave Marshall Street. But with my grandmother dead and my aunt Marlene getting married, I soon found myself being shunted off to a new life. I said good-bye to my friends and shed some real tears with Jerry, but being a kid, I had little to say about the major adjustment in my destiny. I couldn't understand at the time why I was being forced to leave my home, and I was never told where I was going. The only thing that mattered was that I was going somewhere alien to me—end of story.

When I arrived at the Sailors Orphan Home, I went through a period of total denial over my predicament. I honestly figured someone had made a horrible mistake. I was certain I didn't belong there because, unlike the rest of the "inmates" at the orphanage, I still had a father. Sure, he was away at sea for months at a time, but he was still alive, and as long as he was standing his watch out there somewhere, I wasn't an orphan. I knew it would only be a matter of time before someone realized the mistake and my father came to take me home.

It was 1952, and the orphanage was set within the confines of a gigantic estate, or so it seemed to me at the time. The adults who ran the home were caring and supportive of their wards. We kids stayed in large houses along with a regular family. My first residence was called Trinity, and it was occupied by the Brambleses. We called Mr. and Mrs. Brambles "Auntie" and "Uncle." It seemed to please them and established an acceptable relationship that everyone was comfortable with. Uncle Brambles worked at the nearby Dunlop plant, which left Auntie Brambles in complete charge of the everyday operations of the residence. Their son, David, was a natural athlete, and because of him I became very involved in sports. Their daughter, Penny, was a sniveling little twit who demanded unearned respect and attention from everyone in the house. She reminded me a lot of my grandmother—only in miniature.

Even though I had just lost my best friend, Jerry, it didn't take me long to replace him with another boy who shared my interests and my special aptitude for getting into trouble. But Alex Story had a control problem, and we would go through the next few years of our lives continually fighting each other to determine who would be the boss. Neither of us understood why there had to be a boss, but from the first time we had met, it had seemed like the proper course of action. Fortunately, the struggle for control never sullied our friendship.

We often permitted Alex's younger brother, William, to stay around us until we no longer found him amusing. Of course, William was a natural comedian, so he managed to hang around us all the time. Alex and William's sister Evelyn was another matter altogether. She was a full year older than Alex and I, and this led her to believe that *she* should be the boss. It caused Alex and me no end of grief. We knew that if we hit her, we would be in deep, deep trouble with Auntie. The same punishment awaited us if we even argued with her. So, with no other options available to us, we simply ignored her, which wasn't too hard; she was a girl!

It didn't take long to establish a routine and to fit into the home. I was even given a choice as to which school I wanted to attend. I could accept schooling there at the orphanage, or I could go to Endike, about a mile away. I was forbidden to return to the school in my old neighborhood as it was against the orphanage's policy. So I opted to attend Endike. I didn't mind the walk to and from school, but coming home for lunch every day at noon was very difficult. I ended up walking four miles every day, even in the rain or snow.

At the orphanage, we had a set of rules, which everyone lived by. When we obeyed them, everything ran pretty smoothly. Each of us was assigned his or her duties around the home, which consisted of work details that were spread out evenly among the kids. Some were good details; some were pretty crummy. If you really screwed up during a particular week, you got one of the crummy ones. The worst detail was polishing everyone's shoes, and I managed to get that detail on more than one occasion.

The detail I enjoyed most was the garden run. Every Saturday, two of us would take a large basket to the gigantic community garden, which was maintained by an outstanding gardener. We would help him pick the vegetables that we would eat for the following week. On numerous occasions, I attempted to talk the gardener out of putting brussels sprouts in the basket, but always failed. Yet, it never stopped me from trying. The gardener took to calling me Sprout, and he and I became quick friends.

Another one of our friends was Anton Nelson. Anton had a little brother who had fits at the most curious times. One morning, before I knew he had this problem, I was at the breakfast table with about a dozen other kids. I was busily preoccupied eating my porridge—an all-time favorite of mine—when I heard a dull but resounding *thunk*. Looking up quickly, I saw Anton's little brother unconscious, his face buried deep in his bowl of porridge. I didn't know what to do or say, but all of the kids broke out laughing, much to Auntie's disgust. She tut-tutted and ordered Anton to kindly remove his little brother from his bowl of porridge.

After that episode, I found myself waiting for Anton's brother to repeat the performance. He seldom failed to disappoint me. Every other day or so, the little bugger dived head-long into his porridge. The only person who didn't think the seizures hilarious was Auntie Brambles. Even Anton's little brother laughed with us after he finally came to.

Three months after my arrival at Trinity, Anton's brother was transferred to another home where he was able to get medical help for his epilepsy. I didn't think Anton was ever the same after his little brother left us. I know that breakfast was never again as amusing.

Alex also provided months of entertainment at the dinner table. He had become an expert at making uneaten food disappear from his plate. To those who were not privy to his machinations, it appeared that Alex always cleaned his plate, just like the rest of us, but I knew what was going on. My grandmother had lectured me constantly about eating all the food on my plate. Rationing in our household had made me acutely aware of the value of food. Alex's penchant for wasting perfectly nutritious food was alien to me, since I was forced to make do with special items purchased with our ration cards. But I was fascinated with his covert method for disposing of distasteful servings from his plate.

Alex had developed an immense dislike for cheese and several kinds of meat. Although these items were heavily rationed, even in the early fifties, the orphanage seemed to have very little difficulty obtaining an abundant supply. Since we had no dog at the table to pass unpopular foodstuffs to, Alex would simply roll the cheese, meat, or other offending item into a tight, compact ball, then stick it in his pants pocket. He performed this trick at every evening meal, sometimes giggling at the humor of it. It was hilarious, knowing that he was outsmarting the ever-vigilant Auntie who closely watched her charges at mealtime, frequently criticizing them for their table manners. She only caught on to Alex's game when he forgot to empty his pockets on washday. Auntie and some of the girls were doing laundry when they came across a pair of pants with pockets bulging with tightly rolled balls of food. It didn't take Auntie long to discover the owner of the offending pants. Alex soon received a severe scolding and had to sit through the age-old lecture about the poor, starving people of China. Had Alex been a little smarter, he would have escaped with nothing more than a tongue-lashing and the parable, but Alex opined that they could send all of his cheese straight to China to feed all those starving Chinamen. Auntie escorted him directly to the headmaster. One severe caning later, he was a much wiser bloke. Picking up on Alex's silly mistake, I made certain that I frequently queried Auntie if there was some way we could help those poor Chinamen, maybe even sending them some of our own provisions. Although I was quite serious, Auntie took it all as a bucket of blarney.

Alex continued to roll the food he disliked into little balls, but no longer did he put them in his own pants pockets. Forcing us to collaborate in his scheme, he now passed the food balls under the table to me and some of the others to hide them in our pants pockets. When dinner was over, while Alex was being frisked by Auntie Brambles, the rest of us smuggled his unwanted food out of the house, then surreptitiously discarded it around the estate for the benefit of the friendly but underfed animal population. Let the Chinamen starve!

Real fights rarely broke out among us. If two of the kids really got into a serious tiff with the main purpose being total destruction or massive bodily harm, someone in authority would step in immediately to stop it. Both warring parties would be escorted to the gymnasium, where they would be instructed to "put on the gloves." They would then be placed in the center of the boxing ring and left to flail at each other until they no longer possessed the energy to flail. And that would be the end of the tiff. Not surprisingly, Sailors Orphan Home produced some damn fine boxers!

The best fight I ever witnessed was between two girls. Evelyn Story was in the sitting room, holding a doll, when Penny Brambles strolled in and demanded that it be turned over to her. But the doll was community property, belonging to no one in particular and to everyone in general, so Evelyn rightly refused to give it up. Penny, asserting her proprietary rights as the nonorphan resident brat, grabbed the doll. When Evelyn still wouldn't release it, Penny's next ploy was to scream at the top of her lungs, *"You'd better give me the doll or I'll tell me mother!"* Evelyn gave her the doll—backhanded and hard across her forehead. Something had to give with a mighty blow like that one. Fortunately, it was the doll. I had never seen anyone's eyes roll that far back in their head before, but Penny's sure did—just before she crumpled to the floor, out cold. Dick Tiger couldn't have made a better swing! We would be picking up pieces of porcelain for the next two days. Auntie Brambles charged into the room and immediately thought that Evelyn had killed her precious Penny. But when Penny started to come to, and it was obvious that Evelyn's blow had not been mortal, Auntie collected her runaway emotions and began to plot her revenge. Since she was not allowed to strike any of the orphans, Auntie called the headmaster. But when he had heard the full story, he refused to punish Evelyn for striking Penny. Auntie was beside herself and tried to make things hard on the rest of us kids. We reacted by putting up a united front and put both Auntie and Penny in Coventry—putting or sending someone to Coventry meant not speaking to them, shunning them. The city of Coventry housed Britain's large national asylum, and it was where you put people who no longer fit in society. Theoretically, that's what we did to the Brambles females. Some of the kids even stopped talking to David, but most of us refused to participate in that effort. He was a friend and had done nothing wrong. Some of my mates were not happy with my decision to continue talking with David, but that was the way things were. Putting someone in Coventry was a terrible punishment and was not to be undertaken lightly. David didn't deserve it. The shunning went on for the better part of three weeks before Auntie relented and things got back to normal.

Getting back to normal meant resorting to our normal behavior patterns. The "great stone battle" was one of the craziest things we ever did. It started when a bunch of us went around to the different homes on the property requisitioning garbage can lids. We then armed ourselves with BBRs (big bloody rocks) and prepared to do battle. A signal was given, and we began to pelt each other with the BBRs, using the garbage can lids as shields to protect our vital areas.

In the middle of a particularly heavy BBR barrage, Alex—never known for his superior intelligence—decided to pull a reenactment of King Harold at the Battle of Hastings. He lowered his shield and stood up to face the shower of BBRs that were at that very moment descending on his position. I don't know if Alex was suicidal or he suddenly believed that he had become invulnerable, but everyone seemed to recognize his peril but he. We screamed trying to warn him, but it was already too late. Where once stood a happy lad playing warrior, now lay a dazed and bloody mess.

A number of well-thrown BBRs had tattooed Alex severely about the head and shoulders. He had suffered a large number of cuts and gashes, among them an especially bad one just above his right eye, which was now spewing blood everywhere. What did his valiant comrades do? Why, we broke and ran, of course. No one in his right mind wanted to stay around to admit that we had killed one of our own.

I was peeking around the corner of a house expecting any moment to see heavenly angels taking Alex away, when he suddenly stirred and came to. When I saw that he was still alive, I quickly ran over to join him. No one would accuse James William Walker of lacking courage—or good timing. Expecting absolution for my sin, I was soon to discover that I fell into the class of penitents with those other warriors who never returned to the battleground as I had done. All of the parties who were involved in the Battle of Hastings–Part II were given a full week of the crummy detail—that's right, polishing everyone's shoes. And battles with stones were put on the don't-you-dare list.

After Sir Edmund Hillary and Tenzing Norgay conquered Mount Everest, we were all loaded on a bus and transported to a new theater that had just opened, to see a sneak preview of their already famous deed. Most of us felt, "Hey, so what! Bring on the cartoons." We never realized that we were watching history being made before anyone else got to view it.

We orphans were always being transported here and there for special events. I always felt that we had more privileges and more opportunity for group activities than the average kid growing up with two parents.

One time about a dozen of us were transported to York for a special dinner event. We had been assigned to wait on tables and provide gofer (go fer this—go fer that) services at the banquet. There we were in our cute little sailor uniforms running around, working our fingers to the bone. All the adults in attendance couldn't help but notice us—we were *that* cute— and soon took pity on the "poor little orphans." They began lavishing gifts and money on us, never suspecting that we knew exactly what we were doing. I came back from the affair with a pocket full of shillings and enough candy to open a sweet shop. Naturally, we poor little orphans shared our spoils with the kids who had not been selected to attend the affair. Sharing was what we were all about.

It wasn't unusual to receive surprise visits from some of the local people who occasionally stopped by to check out the poor little orphans. Invariably, some of us would be taken home with them—sort of a pet-for-the-day program.

On one of these occasions, I heard a lady visitor talking with Auntie Brambles, saying, "I'll take the cute one home with me," pointing toward me. Her husband nodded in agreement. Their children, standing nearby, were tittering with glee. I felt like a damned puppy being selected from a litter at the local pet shop and taken home to entertain those spoiled brats. But since I knew that I would be given treats and fawned over as if I were something special, I really didn't have a problem going home for the day with the Good Samaritans. Orphans are some of the world's best opportunists. But had I known at the time what was going to happen that same night, I would have demanded to stay at the orphanage.

Like any happy family of five, we took the bus to the downtown area where we enjoyed sodas at an ice-cream shop before making the short walk home. The gentleman of the house worked as a caretaker for a large business, and part of his compensation package was living in a house on the premises. Everything there appeared to be ancient—I'm talking Oliver Cromwell ancient!

I played with their children most of the afternoon. They really weren't bad kids, but they lacked something intrinsic that the kids at the orphanage all possessed. We made the best of any situation. Outside kids couldn't do that. Anyway, I took great pleasure in exploring the old stables and the barn. There were no longer any horses, but there was still plenty of old equipment and tack. Saddles, bits, plows, carriages, and the like were neatly stored away in the stables and barn. There was also an old cottage nearby that I wanted to check out, but was politely told that it was off-limits. When I inquired of my playmates as to why it was taboo, they quickly sidestepped the issue with a "you wouldn't believe us if we told you."

The sunny afternoon was giving way to evening when the

girl looked at her brother and stated we had better go in before "he" came out. When I tried to get them to stay out a little longer, they begged me to go with them into the house. Understanding that I was a guest, I followed them inside. Their parents seemed relieved that we had come in before it got too dark. They told us that they were just getting ready to come out and get us. I didn't know what was going on there, but my curiosity was piqued!

After a small snack, we went up to their bedroom. I had been told to sleep in the same bedroom with the kids, which kind of surprised me. It didn't bother me to sleep in the large bedroom as I was used to sleeping in a dormitory environment back at the Sailors Orphan Home, but I wondered what they had in the other three bedrooms.

We had gotten undressed and changed into our nightclothes when the boy closed the bedroom door. At that time, I had never slept with a bedroom door closed, and I felt a little uncomfortable. So I got up and opened it again. The two kids, almost in unison, said, "You'll be sorry." With that statement, the boy hid his head under the covers. I shook my head and dismissed him as being a little balmy. His sister and I stayed up and talked. Ten minutes had gone by when I suddenly saw an off-white, transparent figure pass in front of the room, then stop by the door. It looked directly at me for a full five seconds, then floated on down the hallway. I never moved so fast in my life. I was out of the bed, across the room, slamming the door, and back in bed in less than two seconds. There was a strong smell of burning rubber in the room, and my feet were still smoking as I pulled the covers over my head.

The girl was giggling uncontrollably. I heard her brother ask if "it" had left yet. Although I was unable to identify the figure, I was pretty damn certain I had just seen a real ghost. Yes, Virginia, there are ghosts!

The following day at breakfast, I learned the full story of the strange happenings of the night before. There was not one ghost, but two. The explanation given me was that they were the wandering spirits of a caretaker and his wife who were murdered there many years ago. The one specter was often seen to kiss his ghostly wife in front of the cottage door before making his rounds of the grounds. The specter would finish the task of walking the property, then make a visit to the main house. He would check every room without fail. The present caretaker and his wife felt a kinship with the friendly apparitions, but the children were petrified. After the previous evening's events, you could add me to the petrified list!

I visited their home on several more occasions, but you can rest assured that I was in the house by nightfall and the bedroom door remained closed. Had there been a lock on the door, it would have received maximum use from me. My precautions worked, for I never saw that ghost again.

It was always a pleasure being invited out by truly caring families, although at times I did feel embarrassed to be the center of attention. They always saw us as poor, underprivileged orphans, but in my mind I was rich. I lived in a big house, had lots of brothers and sisters, wore nice clothes, and ate wholesome meals three times a day.

Most people had the misguided perception that we had nothing. Such was the case when two nuns took me out for the day away from the orphanage. One of the nuns was somewhat aged, but the other was a young, quite attractive lass. At the time, I was about ten years old and was just beginning to feel the urgings of my budding hormones. At least I knew what a good-looking bird was supposed to look like, or so I thought. The younger nun had fire-red hair, a freckled face, and was probably all of twenty years old. When I first saw her, I was instantly head over heels in love.

We went on numerous excursions after that, but the last of our visits is the one I most clearly remember. We had gone downtown to a cafeteria to eat. When we approached the cashier's counter after entering the restaurant, an old man extended his hand, begging for money. All he was asking for was enough money to pay for a meal. This was the first time I had ever witnessed the plight of someone who was *really* poor. Apparently, my existence in the orphanage had sheltered me from the real miseries of the poor. The old tramp was so dirty and pathetic that the only thing I could do was to stare at the floor. The young nun, on the other hand, burst into tears as she thrust her hands in her robes to look for some change. The aged nun scolded her, then told her that the old man was only trying to take advantage of her sympathy. I immediately fell even deeper in love with the redheaded nun and found myself detesting the other as an evil old hag.

After we had finished eating, we went to the bus stop to catch the bus back to the orphanage. It was then that I blurted out to the young nun, "When I get a little older, will you marry me?" It was the most important thing in my life at that moment, and I was dead serious. The young nun was taken aback for a moment, but then she started to laugh. Her older companion, however, had no sense of humor at all. She proceeded to chew me out royally, telling me that they were already married to God, while the love of my life stood to one side, laughing uncontrollably. I guess her answer was no, because I never saw either of the nuns again. I wasn't sure if I had upset the older nun, or if God was punishing me for trying to move in on Him. For over a month after my "great sin," I would sneak into the convent in a vain attempt to see the young nun. I was certain that if I could just see her one more time, I could convince her to marry me!

A year after Elizabeth was crowned queen of England, we received word that she would be visiting the home. We spent an entire week rehearsing what we were to do when she arrived, and much to our surprise, Anton was chosen to give the queen a gift from the orphanage. He was to be dressed as a pirate, and just as the queen's car entered the grounds, he was to jump in front of it as if to rob it, but instead he would present her with a Gurkha knife. Anton's selection for the honor didn't sit well with Alex and me, and we decided to sabotage him. Alex and I started a rumor that Anton was a foreigner from Denmark, and as such, he should not be allowed to present the knife to the queen. We, on the other hand, were true Englishmen with fathers who were serving in the Royal Navy, and who more deservedly than us should be allowed to approach the queen?

We watched silently as Anton made the presentation. Secretly, Alex and I both hoped that when Anton jumped in front of the car, the queen's driver would panic and run him over, but the entire thing went off without a hitch. It was the first time I had been jealous of someone else's good fortune. I had never had to compete with anyone else before.

At the Sailors Orphan Home, it was against the rules for any of the resident adults to strike an orphan. The ultimate means of discipline was left to the headmaster. Any complaints too severe to be handled by the houseparents were given to the headmaster for his disposition.

Over the years, I had managed to get into my share of minor trouble but never to the point of being dealt with by the headmaster. Auntie Brambles was really strict in her enforcement of bed curfew and cleanup. We were each given a certain time to go to bed based on our age. This rule even applied to her own children, David and Penny. It was the bedtime curfew rule that led to my most dreadful sin.

On that particular day, William and I had left the property and had gone to some woods, about two miles away from the orphanage. We were looking for oak nuts and managed to get preoccupied with some of the wild animals that were scurrying around us. Before we realized what time it was, it was getting dark, and we were way past our curfew. We took off immediately for the orphanage and ran all the way to the back gate of the property only to find that it had already been locked. I had no difficulty scaling the wall, but William, who was much shorter than I, could barely reach the top of the wall, let alone scale it. For over an hour, we made desperate efforts to get him over the wall, but the attempt was futile. Finally, we gave up and ran around to the front gate, which was always left open. On the way up to the house, William, for some reason, stopped to pick a flower. When we reached Trinity, Auntie Brambles had already panicked and called the constables to report two of her wards missing. Now she had to call back and explain that she had acted prematurely. She demanded an explanation from us why we had been tardy. I merely shrugged my shoulders and resigned myself to whatever punishment I deserved. Not William! He thrust out the flower and sheepishly said, "We were picking flowers for you, Auntie." I couldn't handle that and burst out laughing. I should have kept my mouth shut and gone along with William's con. He got off without a word said, and I went straightaway to the headmaster for my first and last caning. It was also explained to me that the greatest mortal sin at the orphanage was missing curfew; some years before I had arrived at the home, one of the kids had come up missing and was never found, or so they said.

William had the most unique sense of humor that I had ever seen. Whenever he was around, laughter was sure to follow. One day Auntie told us that, if we behaved, she would take us to the park on a Saturday. We were all determined to be good so we would qualify for the outing. Alex and I even assisted William in building a sailboat that would not perform like a submarine. From past experience, we knew that if we didn't lend our expertise, William's yacht would find its way to Davy Jones's locker soon after its launching. When that Saturday arrived and we discovered that we had qualified for the trip to the park, we were ecstatic. We boarded a bus and soon arrived at the park. The first thing we did was go to the large pond in the center of the park to see if William's new sailboat would float. The foot-long yacht sailed just as it was supposed to. As the design engineers, Alex and I were especially proud. Then we discovered the single flaw in William's new sailboat. When it sailed out of reach, it wouldn't return to port.

Some bloke in his twenties soon noticed our predicament and came to our rescue. He asked William to hold his hand while he leaned out over the pond to attempt to reach the boat. Obligingly, William held on tight as the young man stretched out as far as he could go. Suddenly, William started laughing uncontrollably and released the stranger's hand. We watched in amazement as our Good Samaritan hit the water with a re-sounding splash. He went under briefly, then struggled to the surface. Then he stood there, sputtering and gasping, looking like a drowned duck. William went into hysterics. Then all of the kids started laughing. Auntie arrived on the scene and scolded us into silence for being rude, while apologizing to the waterlogged stranger for our discourtesy. The silence was short-lived as William lost it again and soon had all the rest of us laughing. The kindhearted man walked away, dripping and shaking his head. It was the last time Auntie took us to the park.

On numerous occasions, I sneaked out of the orphanage and returned to my old neighborhood to visit Jerry. It was a breach of the rules, but I wouldn't let that stop me. I missed Jerry. I wondered how he was doing since I left. I managed to get away with my surreptitious excursions for quite a while until the day I made the mistake of taking William with me. I should have known better, because the only way William could keep a secret was if someone were to cut out his tongue. Sure enough, very shortly thereafter, he was talking to Alex about the good time we had on Marshall Street, and he was overheard by Auntie's big-eared daughter, Penny. Naturally, Penny went to her mother. The jig was up. I was given a stern warning about what would happen if I made another clandestine visit to Marshall Street. It had something to do with being struck by lightning.

I must admit that I was a lot better off than most of the other children in the orphanage. Since all of my relatives lived within a mile or two of the premises, I had no problem spending weekends and holidays with them. My uncle Frank and aunt Miriam lived about a quarter mile from the orphanage, and I spent most of the holidays and many pleasant weekends at their house. To their credit, they treated me just like one of the family, and I often went to work with Uncle Frank, collecting feed sacks. He also took me along with him and his son, Frank junior, when they made farm runs. It never made a lot of sense to me how he was able to support his family and pay for petrol doing what he did. We thought it was all fun and games walking through cow and hog manure to get to the barns. We would gather the used cloth feed bags while Uncle Frank negotiated a price with the farmer. We would then return to town, and Uncle Frank would resell the bags to the feed mills. He must have made a good profit doing this, because his was one of the first families on Alexander Crescent to get a television. When the feed mills started using paper bags in place of the cotton ones, Uncle Frank was forced to find other ways to make use of his lorry. But he never grew upset over losing the livelihood he'd had for years. He just accepted it and changed with the times. It was later in life that I realized how extraordinary Uncle Frank was. He was a strong man with high family values.

During these times at Uncle Frank's, my uncle Ronald would sometimes visit when he was on leave from the army. I had been in the orphanage for about two years when Uncle Ronald, a sergeant, gave up his military career to raise a family. He moved into a house on Alexander Crescent with his wife, Jean, not more than a half dozen doors from Uncle Frank and Aunt Miriam. I now had two sets of relatives I could stay with.

While Uncle Frank was lenient and easy to get along with, Uncle Ronald was strict. He was a firm believer that rules were made to be followed and that a man's word was his bond. It was easy to see the influence a life in the military had had on him. I never heard him raise his voice or berate anyone, nor did I ever see him strike anyone. But he had an air about him that demanded respect and attention. I found myself drawn very close to him. When I asked him if he would take me out of the orphanage so I could live with him, I was shocked by his answer. He told me that he had offered to take me into his home and raise me as his own son when he had discovered that my father was going to place me in the orphanage. But my father would have no part of it, stating that I was his son and that he would raise me as he saw fit. Had my father not been so possessive, I would have been raised by my uncle Ron, and my life would have been totally different. Such is destiny!

When another uncle, Alex, got his first telly, Uncle Ron took me over to his house one Sunday for dinner and an afternoon of entertainment. It was while watching the television that I got my first glimpse of America. We watched Lloyd Bridges in "Sea Hunt" and Broderick Crawford in "Highway Patrol." I found myself totally caught up in the rugged and adventurous lifestyle that Americans obviously enjoyed. When I told Uncle Ron that I wanted to be an American policeman, he told me that I would have to be an American to accomplish that. He asked me if I was interested in going to America to live with my mother. Naturally, I said yes. But I promptly forgot that we had ever had the conversation. However, in my fantasies, I constantly transformed myself into Mike Nelson, diving in the depths of some exotic ocean, or Broderick Crawford, chasing down the highway after a fleeing crook. If my school had had a course in fantasy, I would have made perfect scores.

When I got a little older, I made numerous trips by bus to Aunt Marlene's house. I didn't see much of her husband as he was a commercial fisherman and was normally at sea, fishing Dogger Bank. I guess working on trawlers must have been exhausting work, because when I did see him, he was either in bed or getting ready to go to bed. Of course when this happened, I would lose Aunt Marlene's company, which used to upset me greatly. It wasn't long before I was visiting my aunt Marlene and my new cousin. I guess he wasn't that tired after all!

I was spending half of my time at the orphanage and the rest with my family. I felt sorry for a lot of the kids in the orphanage as most of them had nowhere to go except the home. I was especially sorry to hear that Alex, Evelyn, and William Story had not heard from their father in over three years. Yeah, I was pretty well off!

I was getting to the age when I had to make the choice of attending one of two high schools. Again, I could attend high school at the orphanage or continue my studies at Endike High. The choice was easy, and the orphanage came in second once more. I liked Endike, and it afforded me another environment to check out. The orphanage was okay, but it did not offer the freedom that Endike provided. Now that I was in high school, I was given a meal allowance for my noon meal, so my daily trek to the orphanage to eat came to an end. The only other kid in the home who had opted for Endike was David Brambles. I became his protégé.

David was a natural at sports. It didn't matter if it was cricket, soccer, or track, he seldom lost at anything. He played cricket as if he were born to it, and was one of the best wicket keepers the school had ever produced. He spent hour upon hour teaching me the position. When he gave up the position to play on the orphanage adult cricket team, I had no problem filling the spot. I was never as good as David, but I could hold my own.

It was during an important match that I realized that I was in awe of David. The match was on our own home field, and the other team was up to bat. We were changing bowlers when I looked over to our side and saw David. I guess it was destiny. The batman tried to block a bowl and stepped over the line. I had stepped up close to the wicket because the bowler was one of those who bowled slow but could put a heck of a turn on the ball. Before I knew it, the ball was in my gloves, the opponent was over the line, and I knocked not only a stump out of the ground but the entire wicket. The wicket and pegs were still in midair as I yelled at the top of my lungs "How is he?" The umpire waited for a very long second and "ayed" the out. I was in heaven, and the only hero I had known since Batman and Robin was on hand to see the play. I immediately ran to the side and asked David if he had seen the play. With a smile he answered, "Yes, Jim, I saw the play. Don't you think it would be a good idea to finish the match?" I looked around, embarrassed to see both teams waiting for me to return to the game. That year we won our division but got severely bashed at the Hull City finals. In the first round, no less!

When Endike formed its first rugby team, I was in line to try out. Being sports oriented, thanks to David, I was an eager student of the game and had no trouble making the team. I was really looking forward to the rest of my years at Endike.

But the enjoyment and freedom I had found at Endike came to a sudden end when my father showed up and informed me that he was giving up the sea to take care of me. While this turn of events thrilled me at first, it soon turned into a major disappointment. I had been attending a school I enjoyed immensely, and had gone from the B stream to the A stream and was first in my class academically. Now my greatest fears became reality when I discovered that I would have to take three buses to get to Endike High School. It soon became apparent that I would have to change schools.

CHAPTER 2

I had a lot of mixed feelings when I left the orphanage, but giving away some of my most prized possessions helped me to assuage my guilt at leaving my friends. My stamp collection became the property of Alex Story, and my comic book collection went to his brother William. I knew that I would likely never see them again, but this proved to be untrue as I would indeed see them one more time, but on that occasion I would feel like an outsider. Unfortunately, my way of seeing things had changed tremendously, but theirs would remain the same.

My father and I quickly settled into our new domestic life together. It was a drastic change for both of us, and neither of us really knew what to expect. He had purchased a house at 111 Alliance Avenue and had gone out and bought all new furniture, and even a new Pye television set. Most of our neighbors had pay-for-view tellys—the type with a parking-meter slot on the top—from which they could obtain a certain amount of viewing time by feeding sixpence or shillings into the hungry contraption. It wasn't long before I was the most popular kid in the neighborhood; I had a houseful of friends over every day just to watch our telly. Of course, I always made sure the house was empty by the time my father arrived home from work. Had he known that our home had become the neighborhood hangout, he would have been somewhat upset.

My father was putting in rather long hours at a large grocery store, trying to learn the business. He knew no other life than that of a seaman, and he soon discovered that he was totally unprepared for any other type of employment. We both had a number of adjustments to make, especially living together as a family.

The move had forced me to change schools. I had sadly left behind my friends at Endike and was forced to start from scratch at Wilberforce High. The two schools proved to be exact opposites. While Endike was situated on the outskirts of the city and had its own soccer, cricket, and rugby fields, Wilberforce was dead in the heart of the city and didn't have anything but a bunch of inner-city kids who liked to fight. My new life was totally different, but I had little trouble fitting in. I guess being with a number of kids with mixed backgrounds while at the orphanage had helped me to adjust to different situations and diverse people.

Wilberforce, like Endike, was an all-boys school, and being such, things happened there that seldom occurred in the U.S. public school system. I was in my first week at the new school and was paying attention to my teacher, when one of the students sitting next to me prodded me, then pointed to the rear of the classroom. There, in all his glory, was another student with his penis in his hand "whacking off." Before long, a couple of his mates joined him. This was going on while the teacher was occupied writing on the blackboard. Talk about culture shock! Predictably, the participants found it not only amusing, but also exhilarating and daring. I have often wondered just what excuse they would have given for their bizarre behavior if they had been caught. To my good fortune, I discovered that I was now accepted by the class as one of them because I had not snitched on the perpetrators.

All of our teachers were males, which made for a very spartan daily exercise. But just across the way was a girls' school that had a number of very attractive, large-bosomed teachers on staff. At lunch break, a few of us would infiltrate the grounds of the girls' school and "Eye Spy" the ladies' bathroom. It was an almost daily ritual for us to sneak a peek through the window to watch one particular luscious teacher remove her cardigan and bra to wash. To us this was a major X-rated event. Most of us had seen bare female flesh only on the pages of *National Geographic* in the school library. To see the female breast in wonderful living color and in motion . . . well, that was an experience that none of us would ever forget. Unfortunately, we were watching Madam X bathing one day when one of our group decided that it was an excellent opportunity to whack off. He was in the middle of a stroke when another female teacher caught us in the off-limits area of the girls'-school grounds.

It must have been somewhat amusing to the teacher as we all shot off in a flash, attempting to best Roger Bannister's four-minute mile. Unfortunately, our mate was running and trying to hoist his pants at the same time, and he was nabbed before he could clear the grounds. Naturally, he was unable to explain his actions to our headmaster, and I'm certain no explanation was suitable for his parents. There was not enough blarney in the world to save him on this one. Being true to his mates, he never told on the rest of us, but it didn't prevent the headmaster from calling a school meeting in the auditorium. To a subdued student body, it was explained that if anyone got caught at the girls' school again, the culprit would be sent to Dartmouth Prison, or someplace like that!

My grades at Wilberforce, at best, were mediocre. I had gone from the top of my classes at Endike to the bottom quarter at Wilberforce. I took to missing most of my afternoon classes to go to the dock area and visit William Wilberforce's house. I spent hours walking the house, which had been made into a museum. I was fascinated by the displays of items from by-gone days. The theme of the museum was slavery, which William Wilberforce had helped to outlaw in England. I often found myself daydreaming there. When I looked at the stocks and chains, I tried to imagine what it would have been like to be a slave transported across the sea in the belly of a sailing ship, chained and shackled, taken away from loved ones and the land of one's birth. There was even a short essay in the museum about the first slave brought to England. A rich plantation owner had sent the slave to a friend as a gift. The friend, who had never before seen a black man, thought he was merely dirty and attempted to clean him by scrubbing. Of course, no amount of scrubbing would turn the black man white, but the friend would not give up. The scrubbings were a daily routine until the slave finally died of pneumonia. It's hard to believe that the story is true, but it's part of the recorded history of slavery in England. After numerous visits to Wilberforce House, I decided to take school serious again, and my grades soon began to improve until I managed to get them back into the A stream again.

I knew my father was not very happy being away from the sea, but to his credit, he tried his best to make a home for us. But he was spending more and more time at work, and soon began to spend his free time at the local pub. I cannot ever remember him being drunk, but he would imbibe until he came home in a sullen mood. It was obvious that before long he would find an excuse to return to the sea. I really felt sorry for him, but I was afraid that when he went back to the merchant navy I would once again have to move.

One day I was propped up in my father's chair, watching a soccer game on the telly, when he came home with a woman and a couple of children—a boy and a girl. "Son, I want you to meet your new mom," he said to me. I knew I was imagining things, and I only stared at my father as he repeated his words. I had always prided myself on being fully shock resistant, but my father's announcement had quickly shattered that myth.

I had yet to utter a word when my father continued, "This is your new brother, Peter, and your new sister, Mary." My only thought was, Holy shit, Dad, what department store did you find them at? Whichever one it was, take 'em back.

I was still speechless when he ordered me to take my "new" brother and sister outside to show them the yard. Obedient to the end, I led my department-store siblings out into our twenty-feet-by-fifty-feet backyard to show them the two rhubarb plants. We stayed out there just long enough for Dad to lay their mother, which was the only reason we had been sent out on the grand tour in the first place. I was convinced that my new brother was brain-dead when he actually started questioning me about the damned rhubarb plants and how long they took to grow. The three of us shuffled around the yard until my father yelled for us to come in.

My new mother and her children stayed for only a week, but in that short period of time, she had me convinced that she was the most wonderful person in the world. I was wrong about my new brother, too, for he was not nearly as brain-dead as I had first thought. And my new sister proved to be a darling little thing. I was beginning to think that maybe things would work out after all. After the pleasant week had passed, the three of them left to go back to York to pack up their things so they could set up house in our home.

When they had gone, my father sat me down and asked what I had thought of his lady and her children. I told him that I liked her. She had been nice to me and had piled compliment upon compliment on me. It was only then that he told me that their last name was Simpson and that he had not actually married her yet. He said that he wanted my input before he made the final decision. If I had said that I didn't like her, my father would not have gone through with the marriage.

While Mrs. Simpson and her children were back in York, my father decided to buy a used car. He thought that since we were about to increase the size of our family, we would need transportation to get around. No longer would a motorcycle meet our basic travel needs. He bought an older-model black Ford and parked it in the alley behind our house. He then went out and purchased a book on driving. After studying the book for about a week, my father went out on his first drive and promptly sideswiped the wall of the alley. He parked the car and went back to the drawing board to study the book some more. Hitting the wall must have frightened him more than he let on, because he also decided to take driving lessons before he got back behind the wheel.

The week before he was to return to York to pick up our new family, he took me for a ride out in the country. My father should have taken a few more driving lessons, because we hadn't been on the road more than half an hour before he sideswiped a woman riding a bicycle. I was busy daydreaming when I heard the dull thud and looked back to see the lady in a ditch with a bicycle lying next to her. We stopped to see if she was injured. When she refused to go to the hospital, we took her to her house. My dad and she were talking, and she said that it was the first time she had ever been in an accident. My father's poorly thought-out reply was, "There's a first time for everything." I don't know how the lady felt about my father's statement, but I could have crawled under the linoleum!

My father left for York the next week to marry his sweetheart, and I stayed home. I often wondered if he had really gotten married on that trip, since I had not gotten an invitation to the wedding. That seemed strange to me, but my father was always doing some very strange things. But about three days after he had left, he returned with his new wife and my new brother and sister. While I was helping take the baggage out of the car, I couldn't help but check to see if there were any more damages incurred on the trip to York and back. Surprisingly, there were none.

It appeared at first that things would work out well—until I discovered that my stepmother was not all she had seemed to be. I soon learned that she and her offspring were perfect in every way, while my father and I continually fell short of her standards. This became very evident when I took a trip with her to visit her parents—my new grandparents.

There was a river behind her parents' house, and, never one to pass up a chance to fish, I borrowed a fishing pole from my new grandfather and took Peter out to try our luck. We hadn't been fishing more than an hour when Peter slipped on the wet bank and fell headfirst into the dingy water. I started to laugh hysterically. After I had regained my composure, I ran over to help my thoroughly soaked stepbrother to the safety of the bank. Naturally, I could only see the humor in his accident, but Peter could only see the shame, and was soon on his way back home, crying for all he was worth. Out of a well-developed sense of self-preservation, I followed close behind. When we got to the house, he was still crying so hard that he was unable to tell his mother what had happened. When I interceded to tell her that he had slipped and fallen into the muddy river, she immediately became irate. "Peter did not just fall into the water. He must have had a heatstroke," she screamed, at the same time stroking poor Peter's head. It was all I could do to keep a straight face.

When Peter finally stopped crying, he told his mother how mean I had been for laughing at him and not getting him out of the water immediately. He even managed to add, "I could have drowned, Mommy." I knew I was in trouble when my stepmother squinted her eyes for a second, then sent me straight off to the bedroom for the rest of the day.

I was upstairs trying to figure out just what I had done wrong when I overheard my stepmother's father talking. "Now, dear, don't you think you overreacted with Jim?" "No I don't. After all, Jim could have drowned poor Peter," she replied, obviously still very agitated.

I could hear them still carrying on a conversation, but they had toned it down to a point that I could no longer tell what they were saying. A long five minutes later, my new grandfather came to my room to talk to me. He told me his daughter was a pain in the arse, always was and always would be, but as long as this was his house, she was not going to punish me for no reason. I walked down the stairs behind him and made a quick exit through the nearest door. It was only the first catastrophe.

A couple of days later Peter needed a rubber band and went into our grandfather's drawer to get one. To me it was no big thing, but when Grandfather discovered that someone had been in his drawer, he asked who it was. Peter answered that it had been he, and Grandfather merely stated that in the future if we wanted something to ask him for it. Once again, my dear stepmother fell off her broom. "No, Dad, it wasn't Peter. He is just trying to protect Jim. Jim must have taken that rubber band." Even after Peter told her again that he had taken it, she still would not believe that the perfect child of a perfect mother would do such a dastardly thing. A bloody rubber band, and World War III was about to break out in the Simpson household!

When we got back to Hull, the situation with my stepmother reached a climax. At every opportunity she told my father what an evil character I was. My father tried valiantly to keep the peace in the family, but his effort was made worthless by my stepmother's constant troublemaking. I was beginning to feel a lot like Cinderella.

Most of the stories my father heard from my stepmother were outright baloney, and both of us knew it. He would berate me in front of her, then behind her back he would give me money to go to the pictures or do something just to keep me away from her.

My father was still working long hours at the grocery store, which further angered my stepmother. She thought it was below her station in life to be married to a grocery clerk. She felt that my father should own his own grocery store. My father realized that he was not yet ready to go into business on his own, but her continual carping forced him to relent. He found a grocery store for sale not far from our home, and bought it. Since the store had a large living quarters in the rear, he rented out our house on Alliance Avenue to a friend and his family and moved us into the apartment behind the grocery store.

As an owner, my father was forced to spend even more time at the store. The hours grew longer, and the money became shorter. He would be up before first light to buy fresh vegetables at the market, then work all day in the store. My stepmother always found a reason why she could not help in the store. If it was not one thing, it was another. I think her real reason was that she wanted to watch the telly and do her nails. As long as my father didn't disagree with her, their relationship was fine. On the other hand, she never stopped trying to prove to him that I was evil incarnate. It got so bad that I quit playing with Peter altogether because I grew tired of taking the punishment for both our mess-ups. The way I had it figured, if I was going to get berated, it would be for my own indiscretions. I didn't need Peter's help to get into trouble. I could do it very well on my own.

I had new friends from school and the neighborhood who, like me, were particularly gifted at scrumping and having fun. Of course, our idea of fun seldom agreed with adults' ideas of fun.

In our new neighborhood, a brother/sister bully team had the bad habit of taking anything they pleased from the neighborhood kids. A lot of my mates had "bogies"—soapbox cars—that were routinely taken over by this pair of juvenile delinquents. For some reason, I decided to build my own bogie just to see what the bullies would do to me. After a few days of stripping old vegetable boxes and reassembling them, I had a bogie that would tempt any bully. My father bought me the wheels, and the contraption was soon ready for its test run. I took apart one of my stepmother's practically unused brooms and utilized the handle for a pole to propel my four-wheeled monster down the street. I had a friend in the driver's seat as the bogie approached Mach 1—well, it was moving pretty damned fast.

I was amazed at the ease at which the bogie sped down the street, but so were the neighborhood bullies. They stopped the bogie at the end of the street and claimed it under their might-makes-right law. They said they had found it and they were going to keep it. This did not sit well with me at all, and an argument ensued. I ended it rather quickly when I broke the pole I was carrying over the head of the bully brother, then threatened the sister with even worse. Unused to being challenged, they backed down.

I became a minor hero with my mates, but I knew I would be in major trouble with my parents. I was not surprised when I found the two of them waiting for me when I got home. In no uncertain terms, my father told me that I was not to beat the neighborhood kids, especially if their parents were customers of the grocery store. Then my stepmother got onto me for breaking her broom. I felt somewhat dejected until my father came to my room later, wanting to know the blow-by-blow details of the altercation. It was more apparent than ever that he was willing to do whatever was necessary to appease his bride.

My father's business was not doing well, but that didn't keep my stepmother from putting additional strain on him, demanding more and more than they could afford. My father kept giving her what she wanted, and managed to keep a good sense of humor about it.

Once, in front of a number of our regular customers, my

stepmother ordered my father in her demanding way to pick up a pack of cigs for her. With a humble "Yes, dearie" he left the store to run his little errand for her. He returned a few minutes later with a five-pack of Woodbine cigarettes. She immediately became irate and started screaming at him, demanding that he take them back and get her normal brand, Players. Everyone in the store witnessed her tirade. They couldn't understand her outrage, which only fed her anger at being insulted in front of the "common folk."

That night she threatened to leave my father because of his inconsiderate act. I secretly hoped that my father would offer to help her pack her bags, but such was not the case. He relented and apologized, burying the barb a little deeper.

It was no surprise to me that my father's business failed and we had to move back into our house on Alliance Avenue; my stepmother's extravagant spending and my father's lack of business acumen had left us in financial straits. My father was forced to go back to sea to support his family. I didn't like the idea of being left to face my stepmother alone, but I knew that it was the only option my father had left. It was not long before he went down to the Seaman's Hall and got a berthing on a ship.

He went to sea and left my stepmother in sole charge. She soon made the wicked witch in the *Wizard of Oz* look like Mary Poppins. Soon, I was being told how to sleep in bed with my hands inside the covers. How many sheets of toilet paper I could use to wipe my arse, and on and on. Life was becoming a bigger bitch than the one I was living with. I must admit that my trips to York to visit my stepmother's parents were the only highlights of my stay with her. I often wondered how such nice people could have raised such an evil bitch.

School was going pretty well and I was finally at the age where I had to take the fifteen-plus admission test for the merchant navy school. My scores were good but not good enough to get me a higher education, so I decided to go into the army upon graduation from high school. My main goal in life was to get away from that Loch Ness monster that my father had married.

I went to the army recruiter and was sold a bill of goods that I was only too happy to buy, and took the test for R.E.M.E. (Royal Electric and Mechanical Engineers). I passed the test with flying colors. In my mind I had really accomplished something worthwhile, and when the headmaster congratulated me in front of my stepmother, she merely replied, "Just a formality. Anyone can pass that test." Just the support I needed!

My father came home from sea a couple of weeks before I was to report to Hadrian's Camp in Cumberland. He was pleased that I had taken that manly step to serve my country, but I would find out later that he was not too pleased to allow me to come home on furlough.

I said my good-byes, and it was quite obvious that my dear stepmother was only too happy to see me out of her way. I took the bus from Alliance Avenue to Paddington Station as a new adventure was about to begin.

CHAPTER 3

When I arrived at Paddington Station, my train was met by a regular army NCO who had already taken charge of a half dozen recruits before I got there. We grouped together to shoot the breeze and convince each other how brave we were to take these first steps into manhood. Looking back, I realize how naive we really were. The NCO treated us like we were his own kids, asking if we wanted something to eat or drink. He told us that anything we wanted was ours for the asking. I realize now that he was only trying to keep any of us from going AWOL before we got on the train. If we had, it would surely have been his arse.

The ride to Hadrian's Camp was as enjoyable a train ride as

one could want. I should have stayed on that bloody train all the way to Scotland.

Upon arriving at the camp, we were treated to a display of the real army way of life. We were quickly informed that we were nothing but a bunch of ragamuffins and that we were not there for a vacation. Could have beat me! Before we ever saw the inside of a barracks, we were escorted to the barbershop for a haircut. I would later experience a serious bout of déjà vu when I got a repeat of this treatment upon entering the U.S. Army. We were then marched/herded to the barracks for a good night's sleep. I wanted to go home.

As I rested on my bunk, I began to give some serious thought to what I had just done. Here I was only fifteen years old, with a twelve-year enlistment staring me in the face. I would be an old man before I got out of the service.

The shock effect wore off by the next day when I figured out that the crap we had been handed the day before was nothing more than a put-on. I guess they wanted to see how many of us youngsters would start crying for their mamas. The regular army NCOs introduced us to our school NCOs, who quickly explained the pecking order. The NCOs who were our every-day supervisors were students, just like us. When you enlisted in the army in England, you got regular army pay but had to go through a four-year apprenticeship program before you were assigned to a regular unit. It was like college, only better because you got paid. Damn, was I smart for joining the army!

Our day was divided into two separate programs. Half the day was spent in the classroom, while the other half was spent on military training. In the morning, we might be out on the firing range or drilling on the parade field. The afternoon would find us in class learning our military trade. I had asked for and been approved for armorer training, so my main classroom subjects were focused on weapons and weapons systems. This was really neat stuff for a fifteen-year-old. I had a decent place to live, good food to eat, friends to party with, and all kinds of weapons to play with. Life was good. As long as I kept myself out of trouble and obeyed army regulations, I could take pass and play around with the local girls. Since I was in uniform, I could go into any local pub and really make an arse out of myself. I was in heaven, and I hadn't even died yet.

I teamed up with a guy from Northern Ireland whose name was Paddy. He told me that he was five feet three inches, but I had serious reservations about that. This bloke was not only a charmer with the birds but he knew how to have a good time while he was at it. Since my own experience with girls at that point was a pet here and a slap there, I was very interested in learning the proper way to go about things. Paddy proved to be a great teacher.

It wasn't long before classwork began to grow old, and I couldn't wait to do things I was learning about for real. I would sell my soul to go out to the firing range, and took great joy in shooting the Bren gun. Hell, I liked shooting so well that I would actually ask for more ammo in order to fire downrange with the Enfield. Any fifteen-year-old recruit will tell you the Enfield's recoil was so bad that, after he fired a few rounds, he would have to get up and walk back to the firing line. During the first four months at Hadrian, I doubt if I ever lost the bruise on my right shoulder. But I loved it. It got to the point where I was saying, "To hell with the schooling, just let me shoot the gun."

Our first dance at Hadrian's Camp was an affair to remember. The locals had sponsored a dance and had invited us to attend to keep their daughters company. Talk about hiring wolves to guard the lambs! All those young girls and so many horny soldiers in the same place at the same time—it was a recipe for disaster.

I put on my best civvies and let Paddy grease my hair and put that cute curl in the front with the DA (duck's ass) in the back. Not quite a teddy boy, just a poor imitation of one. It had never occurred to me that I had never been dancing in my life. All my energy had been directed toward changing the "untouched" status of my virginity.

At the dance, I had the overpowering feeling that I was making a fool out of myself; however, my dancing partner was convinced she was cutting a rug with Fred Astaire. So who was I to contradict her misconceptions? The more she swooned over me, the more I imagined the night would bring about the fall of my overripe virginity. Paddy had foretold that this was exactly how things were supposed to go, and Paddy wouldn't lie to me.

As the night wore on, she greased my ego so much that I became convinced that I, James William Walker, was a ladies' man extraordinaire. It was time! Nearly choking on my own words, I summoned the courage to ask my lady outside, allaying her fears by claiming that it was hot and stuffy inside. Once outside I quickly stole a kiss, then a longer one, until my hand was finally resting on her breast. The loud slap that followed was heard inside over the noise of the band. So much for Paddy's words of wisdom!

The girl did eventually become my sweetheart, but with the qualification that there would be no sex before marriage. Four more years of celibacy! No thank you! This kid wasn't going to wait around that long to find out if he was a man or not. So I said good-bye to the daughter of one of the wealthiest scions in town, which proved that I didn't have the common sense to pour piss out of a boot if the instructions were printed on the heel.

Just before my first leave, we had to take a physical test. My schoolwork had been up to military standards, and I thought I was physically up to par. But was I ever wrong! Until that time, we had been doing just routine PT. We had no idea that it was not about to prepare us for what the army had in mind. We were marched in formation to a staging area where we were issued rucks, weapons, blank ammunition, water, and gear. We were then broken up into four-man teams and given a map. We spread our map out on the ground to have a look. Somewhat confused, I asked Paddy where we were going. "Well, Jim, we're right here, and we're going there," he said, pointing at a spot on the map. "Screw that, Paddy, how far is it?" I said, not really wanting an answer. "Oh, about twenty miles," he answered.

I knew then that I really did want to go home. Our hike was not to be a walk in the sun but a forced march.

We started off at a run, which eventually became a rapid walk. When I couldn't keep up, my teammates yelled and cursed at me to hurry up. I had already gone about a mile, and there were only nineteen more to do, but I was quite sure that I would never make the end of the hike. It was then that I decided I couldn't let my mates down. I said to myself, "The bloody hell with it! I'll bust my arse to keep up, and if my lungs collapse and my heart stops, so be it."

By the end of the next mile, I had my second wind, and I knew if my muscles could handle the strain, I could make it to the finish. We all made it, and we did it as a team. I had learned a valuable lesson. You never let your team down no matter what the cost to you. It would become a very valuable lesson a few years down the road.

The first six months of training finally came to an end, and we were granted two weeks of furlough. I felt a little bad parting from the guys I had been with during the initial training, but I had the consolation of knowing that we would all be back together in a couple of weeks. The night before we left, we had a hell of a fire in one of the storage areas where blank ammo and weapons were kept. I had witnessed some pretty impressive bonfires during Guy Fawkes Day, but I had never seen anything quite like the spectacle of the ammo dump going up. The firemen could do little but let it burn while they tried to keep the fire from spreading to other buildings nearby. The blank ammo kept exploding in a spectacular display of colors. It was as good as what the Americans celebrated on their Independence Day.

I arrived home on leave only to find out that my father was still at sea. My stepmother quickly pointed out that she thought it would be a good idea if I stayed at my uncle Ronald's house across town on Alexander Cresent. It was no problem for me. Uncle Ron was my favorite uncle, and I would rather spend my leave time with him than watch my evil stepmother practice her craft. At that time, I had no idea that I would never see my father again.

I spent my time at Uncle Ron's between the billiard hall and the movie house, still trying to take care of a nagging case of virginity. I even dated Uncle Ron's good-looking sister-in-law, who was my age, and managed to get slapped a few times. It was during my stay with Uncle Ron that he told me about my natural mother's living in the United States. Once again, he asked me if I wanted to go live with her. I told him that I would. What English kid in his right mind wouldn't want to go to the United States of America and eat hot dogs and hamburgers every day? Hell, I might even run into a real gangster, or even a cowboy!

By the time my furlough was up and I left to go back to camp, I had forgotten the conversation. But a short time later I got a letter from Uncle Ron telling me to make a collect call to a number in the U.S.A. at a specific time on a specific date to talk to my mother. Excitedly, I followed his instructions, and for the first time in twelve years I heard my mother's voice. We had a long conversation, and after all the niceties were taken care of, my mother asked me if I wanted to come and live with her in Gary, Indiana. Naturally, I had no idea where Gary, Indiana, was, but I told her I would except for the matter of a twelve-year enlistment in the army. Before she hung up, she told me not to worry about my enlistment as it was being taken care of. Sure it is, I thought as I walked back to my barracks, and the queen's my grandmother.

I was called into the regular army company commander's office about a month later and told that my enlistment was over. My mother had bought my way out of the army. She had reimbursed the military the expenses it had incurred to train me, and once again I was a civilian. Three days later, I was on a train back to Hull.

I stayed with my uncle Ron and got a job in the Hull Co-op store as an optical engineer. It was a nice title for a kid who ground eyeglass lenses to fit frames. In less than two months, I found myself in London with passport and visa in hand, waiting to board a Pan American jet bound for Chicago, Illinois. Wherever that was.

CHAPTER 4

My uncle Ronald took me to the airport, wished me happiness, and shook my hand before leaving me behind to return home. A short time later, we were notified that the flight was canceled due to dense fog. While that seemed to distress some of the passengers, I was overjoyed because I thought it would give me a chance to look around London. But things just never seem to work out the way we want them to; I soon found myself sitting in a large hotel lobby, waiting to be assigned a room. Three hours later, I was sitting in my room with nothing to do but read the newspaper; my earlier dream of sightseeing in the fog was shattered.

The following morning, December 11, 1960, I was airborne, destination Chicago, Illinois, by way of Boston, Massachusetts. The flight was uneventful except for my tour of the cockpit. I believe the only reason I was granted this privilege was that the crew were all Americans, and they found my accent entertaining.

After a short stopover in Boston, I found myself going through customs at O'Hare Airport in Chicago. A short distance away, I saw my mother pointing toward me and yelling. I was only four years old when she left me at the station with my father. I was now three months shy of my sixteenth birthday.

A dozen hugs and kisses later, my mother introduced me to her brother, Bob, and his wife. I believe she was Bob's second wife or third. Within minutes, we were on our way to Gary, Indiana, about thirty-five miles from Chicago. Because of the snow and ice and the tollbooths, the thirty-minute trip turned

45

out to be an hour and a half. During the journey, Uncle Bob took great pleasure in telling me that his wife was formally a "hillbilly," whatever that was, but that since he had married her he had managed to turn her into a "mountain william." He broke out in laughter when he told me this story, so he must have found it funny. Me, I didn't have any idea what he was talking about.

Our first stop was the Indiana Sandwich Shop in Gary, where I met my grandmother, Mary Taboada, for the very first time. She was the manager of the restaurant and took great pleasure in stacking my plate with french fries and making me a huge hamburger that extended out beyond the edge of my plate. While enjoying my meal, I couldn't help looking around in somewhat of a daze. Here I was in America! I had finally made it.

I took great joy in perusing the price list of the restaurant's fare that was tacked boldly to the walls—big signs that announced the prices of the meals. This was meaningless to the average American, but to me it was my first experience with dollars and cents. I had always been exposed to pounds and pence. I was definitely in America!

I arrived at my new home, 336 Madison Street, and for the first time met my stepfather, Chris Nasoff. He was an unimposing, short, heavyset man with a disarming smile. Through the following years, I would learn to love and respect this kind and affectionate man, himself a former immigrant from Macedonia.

Christmas brought a multitude of presents from my mother and stepfather and their families. My most prized present was a 20-gauge shotgun I received from Uncle Bob. I would spend many a day roaming the fields of northern Indiana, hunting rabbits with Chris and his best friend, Paul Milenkoff.

For three weeks, I had the pure pleasure of doing nothing. If I was not watching the telly, I was visiting with long-lost relatives. Life was good, and I was enjoying it immensely in this strange new land of gangsters and cowboys.

One day ran into the next as my mother and I made up for lost time. On the occasions she was at the hospital working as a registered nurse, I was out running the highways with Chris, visiting with his family and friends.

As all good things must come to an end, so did mine. The Christmas holidays were soon over, and I found myself at Horace Mann High School, enrolling to attend classes once again. The administrator told my mother that since my new school system didn't recognize my high school in England, I would have to enroll as a freshman and go through another four years of secondary schooling before I could graduate. I guess after America had won its independence from the British, they must have figured we had gotten real stupid.

I was in for one hell of a culture shock when I walked into Horace Mann High School for the first day of class. It was coed, and it didn't take me long to discover that more girls were enrolled than boys. This was a great blessing for me, and I soon found myself more interested in the girls than in what the teachers were saying. At times, I spent the entire class passing notes to girls. My accent and the fact that I was different from the local boys led the girls to find me attractive. This was the same James William Walker who would have put a squirrel on his head to get a little female attention back in England. Unfortunately, my newfound popularity seriously overinflated my ego, and before long I was bumping heads with some of my teachers. I was caught chewing gum in class by one of the teachers, who scoffed at me in front of the class by saying, "Just because you're in a free country doesn't mean you can chew gum!" Where did this fool think I had come from—Red China?

I soon discovered that a number of my teachers were still a little upset over the Revolutionary War and frequently took great pains to point out to me who the final victor was. I didn't have the heart to tell them that we called their "revolution" a "rebellion." It probably wouldn't have scored any points for the British Empire.

During the school year, I discovered that Texans were still mad at the Mexicans, the Yankees up north were still mad at the Rebs down south, the Japanese were still Japs, and the

Germans were still Krauts and Nazis. Americans were quick to rile and slow to forget.

To my male classmates, I soon became the English kid who was trying to make time with all the ladies. Before long, I was knocking heads with some of the bolder ones who took exception to my flirting with "their" girls. Fortunately for me, the young ladies didn't appreciate being labeled someone's property, and seemed more drawn to me than before.

I never claimed to be a pure and innocent soul, but I tried to keep my profanity in check in my new country. Sure, I still occasionally used words like *bloody, sod, bugger*, and *shag*, but they never seemed to bother anyone. Besides, no one knew what they meant, so they never threw them back at me. But the first time someone called me "motherfucker," I only stared at the kid with a confused look on my face. I had no idea what he was talking about. Jimmy Meyers, my best friend, pulled me aside and informed me that I had just been dealt a most grievous insult. Another friend, Jimmy Jenkins, encouraged me to knock the kid's block off for insulting me in such a manner. I was reluctant to punish the lad, because I was truly not offended by the name he had called me. I told Jenkins that maybe he thought he was paying me a compliment because he had probably fucked his own mother. But when I repeated this to my antagonist, he took offense and swung at me. I was forced to give him a sound thrashing. He never called me a motherfucker again.

I took a lot of profanity from a lot of kids, because it didn't really offend me. They didn't understand that what was offensive in their culture was meaningless in mine, so we traded a lot of horrible insults without anyone's really getting offended.

The day came when I finally lost my virginity to a girl named Mary. I was immediately head over heels in love and swore that I would never point my wanker at another. As fate would have it, former virgins should never make promises they cannot keep. But at the time, Mary was my girl, and she would be mine forever. Needless to say, school was no longer the boring place it used to be.

I was in my junior year at Horace Mann High School when

integration took place in the United States. That's right, racism and segregation were still alive and thriving in the North in 1962. This new turn of events had the school and the white parents in an uproar. Many parents pulled their kids out of the public school system and put them in private institutions. Being an outsider, I guessed that the American Civil War had been fought for naught.

During this major change in the federal law, I was still madly in love with my Mary, and soon took exception when a black kid named Johnny Spears informed me that he wanted to fuck her. I had been in the United States long enough to know that even alone, that word had evil connotations. Spears and I had a major altercation right in the middle of study hall. It started and ended when I picked up a desk and hit him over the head with it. The incident did not sit well with the principal, and I was kicked out of school. If I had hit a white kid, I would have been given a three-day suspension, and that would have been the end of the matter. But with the new integration policy in effect, the school decided to make this a racial issue, even after I told them it wouldn't have made a difference what color the lad had been—nobody insulted my girlfriend. They were unimpressed.

My parents were also unimpressed and assumed that I would immediately go to enroll in another school. Instead, I went down to the army recruiter to see if I would have any problems enlisting. It appeared that the quick trip across the Atlantic had erased all memories from my past life. I was doomed to repeat the same mistake I made in England.

The recruiter told me that not only would my British high-school diploma be recognized, but I would be given my choice of training. I believed him. No one offered to tell me at the time that the ability to fog a mirror was the only requirement for securing an enlistment in the American Army.

But there was still the problem of my age. I was only seventeen years old and I would need parental consent to enlist. It took me two weeks to convince my mother to sign the necessary paperwork. I had to tell her that I would not enroll in another high school, and if she didn't let me go into the service right then and there, I would become a bum until my eighteenth birthday when I could enlist without her approval. She signed the enlistment papers with the promise that I would get an American GED as quick as I could. She was not as impressed with my English high-school diploma as my recruiter had been.

CHAPTER 5

It was a chilly day in October 1962 when my parents dropped me off at the Gary, Indiana, Selective Service Board. From there I would be transported, with other draftees and volunteers, to a Chicago, Illinois, Selective Service Office for physicals and swearing in. Some of the draftees with us were tearfully saying their good-byes to family and girlfriends. During Basic, those poor saps would be constantly informed that some dude named Jody was banging their girlfriends while they were away defending their country against enemies both foreign and domestic.

By 10:00 A.M., we were on our way to Chicago. It didn't take a genius to distinguish the draftees from the volunteers. The volunteers were cheering and horsing around; the draftees were sitting by themselves, looking as if they were headed for the gallows.

I had been through this routine in England, so it came as no surprise to me when, upon our arrival, we were greeted by an oversize, horribly ugly NCO with a bloodline that likely included Neanderthals and mountain gorillas. He began screaming at the top of his lungs for us to dismount the bus and form up ranks. Naturally, few of the recruits on the bus had any idea what

Attila was talking about. It took time and a major effort for these poor civilians to form anything that would remotely resemble a line. Ranks were totally out of the question.

We were finally herded into a large room and ordered to undress down to our undershorts. We were given a plastic bag for our valuables, then formed back into lines to begin receiving our physicals. We were told to follow the yellow line painted on the floor that led from station to station, where we were prodded, poked, goosed, gored, grabbed, and gabbed at before being forced to respond to inane questions designed to determine if we were mentally and emotionally capable of killing our country's enemies. I was quite certain that the examiners paid little attention to our answers, because I heard one draftee admit that he would rather "play" with boys than with girls. But it did him no good, for not long after that he was standing right beside me saying "I (state your name) do solemnly swear . . ."

We were rushed through the series of stations, carrying our physical folders in our hands, as clerks, medics, and doctors scribbled short notes that would determine the next two or three years of our lives. I would discover a short time later that the only thing quicker than an army physical is an army meal.

Finally, we were all lined up in the last room, where we were ordered to drop our drawers and bend over. This was my first exposure to "blind trust." We held this vulnerable pose until someone disguised as a doctor passed down the line to our rear checking our exposed posteriors for foreign matter, microscopic wildlife, ass-teroids, and other debris from inner space. If you were found to be pure and "holesome," you received a slap on the rump, which meant that you had just passed your army physical. I was both relieved and excited when I received my brand. We were then lined up in even rows while a lieutenant entered the room to give us a short but well-rehearsed speech about how we were about to join the finest army in the world, etc. When he finished with the PR pitch, he called us to attention and administered the oath of allegiance. In seconds, we were officially members of the United States Army. To welcome us to our new lives, we were each given brown-bag lunches and ordered not to leave the building.

We then received our first set of instructions as U.S. Army soldiers. We were taught how to hurry up and wait for a long time. After we had mastered that, stylish green buses were sent to transport us to the railroad station for the trip to our first training center, Fort Knox, Kentucky.

I could hardly wait to begin training. My recruiter had generously given me a written contract, so I knew what lay in store for me. I was guaranteed Basic Combat Training, Advanced Individual Training, then an assignment to Europe. Those poor, stupid draftees didn't have any guarantees at all. Well, that's what they deserved for not being smart enough to enlist. Crowded into the passenger cars, our journey to Fort Knox began. Once again, the enlistees cheered and horsed around; the draftees cried.

We soon discovered that the army took great pains to make sure that all recruits arrived at training posts during the hours of darkness. I believe that this was designed to keep us from being overwhelmed by the excitement of seeing all the wonders of a military post at one time. Some of the draftees said that it was so we couldn't identify escape routes. Anyway, we arrived at a railroad station in Kentucky at about two o'clock in the morning and were transported to the post in large, open trucks affectionately called "cattle cars." It was amazing how many of us fit into one of those trucks. By 4:00 A.M., we were lined up and introduced to the NCO who would serve as our drill sergeant for the next eight weeks. He was another one of those really large, ugly NCOs with dubious antecedents. I had no idea where the army found those guys.

Our drill sergeant looked over our hastily organized formation, then informed us that he had never seen such an inept bunch of scumbags in his life. He wanted to know what we were doing in "his" army. I think it was a rhetorical question. There was some muffled sobbing from deep within the ranks, but in all fairness to the draftees, I did hear a fair amount of snickering, too. Welcome to Fort Knox, Kentucky.

We were then transported to a supply building where we

were issued bedding. This unexpected act of kindness restored our faith in humanity. But just when we thought we would be able to get some sleep, we discovered that the bedding had been issued just so we would have the proper tools to make our bunks. As a matter of fact, our beloved troglodyte of a drill sergeant let us make up our bunks about twenty times until he was satisfied that we had exceeded his and the U.S. Army's specifications. I believe that this was the last time we saw our drill sergeant happy.

By the time we had completed Bunk Making 101, it was daylight and the beginning of our first real day in the army. We were ushered outside, placed in formation, then marched to a building where we had our financial needs taken care of. Each recruit was given twenty-two dollars temporary pay to get us through until payday.

We were then ushered to the next building, where we formed four lines for haircuts. The civilian barbers buzzed through our hair like Australian sheep shearers. When they were done, they charged us fifty cents for a haircut that a blind man could have done.

At the next building, we were fitted for and issued our uniforms. The fatigue, khaki, and class-A green pants had to have their seams sewn, for which we were charged another fifty cents each. We were beginning to discover why they called it temporary pay—you were only going to get to keep it for a little while.

When we were finished, we stored our clothes on our bunks and were led to the PX, where we bought all the toiletries and personal items that we would need, and some others that we would not be allowed to use. These items, such as tooth powder, toothbrush, shoe polish, and handkerchiefs, were to be used only for our footlocker display. By the end of the day, each of us was down to about $1.50 of our original $22. Not bad for a whole day of shopping! But after all this running around, our DI still wasn't finished with us. A box had been placed on each of our bunks, along with a piece of paper, an envelope, and a pencil. We were ordered to put our civilian clothes in the box, secure it, and put our names on it. The army would store the boxes for us until we finished basic training. Our DI then ordered us to write letters to our mothers and tell them everything was fine and that the army was taking good care of us. We were told that we would write a letter to our mothers each and every week that we were in basic training, and God help the poor soul who neglected to do so.

The following eight weeks seemed to run together as we learned to distinguish between the civilian way, the right way, and the army way of doing things. The first two weeks, we learned to get into formation without our DI screaming and berating us. We also learned that in the army every sentence began with a form of the word *fuck*. By the third week, we could actually march in formation without tripping over each other. We could even turn in different directions on command without causing a one-hundred-man pileup.

When the day finally came for us to go out to the rifle range, I was ecstatic. Thank God they had gotten us halfway into some kind of shape, because we had to climb both Agony Hill and Misery Hill on our march out to the ranges. By the time we reached the firing lines, carrying our M-1 rifles, the calves of our legs were screaming for a break.

Within a week, nearly everyone in our training company had an "M-1 thumb," a condition caused by a recruit's inability to coordinate the removal of his thumb from the receiver of the M-1 prior to the bolt's slamming home. It was the same principle of physics that made the guillotine so effective in eighteenth-century France. Some incredibly slow recruits had M-1 thumbs on both hands. This was mentally comparable to being beheaded twice in eighteenth-century France.

The following week, we learned how to shoot and maintain the BAR, or Browning automatic rifle. We didn't realize at the time that we were training on obsolete weapons that were being turned over to National Guard units all over the country even as we were training on them. Active duty units were busy phasing in the M-14 rifle and the M-60 light machine gun. By the eighth week of training, we could fieldstrip the M-1 and BAR blindfolded. We were finally beginning to look and feel like soldiers.

Just before graduation, our battalion was assembled in a movie theater that was used as an auditorium. On stage stood a giant of a man, a soldier who stood head and shoulders above any other soldier I had yet seen at Fort Knox, Kentucky. He told us that he was an Airborne infantryman, better known as a U.S. Army paratrooper. The more he talked about the history of the Airborne, the more I knew I wanted to be a paratrooper. When he mentioned that the army paid an extra fifty-five dollars per month in hazardous-duty pay for anyone who would repeatedly jump out of perfectly good airplanes, I was sure I wanted to be a part of that. My brain kicked into Vapor Lock Mode 1, and I signed on the dotted line. Of course, doing so canceled the army's contractual obligation to send me to Europe after AIT. It was right there in the fine print.

We stood in formation after graduation while our DI read our next training stations. I was one of three who got orders for Advanced Individual Training at Fort Polk, Louisiana. Since I had signed up for airborne infantry, I was now going to be trained in the fine art of infantry warfare. At the end of all my training, I was going to be Airborne infantry—all the way. Since it was close to the holidays, the army gave me a two-week Christmas leave before I had to report to Fort Polk. I often wondered how many recruits failed to show up for the beginning of their AIT.

The weather was so frigid during Christmas and New Year's that I could hardly wait to get out of the Gary area and report down south at Fort Polk. The train ride to Polk seemed longer than the trip from Chicago to Fort Knox, but it should have been since Polk was a lot farther away. And if I had known what was in store for me once I got there, I would have wished for the trip to take a lot longer.

Once again, it was totally dark when we arrived at Fort Polk. However, it was not so dark that I couldn't tell the terrain was flat and sandy. To make matters worse, the temperatures were hovering at zero, and the sand was frozen solid. The barracks were not like the brick buildings I had encountered at Fort Knox. These were pre–World War II frame buildings that had clearly been put up by the lowest bidder. I could see the back door from the front door, with the front door closed. I had the feeling that the following eight weeks of training would not be among my more pleasant experiences. Before long, we were calling Fort Polk "Fort Puke," just like the trainees who were getting ready to graduate.

I was blessed with being able to go through AIT with a bunch of Texans, most of whom were serving with the state National Guard, with a few draftees mixed in for good measure. There were only three volunteers in my entire training company, and one of them was me.

Since all of us were able to get from point A to point B in formation, and were able to dress ourselves like real soldiers, we went directly into training. Most of the Mickey Mouse harassment I had seen so much of in basic training was a thing of the past in AIT. The army was now more interested in training infantry soldiers than in trying to convince a bunch of kids how pathetic they were.

We were each issued an M-14 rifle, which would be ours for the duration of training. Between classes, we would be taught to clean, caress, and love our weapons. It would be our constant companion while we were in the barracks during duty hours. The army was forcing us into an unnatural love affair with a clunky but faithful inanimate object, the M-14 rifle. Little did I know that after AIT I would never touch an M-14 again. While I was in training, the Airborne units were being rearmed with the M-16 rifle.

We also qualified with the M-60 light machine gun, and familiarized ourselves with the M-79 grenade launcher and the .50-caliber Browning heavy machine gun. Life was good. We were being paid to rock and roll with all those deadly mistresses.

There are some things in life that must be taken for granted because they are tradition and will never change. One of those unchangeable traditions is that the Texas National Guard and all other Texans will, always, remember the Alamo. Another is that they definitely know how to party. Beside them, I was a rank amateur. They quickly taught me the fine art of doing "shooters"—tequila and beer—and puking without hitting the tops of my shoes. I also learned how to talk to local cops while fully smashed, and at the same time convince them that I had a speech impediment. It was not long before those long, tall soldiers from the Lone Star State had not only accepted me, but had even sworn me in as an honorary Texan. Sam Houston was probably rolling in his grave.

The temperature never rose over forty degrees the entire time we were at Fort Polk. Sitting in the bleachers in our warm winter clothing during most blocks of instruction, it took almost everything we had to keep from falling asleep. I just knew that if I did, the snow snake the DI talked about would crawl up my ass and freeze me to death!

During AIT, I attempted to get some of the guys I was hanging out with to join me in signing up for the Airborne, but I couldn't get a single taker. They failed to see the Airborne as an adventure. Maybe we were both right!

When AIT finally ended after eight weeks of intensive training, I had been in the military for a total of four and a half months. I was promoted to private E-2 and was set to depart for my greatest challenge, Airborne training at Fort Benning, Georgia. If I could make the grade, in four weeks I would be standing tall as a U.S. Army paratrooper.

I felt a sense of great sadness saying good-bye to my friends at Fort Polk. I had just under two years and eight months left to serve on my enlistment. Most of my National Guard friends had only two months of active duty remaining. I would serve my time in two different combat zones over the next three years, while they would continue the party they had started in AIT.

The trip to Fort Benning began at four o'clock in the afternoon, ensuring that it would be dark when we arrived in Columbus, Georgia. They told us that we were getting a late start because the buses were late, but we knew by then that it was just the normal course of travel in the army. Once again their planning was perfect, and we arrived at Fort Benning around two o'clock in the morning. In the past, we had always been greeted on our arrival by the biggest, ugliest NCOs on post. There was no difference at Airborne School except for the black baseball hats they wore and the fact that they screamed like banshees. Would this kind of insane treatment ever end?

When we dismounted the bus, we incorrectly assumed that we would be marched to our barracks, which were surely nearby. It was pitch-black, far too dark to see anything around us. We were ordered to shoulder our duffel bags and march off to a new location. Then the order came to "Double-time, march." That heralded the normal mode of transportation for us the next four weeks. Two miles and fifty push-ups later, we arrived at some old wooden barracks, very similar to the ones we had stayed in at Fort Polk. Once again, we would freeze our buns off at night.

They assigned us bunks, issued us bedding, then gave us a couple of hours to get our gear put away and grab some sleep. Our trials were to begin early the next day.

It seemed that my head had just touched the pillow when some noisy young corporal strolled through our barracks banging two trash can lids together. He was screaming at the top of his lungs about what a bunch of "stinking legs" we were. Part of the description was familiar to me, I knew what "stinking" meant, but the term "legs" I did not fully understand. Well, it didn't take us long to discover that a "leg" was the foulest creature to walk the hallowed grounds of Airborne School—an individual who had not yet qualified to wear the silver jump wings of a U.S. Army paratrooper.

During our first formation, a muscular black corporal strolled through the ranks to intimidate us. Occasionally, he would stop in front of one of the terrified students and ask, "Would you fuck my mother, leg?" If the soldier answered "yes" the DI would get in his face and scream, "So you think my mother's a whore. Drop and give me twenty push-ups, leg." If the soldier answered "no" the DI would get in his face and scream, "What's the matter, my mother ain't good enough for you? Drop and give me twenty push-ups, leg."

This went on for a full five minutes with half the formation down on the ground doing push-ups. It was obvious that there was no right answer to his query. Then he reached one of the last soldiers in the formation. Nose to nose with the wide-eyed young troop, the corporal screamed, "Would you fuck my mother?" The young private hesitated for a second, then screamed back, "No, Corporal, I'm not a motherfucker."

The black corporal stood there for a full minute, saying nothing in response. Finally, with the hint of a smile on his face he said, "That's good, leg. At ease. Better have a good one for tomorrow." The system could be defeated. There was hope for us yet.

When the young DI finally got to me, I had already made up my mind that any answer I could give would be counter-productive. For the sake of originality, I dropped to the ground and started knocking out push-ups.

After we had all managed to qualify for a couple of rounds of push-ups, a bullnecked staff sergeant stepped to the front of the formation and ordered us to strip to the waist. When we had complied, he began walking through the ranks looking for Air-borne tattoos. Unfortunately, a couple of fools in our class were already sporting Airborne tattoos on their arms. They became marked men for the rest of the cycle. We soon learned that Air-borne School had the copyright on military harassment, and our sentence would last four full weeks.

The first week was called "detail week." It was the seven-day period set aside to accommodate the arrival of the students who were showing up for the next cycle. While the DIs waited for the entire class to show up, those of us who had been unfor-tunate enough to arrive early were being loaned out to anyone who needed a job done. Most of us were sent to pull KP duty at the mess hall, without a doubt the worst detail on post. Paint-ing things like ornamental rocks and barrier poles, conducting numerous police calls, and pulling or cutting weeds were just a few of the other assignments we were given.

My name seemed to have found a permanent spot on the KP roster. We were up long before daylight, stood an early-morning formation, suffered through another bout of verbal harassment by our DI, dropped for more push-ups, then double-timed off to some unknown unit where we would spend the rest of the day up to our elbows in grease or leftover food. We couldn't wait to start training, just to get the hell out of Fort Benning.

It was SOP that all Airborne trainees were restricted to their areas for the first two weeks of training, but when my uncle, SFC Airborne Eddie Chiasson, showed up, he had no problem getting me a weekend pass. I had no idea at that time that he and the first sergeant of the Airborne School were Korean War buddies. None of my fellow students could understand how a lowly private had the pull to obtain a weekend pass in his first week of the cycle. Even though none of our cadre seemed to mind when I left for the weekend, I would later pay in spades for my special privileges, and became the class whipping boy for the remainder of the cycle. Anyone passing by our parade ground during the day would likely see me in the front-leaning-rest position. By graduation, I was up to about three hundred push-ups a day.

We began airborne training during our second week. This was a lot of fun for those of us who had been assigned right out of basic or AIT, but for those who had come from regular leg units it was pretty tough. The push-ups and the running were quickly wearing down those out-of-shape garrison troops. Soldiers who didn't know how to push themselves away from the meal table paid a heavy price. Yet everyone seemed to hang in there through the toughest part of the training. It wasn't unusual during the morning runs to see one or two of those old-timers falling out of formation to toss up their previous meal along the side of the road, only to sprint back a few minutes later to catch up with the rest of us to finish the run.

It was during this first week of training that we were introduced to the hand-to-hand combat pit. "The Pit," as it was called, was a small, circular arena filled with sawdust. We entered it, two at a time, to do battle, i.e., toss each other around to the cheers and encouragement of our comrades. One time, I had just thrown my partner over my shoulder, and he had come up spitting some sawdust from his mouth. One of the instructors saw him spit and came unglued. He screamed and ordered him to remove that wad of spit from "his" pit. When my partner bent over to pick it up with his hand, the angry sergeant bellowed at him, "You didn't put it there with your hand, so don't remove it with your hand." My friend was forced to get down on his hands and knees to pick up the spit with his mouth. It never paid to screw up in front of the training instructors.

Besides the constant harassment and tough physical training, we quickly got down to what it was all about—Airborne training. We learned what a PLF or parachute landing fall was, and practiced it so that we would do it automatically anytime we touched the ground with both feet at the same time. "Upon contact with the ground, you will hit first on the balls of your feet, then roll to the side so that your calf, hip, and shoulder make contact, in that order," the instructors constantly drilled us. "The only thing worse than a streamer is a bad PLF," they warned.

When the first week of training was over, my body was screaming for relief. My mind, already numb from the frequent pain messages being forwarded by my aching muscles, refused to respond. It had been fun in a sadistic sort of way, but the constant stress and strain were taking a heavy toll. Unlike most cycles going through Airborne School, no one had dropped out of our class during the first week. I began to think that maybe our class was a little different from those who had come before us.

I spent a relaxing weekend at my uncle Eddie's, knowing full well that I would catch more hell from the Black Hats when I returned, but the rest and relaxation made the added harassment worth every penny. Sure enough, when I got back to school I was selected first in my class—first to do push-ups, first to run around the parade ground, first to do pull-ups. I loved it. It made me feel wanted. The more the instructors pushed me, the more I got with the program. Jump school was really beginning to be fun.

But during the second week of training we were introduced to the Airborne's answer to the medieval rack. During the Middle Ages you had to have committed a major transgression to earn a turn on the rack. You only had to volunteer for Airborne training to get a session on the "hanging agony." The sadists who had developed the hanging agony had not come from the ranks of the mentally enlightened. The device was actually a very simple application of the military parachute, with the ordinary parachute harness suspended from overhead rafters. This doesn't sound like anything unusual; after all, thousands of paratroopers use them every time they exit a troop-carrier aircraft. However, it is the misapplication of the ordinary parachute harness that makes the hanging agony mankind's greatest physical torture. During a normal parachute fall, the descending chute counters the pull of gravity to prevent the parachute harness from completely cutting off the flow of blood to the jumper's groin. While suspended in the hanging agony, the pull of gravity is no more, no less than in an actual parachute jump. However, the rafter supporting the parachute harness does not descend as does an open chute. This phenomenon allows gravity to combine with the weight and mass of the jumper to totally cut off not only the blood supply to the jumper's groin but also the nerve receptors that enable the jumper to scream. Prolonged suspension in the hanging agony results in impotence, crossed eyes, and sometimes death.

During our third week, we were introduced to the 34-foot and 250-foot towers. The 34-foot tower was nothing more than a mock-up of an aircraft fuselage with an opening comparable to the door in a troop-carrier aircraft. A student, again wearing a snug parachute harness, would snap-link the overhead harness to a cable extending from the tower to an earthen berm approximately 150 feet away and 10 feet high. On the command "Go!" the student made a tight exit off the platform, falling approximately seven feet before the slack was pulled out of the overhead harness, resulting in a bungeelike reaction that caused additional damage to the student's already swollen and lacerated groin area. Due to the elastic give in the running cable, the student was then subjected to a number of additional, but ever-decreasing jolts to the injured area of his groin as gravitational pull caused him to sideslip down the cable, picking up speed until collision with the earthen berm stopped all lateral motion. The impact with the earthen berm was designed solely for the purpose of restarting the jumper's normal heartbeat. To pass this phase of Airborne training, the jumper had to remember to look up to check the opening of his imaginary chute after completing a three-count that began at the exit from the door and ended just after the simulated opening shock of the parachute. This maneuver had to be performed successfully three times to the satisfaction of the instructors before a student could move on to the 250-foot tower. It took a real man to remember to look up to check his chute immediately after having the inertia of the entire weight of his body, in full free fall, stopped by the tiny round fleshy orbs that used to be his testicles. The rumors concerning the army's use of saltpeter to control the sex drive of its combat troops is totally untrue when applied to Airborne infantry. It was not needed.

The 250-foot tower was the easiest part of airborne training. This required allowing oneself to be strapped into a parachute harness that was attached to a standard parachute, held in full deployment by a metal frame. A cable lifted the student 250 feet straight up, to where the chute was released, allowing the jumper to float gently back to earth. The only danger came from occasional wind gusts that could blow an unsuspecting jumper on the upwind side of the tower directly into the structure. If that occurred, the jumper's chute could snag on the tower, where he would hang stranded and helpless until the instructors ascended the tower by means of an internal stairwell, then crawled out and rescued him. Due to the high winds and the constraints of time, the aspiring paratroopers were permitted only a single drop.

In the final week of training, we were loaded on C-119 Flying Boxcars in two "sticks" of fifteen jumpers each. The aged planes then struggled down the runway and shuddered into the air. Somehow they vibrated their way to the proper elevation by the time they reached the drop zone, somewhere across the Georgia border into Alabama.

My throat was parched, and I prayed that no one could see or smell the fear that I was feeling. The flight seemed to take thirty minutes, but I'm sure it was nowhere near that long. Then the jumpmaster shouted *"Stand up!"* One of the trainees in my stick refused to move. The jumpmaster hollered again, *"Stand up!"* Again the reluctant trainee refused to move. After all of the training and harassment we had gone through, he was not going to jump. The jumpmaster stepped up and pulled him away from the rest of us, telling him to go and sit in the front of the plane where he could watch the rest of us. Then the jump-master returned to his spot and continued with the jump commands. *"Hook up! . . . Check equipment! . . . Sound off for equipment check! . . . Stand in the door!"*

It felt like an eternity before the red light blinked out and the green light came on. The jumpmaster yelled, *"Jump!"* Like a worm disappearing into the ground, the stick of trainees followed each other out of the plane, each man hesitating briefly in the door before leaping into the prop blast.

When my time came, I jumped out in a perfect "night" jump—my eyes were closed tight. I forgot to count to three, and was jerked into reality by my chute's opening above me. I floated slowly down to earth, the wind pushing me backward. At approximately three hundred feet I looked down and recognized a number of my instructors. They were running around yelling instructions at us. I was still drifting backward as my favorite black corporal yelled at me at the top of his lungs. I ignored whatever he was trying to tell me, trying to concentrate on making a perfect PLF. Then it was Thump . . . thump . . . thump as I hit the ground with my heels, ass, and head—definitely not a perfect PLF.

The corporal stood not more than twenty feet away, yelling through his megaphone, challenging my family heritage. He then lowered the megaphone to his side and softly ordered me, "Give me twenty, you fucking moron." Hell, I was happy to give him twenty—I was still alive.

My next four jumps were a lot better than the first one, and on that "special" day at the end of the week, I was proud to have my uncle Eddie pin on my jump wings. I was now officially a United States paratrooper.

CHAPTER 6

It was easy to say good-bye to Fort Benning. Enough was enough! I had been called a dirty leg for a month, but now I was finally Airborne qualified. I proudly displayed my silver wings on the left side of my uniform, and earned myself a new title—*cherry*. That's the way it worked in the military. You fight your way to a pinnacle, only to discover there's another distant mountain to conquer, one even higher than the one you had just beaten.

I had hoped for an assignment to the 101st Airborne Division stationed at Fort Campbell, Kentucky, but had already resigned myself to the fact that I would be going to the 82d Airborne Division at Fort Bragg, North Carolina. It was, at last, a permanent duty station for me—no more training assignment—and it was a long way from home.

The cherries who had been assigned to the 82d Airborne Division piled onto a couple of Trailways buses. I thought it would be another one of those long, dull bus rides, but within a half hour, pint bottles of spirits, wrapped to the neck in brown paper bags, were being passed back and forth. Not long after that, decks of cards came out, and everyone was involved in one game or another. Every time we stopped at a bus station for a break, we found a liquor store and replenished our supply.

By the time the buses pulled into the home of the 82d Airborne, there was nary a sober trooper aboard. They unceremoniously dumped us in front of division headquarters, where we were greeted by a number of high-ranking NCOs. The medals and chevrons displayed on their uniforms gave one the impression that these boys had won World War II all by themselves. The only problem was that not one of them was smiling.

No sooner had they got us into formation than they began pulling us out again and posting us to our assigned units. I was going to Company C, 2d Airborne Battle Group, 501st Infantry. The top NCO for Charlie Company was First Sergeant Wimple, and like all senior NCOs of that era, he was a veteran of both World War II and Korea, with a full chest of ribbons and combat jump devices on his master parachutist wings. He was a sight to behold. I was soon to learn that to mess with First Sergeant Wimple was to mess with God.

We "lucky ones" who had been assigned to First Sergeant Wimple's company were marched to the unit area and assigned to a platoon. I went to 3d Platoon under the guidance of Staff Sergeant Beauchamp. My squad leader was Sgt. John Jakovenko.

It soon became apparent that training was a God-given absolute requirement in the 82d "All-American" Division. Slack time was unheard of; that was something reserved for pussies in leg units. Paratroopers were a couple of breeds above the ordinary soldier.

First thing every morning, we performed the daily dozen followed by a two-mile-plus run—depending on the mood of our platoon sergeant. When we finished the run, we ate breakfast, then spent the rest of the day in training. That could involve weapons training, classroom instruction, fieldwork, or any number of other education blocks. If nothing else was scheduled, we drew our weapons and cleaned them. It didn't matter that they were already spotless, the important thing was that every minute of our workday was taken up with something military or something constructive.

Our day ended at 1730 hours, and if we had performed satisfactorily, we were allowed to go downtown to play with the local populace. It didn't take us long to realize that the good people of Fayetteville liked the money we spent in their community a lot more than they liked us.

I made my first trip into Fayetteville in early April 1963, and I was amazed to learn that the color barriers were still in existence. I had expected to see that in Georgia and Louisiana, but was utterly surprised to find WHITE ONLY signs posted all over Fayetteville. The restaurants wouldn't serve blacks. They could go to the local movie theaters, but they had to sit up in the balcony. If they wanted a drink of water, they had to get it from a "colored only" drinking fountain.

Personally, I resented making friends with black paratroopers in my company, then being unable to associate with them once I left post. But that's the way it was in Fayetteville, North Carolina, in 1963. I was there in 1964 when the color barrier was lifted. It gave me great pleasure to see the local bigots eating crow.

In February 1964, my unit was changed to Company C, 1st Battalion, 504th Infantry Regiment, and then in May of 1964 it was changed again, to Company C, 3d Battalion, 325th Infantry Regiment. I had been a member of three infantry companies in just over a year and was still sleeping in the same bunk.

We normally trained during a five-and-a-half-day week, although every now and then we got lucky and got the entire weekend off. Training was intense, and time passed very quickly. Once a month, we had "field week," at which time we would spend five to seven days in the field, attempting to outmaneuver the Soviet troops we were sure to be fighting someday. Once every two months, we were the alert company, and we weren't allowed to leave our company area. We were ready to leave for destinations unknown on a minute's notice. During this time, we thought it was a joke, but it wouldn't be long before we discovered that it was not.

Once a year, the division participated in multiunit war games. The biggest of all was SWIFT STRIKE in 1964, which was fought on a battlefield that encompassed parts of North Carolina, South Carolina, and Georgia. The mock battle pitted the 82d Airborne Division against the 11th Air Assault Division. Normally, the 82d kicked the crap out of any unit it took on in the annual war games, but it became obvious on the very first day of the battle that the 11th Air Assault Division was not just any unit.

We parachuted into a cotton field that straddled the border between North and South Carolina. The jump went in with a number of injuries. In my company alone, three men were evacuated: one had come down through a greenhouse; another had slammed into the roof of a house; the third broke both his legs when he hit a donkey. The games were put on hold while we transported our injured out of the area.

No sooner had the games restarted than we were up to our asses in helicopters. I had seen Huey helicopters before, but not a hundred of them at one time. Every time we looked behind us, we were being pursued by dozens of flying machines loaded with Air Assault troops. If all the maneuvering had been done on the ground, we could've kicked their asses, but that was not the way the 11th Air Assault fought; they located our units with scout helicopters, and before we knew it, we had company by the hundreds. I always enjoyed participating in war games, but it was no fun when we were the ones who got our asses kicked.

Right after the war games, Gary Timikouski and I decided to hitchhike to Fort Stewart, Georgia, to see if we would have better luck with the girls. We were picked up by a gentleman in a suit, driving a new Plymouth station wagon, and immediately thought what a couple of lucky guys we were. We hadn't driven more than an hour when our driver said he had to stop to use a rest room. We pulled over at a break area, and I went into the building to take a leak while Gary and the driver stayed outside to talk. When I had finished, Gary and the driver went inside. I didn't find that strange, since there were five or six stalls in the latrine. A short time later they came out, and we got back in the car and left. At the time, I didn't notice that Gary was pretty upset about something.

We hadn't gone a mile when Gary picked up a typewriter that had been sitting in the back of the station wagon and whacked the driver over the head with it. We were going seventy miles an hour down the highway when Gary flipped out.

The driver got his car under control and slowly pulled to a stop along the side of the road. All three of us jumped from the vehicle and the driver immediately screamed, "If there's one thing I like better than sucking dicks, it's kicking young paratrooper asses." Without waiting to see if he was a man of his word, we both turned and took off running down the highway. If he could take a Remington typewriter across the top of the head without flinching, he could sure as hell take a fist.

We continued running until we were certain that the mad homosexual had turned around and was going down the highway in the opposite direction. When we knew we were safe, I asked Gary what in the hell was going on. He said that when he and the driver had gone into the latrine, the driver lay down on the ground and asked Gary to urinate on him. When Gary refused, he offered him ten dollars to suck his dick, which Gary also rejected. Gary was still upset when he returned to the vehicle, but he knew we needed the ride. But sitting in the back seat, mulling over what had just happened, Gary got madder than hell and decided to kick the guy's ass. I didn't blame him for what he did, but we were still on the highway two hours later trying to get to our destination. When we finally managed to reach Fort Stewart, we discovered the situation was the same there as it was at Fort Bragg—the civilians were just money-grubbing carpetbaggers.

I was in Fayetteville at a local watering hole when an MP came into the bar and announced that all 82d Airborne personnel were to assemble outside on the main street. I went out and was surprised to see a large number of deuce-and-a-half trucks parked along the curb waiting for us. Within the hour, each truck was filled with paratroopers and had departed for Fort Bragg.

When I reached my platoon area, there was already a line in front of the armory. Since I was the platoon RTO and the platoon armorer, there was no way they could get their weapons until I showed up. It was a bad system, but that's the way it worked.

After everyone had been issued his weapon, I went to the barracks, got my gear together, and reported to my platoon leader. When I showed up, he just smiled and announced, "We're going to war." My eyes must have bugged out of my head. Holy shit, I thought, the Soviets have finally attacked us.

The entire company filed outside in full combat equipment, minus ammo, and loaded onto vehicles. In less than thirty minutes, we were on the tarmac at Pope Air Force Base. We hadn't been waiting more than an hour when we were ordered to line up and draw ammunition and grenades. It wasn't a practice alert this time. We were going to war.

Just before we loaded into C-130 aircraft, a second lieutenant approached us with blackboard in hand to explain that a revolution had broken out in the Dominican Republic and was on the verge of overthrowing the government. We were to put the revolution down before it succeeded. None of us understood why we were invading a little banana republic, but what the hell—a little war was better than no war at all. That was what all our training had been about.

I had been in downtown Fayetteville drinking a cold beer less than twenty-four hours before, and now I found myself standing on the tarmac at the San Isidro Airport in the Dominican Republic waiting to shoot someone. Progress is truly an amazing thing!

It was hot, humid, and dusty as I stood there, watching planes landing every ten minutes. There was no doubt that we were serious about putting down this revolution. We had come in force, and we had come to stay.

An hour passed, and we were still sitting on the ground, watching the buildup, when a jeep drove by. It hadn't gone a hundred meters past us when it exploded. We jumped to our feet, grabbed our weapons, and chambered a round, fully prepared to fend off an attack. When nothing happened, we stood milling around trying to figure out what was going on. An hour later, an officer came by with green tape and told us to tape down the handles of our grenades. It was then that we discovered that the young lieutenant from B Company had inadvertently pulled the pin on a hand grenade and dropped it on the floor of the jeep. It had exploded, killing the officer and severely wounding the sergeant who was driving. To this day I still haven't figured out how anyone can inadvertently pull the pin on a grenade. It must have been a case of terminal daydreaming.

We spent that first night in abandoned brick houses not far from the airport. Every now and again, a shot would ring out as a paratrooper fired at some phantom skulking in the shadows. Everyone was suffering a bout of itchy trigger finger. It would take a couple of days for the nervousness to subside.

The next morning, we drove to the San Duarte Bridge, which spanned the Ozama River. Still-smoking vehicles were strewn along both sides of the bridge. Nearby houses had taken multiple hits from large-caliber weapons. But it was so quiet that the only noise we could hear was the sound of our own footsteps crunching on the debris as we patrolled across the bridge.

After we reached the far side, the company broke into two sections. The 3d and 4th Platoons patrolled together and turned left to parallel the Ozama River, while the 1st and 2d Platoons went right.

About a mile down the river, the 4th Platoon dropped off, and we continued on alone. Thirty minutes later, we came to a halt when we reached a tall metal gate. Security police opened the gate and allowed us inside the Santo Domingo power plant. We were to protect the plant from a suspected rebel attack.

It didn't take long to convince us that we had arrived just in time. Every ten or fifteen minutes a shot ricocheted over our heads, so we knew that the guerrillas were already in the vicinity. The shots were not very close. The guerrillas were just trying to warn us to get out of their way or they were the worst shots that I had ever seen.

If we spotted the smoke from the guerrillas' weapons, we would answer it with a fusillade of forty or fifty shots in return. Within a day, the snipers were either dead or tired of getting their houses shot up. There were at least a dozen houses with their windows shot out where the snipers had been active.

We had been at the power plant about three days when two squads were ordered out on patrol. Since I was the platoon RTO, I was automatically selected to go when the platoon leader decided to lead the patrol himself. Our mission was to find and secure the SS *Santo Domingo*, which was supposed to

be filled with ammunition and firearms. The dock we were heading toward was less than a half mile away, but we couldn't see
it because of all the buildings in the way. Theoretically, we
should have been able to reach the dock, secure the ship, and
be back on the verandah at the power plant drinking *bueno*
Coca-Colas—a half-bottle of Coke and half-bottle of 151-
proof rum—within two hours.

We moved out cautiously toward the pier where we
expected to find the *Santo Domingo* docked. Unfortunately, we
moved *soooo* cautiously that we gave the rebels time to secure
the ship and sail it away, then lay an ambush for us.

When we arrived after two hours, the ship had already
sailed. The lieutenant got on the radio and was explaining the
situation to battalion headquarters when the first shots rang out.
I jerked the handset from him and dove behind a stack of
boxes, leaving him standing in the open with his mouth ajar. It
took him a full fifteen seconds to snap out of his shocked
stupor and join me behind the cover. By then, the shooting was
all around us, mostly outgoing. Not more than twenty meters to
my front, I spotted a figure, holding a carbine, slowly walking
around on a second-story verandah. I let loose with an entire
magazine, twenty rounds, and saw him go down. I was looking
up as I was loading another magazine and saw Sergeant
Jakovenko cut loose with twenty rounds at a brick wall as he
screamed, *"Come on, you motherfuckers, show your faces."*
Man, was he pissed off because he couldn't shoot anyone. The
lieutenant grabbed my radio handset and called the company
for instructions. We were informed that our weapons platoon
had just sunk the SS *Santo Domingo* with a recoilless-rifle shot
below the waterline. We were ordered to withdraw. It didn't
take us more than fifteen minutes to sprint back to our base
of operations.

We were at the power plant less than a week when we were
relieved by another unit and ordered to rejoin the rest of our
company. Our next assignment was to man a barricaded street
not far from a local high school. Our CO, never one to remain
idle, had us rappelling off the school building during our slack
time. It was during this period that General York, commander

of the 82d Airborne Division, was relieved of command—if one believes the rumors, that is.

The division had taken a number of casualties during the incursion, and it angered General York to lose any man to enemy fire. It was rumored that if another one of his troopers got shot again, he would abandon our static positions and take the entire city by storm. Well, it didn't take long before we had another paratrooper shot and killed, and the general immediately ordered us to move out and to take the rebel positions by force.

We had covered about ten blocks, really shooting up the neighborhood, when we received orders telling us to return to our sandbagged defensive positions. Shortly after our brief attack, General York was recalled, and we had another commanding general. General York had been liked and admired by officers and enlisted men alike.

As the action began to wind down, we were ordered to patrol the street in pairs. Each pair of troopers would be responsible for about four square blocks. The highlight of these patrols was the frequent stops at the local cantinas to drink a quick *bueno* Coca-Cola. As far as I knew, the officers who came to check on us never had a clue that the Coke bottles we were drinking from contained about six ounces of 151-proof rum.

It was on one of these routine patrols that I finally figured out what life was all about on this tropical island paradise. My partner and I had just walked out of the cantina and were scanning the street for rebel activity when a Dominican civilian walked by us. There was nothing strange about him, and he had the customary half pint of rum in his back pocket. He walked about half a block down the street, then propped himself up against the wall and took a long, slow drink from the rum bottle. Just as he was doing this, a vehicle with two Dominican national police drove by. The civilian saw them and took off running. The police backed up their vehicle, and when they realized that they could not catch up with the fleet-footed sprinter, they bailed out of their vehicle, drew their weapons, and shot him dead. I made a mental note to avoid running from the Dominican national police, especially if I was drinking rum.

It soon became obvious that the division had nothing for us to really do when they suddenly ordered us to sweep the streets. The Dominicans had a real bad habit of just throwing the garbage outside their doors, and with no one to pick it up, it was beginning to smell to high heaven. But we all resented the fact that we were the ones who had to sweep up this junk.

On one particular day, my squad drew the garbage detail, and Staff Sergeant Beauchamp decided to give Sergeant Jakovenko a break. He was supervising the detail, and we were halfway through sweeping one side of the street when a door flew open and a woman threw out a can full of garbage right behind us. Staff Sergeant Beauchamp suddenly became enraged, pushed open the door, and not only threw her garbage back inside but proceeded to shovel in the rest of the garbage we had collected during our cleaning detail. By the time he had finished, the woman's entire living room was piled two feet high in nasty, week-old garbage. We were all mighty proud of our platoon sergeant, but our commanding officer thought it was insubordinate and in poor taste. It wasn't long after this episode that Staff Sergeant Beauchamp was relieved of duty and whisked back to the United States. He was soon replaced by another NCO.

The highlight of our tour in the DomRep was when I had the opportunity to attend a Bob Hope show. I don't think anyone expected the famous comedian to come down to entertain the troops during our little revolution.

It wasn't more than a month after the show that I was called into the company commander's office and informed that I would be returning to the States. My stepfather, Chris, was in the hospital in critical condition with leukemia. I was still in shock when I arrived at Fort Bragg the next day, but more bad news followed me. I would not make it back in time to say good-bye to my stepfather and good friend. He had already passed away.

I returned to Fort Bragg after the funeral, and because I had only a few weeks left in the military, I did not have to return to the Dominican Republic. Chances were that if I had gone back to the DR, I would have reenlisted. On 10 October 1965, I said good-bye to military life and became a civilian once again.

CHAPTER 7

At first it felt strange being a civilian, but before long, I had it down pat. Do what you want, when you want, however you want to do it. I think they called it "freedom" or something like that. The only problem was that I had to get a job if I wanted to enjoy all those freedoms. My uncle Bob was working for a major auto manufacturer in Chicago Heights, Illinois, and arranged a job interview for me. At the time, I was living with Uncle Larry and Aunt Betty. Uncle Bob's house was just a few miles away. Uncle Bob took me to the interview and explained to the interviewer that I was an army veteran who had just returned home from "the war." Evidently, the interviewer was impressed with Uncle Bob's bullshit introduction. I was hired immediately for a high-paying job. My starting pay was $3.27 an hour. I would have been well on my way to Easy Street if fate hadn't stepped in right then and dealt me a cruel blow.

I had been working all the overtime I could get and had managed to fit in pretty well with my coworkers. My biggest problem was that I still had a lot of "kid" left in me and thought that work should be fun. Nearly every time my supervisors saw me, I was either laughing or clowning around, so they immediately got the impression that I was up to no good. This was not the fact at all, and the more they watched me, the more they came to realize that I was doing a good job. They gave me all the overtime I wanted. Unfortunately, this really upset one of my supervisors, who had taken a dislike to me.

I had been on the job about six weeks and had been working the entire time on the assembly line that made doors. All I had to do was stack the finished doors on a dolly as the machine stamped them. It was real "metal work," if you know what I mean. We had been working most of the morning when the inspector closed down the line because of some metal defect. I was sent to another machine with a younger employee.

We were assigned to the printing machine that printed "widgets" or something. I didn't even recognize the finished product. We would put this piece of sheet metal in the machine and then simultaneously press our individual control buttons. The upper part of the machine would descend and compress the metal into a mold, then it would return to its prior position while small kicker arms would push the finished product out of the mold. We were on the machine for about an hour when it malfunctioned. The sheet metal was put in the machine, the kicker arms came out, and the machine pressed the kicker arms into the metal mold. My partner and I were taken by surprise, and we started to laugh. This didn't please our supervisor, who gave us an ass-chewing for laughing, then called in the millwright to fix the machine. When the machine was fixed, we resumed making our widgets. It wasn't more than thirty minutes later when the machine malfunctioned and trashed another set of kicker arms and molds. We made the serious mistake of laughing again. Within fifteen minutes, I was in the company's employment office becoming very unemployed. The union representative could do nothing for me as I had not been on the job for the required ninety-day probation period. He swore to me that he would work on my case as I had been terminated unfairly. At the time, I thought the man was full of shit.

I was somewhat disgruntled and found myself pounding the pavement in search of work. At every job interview, I was told one of two things. I was either unemployable because I had been fired or they couldn't pay me the wages I was used to. My money was running out, and my future was beginning to look pretty dim, so I decided to go back into the military. Besides, there was a new little war going on over in some place called Vietnam.

My cousin Sam was thoroughly amazed that I was going back into the military. He was rapidly approaching draft age and was researching every avenue he could find to keep him out of the service. I went back down to the Gary, Indiana, enlistment center and re-upped for another three-year hitch in the army. But this time, I shunned both the Airborne and the infantry, choosing instead the somewhat dubious honor of being a straight-leg military policeman.

Because of my prior service, I was selected to escort a batch of new enlistees to Fort Polk, Louisiana. So when I went to the Chicago induction center, I was already in full uniform. I had just finished taking my physical exam when I was approached by an army captain who asked me if I was interested in becoming a helicopter pilot. I was excited about the opportunity, but when I told him that I had a problem with color blindness, the offer was quickly withdrawn. Hell, if it hadn't been for poor color vision, I might have become an officer and a gentleman!

After I had turned over the new recruits to the drill sergeants at Fort Polk, I was assigned to the replacement center to await orders for military police training at Fort Gordon, Georgia.

I was made a company clerk and discovered very quickly that there were great opportunities to make some money in the military. People assigned to the company asked me all the time to keep them off details on certain days, especially on weekends. They offered cash or liquor just to bypass their names on the duty roster. But I guess I was dumber than the average bear, because I refused to bend the rules. What a moron! I could have been a king.

It was a great relief when I finally received orders assigning me to Fort Gordon. Serving as company clerk was a real bore. I realized that my "easy" days were soon going to come to an end, but I was impatient to get on with my training. More important, I would be heading for another duty station, which meant another adventure.

Because I was a private first class wearing Airborne wings and a Combat Infantryman's Badge, I was immediately selected as the trainee platoon guide for my training class. It would have been a great job except for the fact that I was continually under the microscope. The training staff used me to keep their thumbs on the pulse of the unit. I was the yardstick, the standard, the model for the rest of the platoon. So goes Limey, so goes the platoon. I didn't like the pressure it put on me. It forced me to work twice as hard to be a model, which is the last thing in the world I wanted to do. I had to study longer, shine my boots better, and press my uniforms more often than anyone else. What I had first imagined as a really easy job had become a major chore. But it kept me out of trouble, and evidently I performed well enough; I wound up the honor graduate of my MP class.

Since I finished number one in my class, I was given my choice of assignments. I had never paid much attention to "dream sheets," but since they were offering, I decided to fill it out. I selected the Dominican Republic as my first choice and the Republic of Vietnam as my second. They must have seen me coming a mile away. Here was a guy who had been offered a chance to go anywhere in the world where there was a U.S. Army MP detachment and the idiot picks DomRep and Vietnam! Two days later I was told that, along with about a dozen other trainees, I was being assigned to the 218th Military Police Company, Santo Domingo, Dominican Republic.

I was delighted to return to the Dominican Republic, but I soon discovered that things were a little different this time around. The 218th MP Company's area was located in the rear garden of the old presidential palace. Our barracks were large, all-purpose canvas tents with wooden floors, but we had our own bar and an Olympic-size swimming pool!

In less than a month, I was promoted to specialist four. I guess that my new company commander was impressed with my training record from Fort Gordon.

Our two-man patrols were tasked with making sure the U.S. troops stationed on the island followed the military rules and regulations. Rule number one was that *all* houses of ill repute were off-limits. Naturally, that was the first rule broken by nearly every soldier on the island. We MPs had our own whorehouses that we knew were safe, and even the officers frequented one out near the airport, the "Pink Palace." MPs didn't arrest each other, and the officers seemed immune to the rules; the ones who got the shitty end of the stick were the ordinary troops, who were forced to defy the rules to get their lay in the hay. As usual, the grunts got the C rats, while everyone else was getting steak and lobster.

It wasn't unusual for us to pull a raid on a combination bar and whorehouse and find a GI under the bed in each and every room in the building. If the soldier took the bust in stride and didn't try to prove his manhood by fighting us, we just escorted him out of the building and sent him on his way. If the offender got abusive or was a smart-ass, he would be cited with a DR (delinquency report), then be escorted back to his company area. For every ten GIs we caught, we had to cite maybe two.

Duty in the DomRep was the best I had encountered in the military. Serving with the 218th MP Company was almost like having a civilian job. We worked an eight-hour shift, got off on a pass into town, or stayed behind and spent the rest of the day snuggled up to our very own bar, where the beer and liquor flowed freely at a very cheap price.

My hope that I would spend my entire three-year enlistment at DomRep came to an end in September when we were told that we would be leaving our tropical paradise in October. Our next duty station was being kept secret. During our final month in DomRep, we cleaned and inventoried our gear and equipment, and patrols took a backseat to administrative duties. We made the deadline with all our equipment in order with only a few days to spare.

In appreciation of the fine job we had been doing, the CO held a going-away party for his troops. Had we known where we were being assigned, I don't think we would have been all that dedicated.

We were on an LST sailing for Cherry Point, North Carolina, when the CO informed us that we were being assigned to Fort Bragg. My new assignment was to Co C, 503d MP Battalion. What a nightmare! I was going to be part of a leg MP unit in the middle of an Airborne military post. The 503 MPs were stationed right next to the XVIII Airborne Corps headquarters.

I wasn't with my new unit more than two weeks when a call went out for volunteers to man a new MP company. The 218th MP Company was being reorganized to be sent to Vietnam. It didn't take long for me to throw my name in the hat. I had wanted to go to Vietnam anyway, but better than that, I had wanted to go over with the unit I had served with in DomRep. Things were sure looking up for me.

CHAPTER 8

In mid-November 1966, the company received a fourteen-day leave before we were to depart for Vietnam. Since the entire unit was made up of volunteers, I figured they weren't too worried about any of us going AWOL.

I was at Uncle Larry and Aunt Betty's house listening to another scheme that my cousin, Sammy, was cooking up to keep himself out of the draft, when another cousin, Mary Beth, changed the TV channel. It was a special program on Vietnam and the songs of Special Forces NCO Barry Sadler. I tuned out Sammy's insane ramblings and pulled up a chair to the TV. I was just getting into the show when my aunt Betty walked in and switched the channel again, saying, "We don't want to watch this garbage."

I was somewhat taken aback by her statement and told her that in a month I would be going to Vietnam and would like to watch the program. She repeated in no uncertain terms that in *her* house they didn't watch that "kind of garbage."

I couldn't understand her attitude. After all, I was getting ready to leave for Vietnam, and her brother, my uncle Eddie, was already there. Maybe that was the reason she didn't want to hear anything about the war—hoping that if she didn't pay any attention to it, nothing bad would happen to her brother. Well, with my departure just days away, I couldn't handle that kind of attitude, so I cut my leave short and returned to Fort Bragg.

On 21 December 1966, I first laid eyes on our transportation to Vietnam. The army was trying to sell us on the idea that the USNS *General Darby* was a ship, when it was nothing more than a bucket of rust. I had heard many tales of the famous Col. William O. Darby and his army Rangers; I hoped that the floating scrap heap hadn't been named after him. I didn't think that William Darby had been promoted to general before his death, so maybe the old transport had been named after some Civil War general who had lost some famous battle or something.

We were marched onto the *Darby*'s decks single file, then led to our sleeping quarters below, which were worse than I could ever have imagined. The bunks were constructed of nylon webbing strung from pipe frames and stacked in tiers, four bunks to a tier. Never in a million years would I have thought this was the way I would go to combat. My first battle would be just to reach the war zone.

But the worst was yet to come; since we had arrived ahead of schedule, we were to pull KP for our own and the other units just beginning to arrive. I guess that was our reward for being so efficient. I knew it was going to be a *very* long trip when people began to develop seasickness while we were still tied to the pier. I was no exception. It took all my strength not to join my sick comrades at the rail. Many became sick leaving the chow line with a tray of food. Even the proximity of food had many of them upchucking all over the place. And the poor souls assigned KP duty drew the unsavory work of cleaning up all the vomit. To be told that you were on the KP roster was like being told you were going to be shot at dawn. But with the arrival of a pair of infantry companies, our mess hall duties finally came to an end. We were then assigned deck patrol and deck watch. On 26 December 1966, the *Darby* set sail for Vietnam.

Once we were at sea, it didn't take long to realize that those who voluntarily sailed for a living were about a sandwich short of a full picnic. The *Darby* rolled and tossed with every undulation of the sea. With nothing to look at but sky and water, boredom soon began to take its toll.

We got a taste of excitement as we passed the Hawaiian Islands. It was about nine o'clock in the morning when the speaker blared loudly, "Messman Martinez, report to the galley." This message was repeated for the better part of an hour before we began to realize that our ship was circling. Evidently, old Martinez had become more bored with the trip than the rest of us and had jumped overboard. Or he had really pissed someone off and had been thrown overboard. A rumor soon filtered down to where we were gathered that a lifeboat and lantern were missing. It turned out to be just that, a rumor. After about four hours of circling aimlessly, we headed west and continued to Vietnam.

We were not allowed to remove our weapons to take up some slack time, and polishing boots would have been asinine, even for the army, so the old man decided to schedule boxing matches. We spent a lot of time watching guys beat the hell out of each other. There were not many good boxers aboard ship, but there were a good number of tough street fighters.

One boring day ran into another until we finally got the word that we were within a day of the coast of Vietnam.

CHAPTER 9

My first impression of Vietnam was as seen from the deck of the *Darby* when it dropped anchor in Nha Trang harbor. I was standing at the rail with a group of guys, looking shoreward, when Jeep said, "You ain't gonna believe this shit!" Handing me the field glasses he had been looking through, he pointed toward a road on shore, five hundred or six hundred meters away. While I was trying to focus on Jeep's point of interest, I heard him remark to some of the soldiers lining the rails, "Hey, guys, we may have found Walker the love of his life."

At that moment, I located the subject of my attention. There, on the side of the road, a female Vietnamese in native garb had dropped her pants and was busily engaged in natural recycling. I was amazed. Nothing in my past life in England and America had prepared me for this lesson in field expediency. It would be the first of many surprises I would receive before leaving Vietnam.

We remained at anchor for twenty-four hours while the infantry off-loaded. The field glasses were never far from my reach; along the bustling shoreline there was a constant flow of sights to see.

When we had still not unloaded by the second day, the rumor mills began to run wild. We were supposed to have been attached to the 630th MP Company in Nha Trang, but now the word was that we were going up north in response to increased enemy activity there. Another rumor said that the North Vietnamese had surrendered and that we were going to Hanoi as an occupation force. Rumor mills had a way of obfuscating the facts.

The following day, we were informed that we were going to Cam Ranh Bay. The *Darby* raised anchor and put out to sea for the short run down the coast. It didn't matter to us where we landed, as long as we got off the damned boat.

Cam Ranh Bay was an amazing scene. Hundreds of ships were anchored offshore, waiting for their turn to move in and unload their cargoes. But since we were a troopship, we were considered a priority vessel, and sailed past the other ships to an anchor point two hundred meters from shore. We were given orders to change into clean fatigues and to make sure that our boots were polished to a high gleam. Even in a combat zone, the brass still loved to put on their dog-and-pony shows.

We left our belongings on board the *Darby* and off-loaded into landing craft. After the inevitable hurry up and wait, we finally chugged toward shore. The front-loading ramps of the landing craft dropped into the fine, white sand, and we marched onto the beach, in formation with flags flying, to the sound of a military band playing the national anthem. Boy, was I impressed!

We stood in formation at parade rest while some general, wearing heavily starched fatigues and jump boots that someone had gone to one hell of a lot of trouble to spit-shine for him, gave a long and boring speech. The ceremony had to be for his edification rather than for ours. He railed on about the evils of Communism and the goodness of America until we couldn't stand it any longer; we were just a bunch of kids who had traveled halfway around the world on a slow boat to land on the shores of this foreign and exotic country, and the last thing we wanted right now was to be forced to listen to this overinflated charlatan. Besides, the temperature on the exposed sand was well over a hundred degrees Fahrenheit, and we were beginning to melt. I couldn't see the face of our commanding officer, but our first sergeant was making no bones about his interest in the general's speech.

Finally, the officer realized that the heat had ruined his timing, and he put an "amen" to his long-winded sermon. Our CO saluted the general, then did an about-face and told us to be at ease. He said we could smoke them if we had them. We had them.

Within minutes, we had broken ranks and were milling around, bullshitting and wondering what was in store for us next. A short time later, the first sergeant grabbed a group of unlucky souls and ordered them to return to the *Darby* to retrieve our equipment while the remainder of us were put into platoon formations and marched off to find our new homes.

We finally halted in the middle of a great expanse of white sand and were told, "This is it." They couldn't mean that *this* was our home. Nothing was there but us and the sand. Then we spotted a number of pallets, containing what appeared to be a large number of canvas tents.

During our first week in Vietnam, we occupied ourselves with constructing the company area. Until it was complete, we were restricted to the immediate vicinity of the compound. For seven days, the 218th MP Company toiled in sand and sun to build our new home. We completed the task just hours short of a mutiny. Our CO realized that our morale was lower than whale shit, so when he was satisfied the camp met the standards of the powers that be, he authorized passes into the village of Cam Ranh.

By this time in my life, I had been around the block a few times. I had visited a couple of the border towns in old Mexico, and I had left DNA samples at every house of ill repute in Santo Domingo, but I must admit that I was not ready for the village of Cam Ranh.

When you entered the village, the first structure you encountered was a brick building that housed the local QC, the South Vietnamese military police. This building also contained the first of many whorehouses that lined the main strip. It soon appeared to us that we were in the heart of the red-light district, where there were at least three whorehouses for every retail shop, and a massage parlor for every whorehouse. If there was a special place for sins of the flesh, we had just discovered it. The most amazing part of our discovery was that after we got settled in, our first assignment in Vietnam would be to patrol and control this erotic sin city.

CHAPTER 10

When all was finally said and done, I guess that week of busting ass was not so bad. After all, the old man was kind enough to reward us for our hard work by giving us the opportunity to avail ourselves of all the sex we could handle. During the first week of no restrictions, most of us had managed to find a long-term girlfriend who would "love us tooooo much." Being an MP had its advantages: We were all "Numba One GIs," and the rest of the REMFs at Cam Ranh Bay were "Numba Ten GIs," even though they paid for the favors of the fair maidens of Cam Ranh village.

Between exploits in the village, we continued readying our equipment for our upcoming duties. We had already been alerted that, in addition to patrolling the village for evildoers and law-breakers, we would also have the pleasure of escorting convoys from Cam Ranh to Phan Rang and Nha Trang. There would also be the no-brainer duty of manning checkpoints.

I was assigned the first convoy escort to Phan Rang during my third week in country. I was so excited that Jeep finally told me to calm down: "It's just a short trip up Highway 1. No big deal."

"But, Jeep," I said, "we are going into combat."

Jeep only shook his head and growled, "Boy, are you out of contact with reality!" I would discover later that we were both out of contact with reality. We were dealing with a country club, not a combat zone.

On the way out to the firing range to zero our weapons, I swung the M-60 around on its swivel in the back of the jeep and pretended to mow down the hordes of Commies trying to overrun the convoy. How damned stupid!

After putting a hundred rounds through the M-60, we test-fired our .45s by shooting at targets that didn't move or shoot back. When we'd finished, we returned to the company area for a final briefing. It was at this briefing that I first began to realize that we were to follow rules that didn't make a lot of sense. The brass called them "rules of engagement." They were nothing more than a set of unilateral restrictive covenants, subscribed to for us by our fearless leaders, that established standards by which combat was to be conducted. The only problem was that the other side failed to establish its own rules of engagement or abide by ours. This led to our soldiers being forced to wear gloves and fight with one hand tied behind their backs, while the enemy got to take his gloves off and duke it out with both hands. It made it really tough to win the close ones.

One of my favorite rules is worth sharing. On the west side of the road, just before Phan Rang, was the Michelin rubber plantation. We were ordered that, under no circumstances, were we to return fire at the enemy if they were on the Michelin rubber plantation.

Another rule that we all had a terrible time obeying was the rule that we could not bring enemy soldiers under fire unless they opened fire on us first. Don't think the VC didn't have fun with that one!

A third rule was that we were there in Vietnam as the guests of the Vietnamese government, and as such we would not return fire if it was *possible* that innocent civilians were in the line of fire.

Of course, there was nothing secret about the rules of engagement. So a particularly smart VC commander would set up his base camp in the Michelin rubber plantation, send out unarmed soldiers to plant mines in the roads with instructions to wave at any Americans they ran into, and set up ambushes only in occupied villages and crowded marketplaces. It made perfectly good sense to me.

We traveled at the head of the convoy, leading it the half mile down the dirt road toward Highway 1. When we reached the graveled, pothole-filled main highway we turned left and headed south for Phan Rang. At the intersection was a combination massage parlor, bar, whorehouse, and car wash where you could get yourself and your vehicle taken care of at the same time.

One mile south of the intersection was a village on the right side of the highway with a regular red-light district. On the left side of the highway was an ARVN compound.

A little farther down the highway, we were passing the Republic of Korea White Horse Division compound when a tremendous amount of heavy machine-gun fire sounded just ahead. We rounded a bend in the road on full alert, expecting at any minute to drive into an enemy ambush when, to the side of the road, I spotted a flatbed truck with a quad-fifty—four .50-caliber machine guns—mounted in the back. Its crew, concentrating on pulverizing the countryside, ignored us. We stopped the convoy and dismounted to find out what was going on. The quad-fifty never stopped firing as an ROK (Republic of Korea) soldier swept the spent brass from the back of the flatbed. An officer was sitting in the front of the truck, with his feet propped up on the dash, smoking a cigarette. When he saw me approaching, he got out of the truck and smiled.

Over the din of the quad-fifty, he explained that a sniper had fired a shot into their compound the night before, and there was no way they were going to put up with it. He smiled again and calmly lit another cigarette as the quad-fifty continued to chop down trees and other things in its path. Now, to me this made a lot of sense. The ROKs knew how to establish rules of engagement: Screw with us, you're dead.

During the trip down to Phan Rang, I was amazed at the wreckage that littered both sides of the highway. There were about an equal number of civilian and military vehicles that had been destroyed on the road in heavy fighting. I wondered how many lives had been lost along that short span of road while the casualties were observing someone's rules of engagement. But except for a few rounds popped at us as we passed the rubber plantation (surprise!) the entire trip was uneventful. Rules or no rules, I had already made up my mind to fire up the plantation if we took more than a couple of rounds of sniper fire.

During our first month at Cam Ranh Bay, we lost two of our four platoons. One was sent to Phan Rang, the other to Dalat. We were told that we would rotate duties between the platoons, but that never quite materialized. It appeared that I would be doomed to pull my tour in the sandbox of Cam Ranh Bay.

My duties alternated between village patrol and convoy duty until I managed to do something stupid, getting caught in the village after hours by a civil affairs officer. Since I had previously been a good little MP, my punishment was light—one week of checkpoint duty along Highway 1. My first sergeant privately informed me that if army regulations had not prohibited it, my punishment would have been a good, old-fashioned ass-kicking for allowing myself to get caught by an officer. The first shirt was not overly fond of officers.

Now, I'm not saying that officers in the United States Army are stupid, but a survey taken from a random sampling of enlisted men with at least one year of active duty service would probably indicate an overwhelming opinion that the officer corps' collective allotment of common sense would hardly fill a canteen cup.

The ROKs manned a checkpoint directly across the highway from their compound, leading some ranking U.S. officer from the Cam Ranh Bay staff to think that we should have our own checkpoint farther south, toward Phan Rang. No one determined why we should man such a checkpoint, or even why there should be another checkpoint. But I soon found myself sitting in an eight-foot-by-ten-foot guard shack with my M-16 and a basic load of ammo, wondering what the hell I was supposed to do. I didn't know about the other MP with me, but I did know that if a company of armed VC came marching down the highway, I was getting the hell out of Dodge. They could have the guard shack and the highway. Neither one belonged to me!

This short week on shit detail got me somewhat disgruntled with the 218th MP Company. It was a damn good unit with better-than-average officers and NCOs, but they had no control over the moronic schemes developed by the grand wizard of Cam Ranh. Not long after I had been paroled from the checkpoint, it came under direct fire from Charlie. No one was injured, but I knew the asinine detail would eventually claim the life of one of my comrades.

Between convoy escorts and village patrols, we did manage to host a number of beach parties. We would take a truck, back up to the back gate, load it full of girls, then pull down the tarp and head off to the beach. Life was pretty good at Cam Ranh Bay. As far as we were concerned, the war was in another country.

As we saw it, our sole mission in life was to get through our year without contracting the dreaded "black syphilis," which—according to rumor—resulted in eternal exile to some desert island in the South China Sea. The rumor must have been true, because no one I know ever met a person who had gotten off the island.

Yet something was missing for me. I had gone to Vietnam

to fight a war, and I had yet to even see one. Things started to change drastically for me when I committed the unpardonable sin of shooting up the Michelin rubber plantation. I was on convoy duty, as I had been a dozen times before. And just like a dozen times before, as we passed through the evenly spaced rubber trees, the VC opened fire on us. But instead of the one or two wild shots they usually fired at the lead jeep, the dumb ass fired an entire magazine. I lost control and overheated my M-60 burning through a full ammo box of linked rounds, then I realized that I had just stepped on my manhood with both feet. Checkpoint duty was for minor infractions. This time, I would be lucky to get away with nothing more than a firing squad.

My punishment was worse than a firing squad: no longer would I patrol the village, no longer would I pull convoy escort, no longer would I pull checkpoint duty. From then on I was relegated to the role of the company commander's driver. I had been turned into a gofer!

I tried hard to be a good gofer. Without complaining, I repainted the old man's jeep, washed it at the car wash, then polished it. Really, it was a choice assignment on the fast track to making sergeant, E-5, but I was miserable. My buddies were traveling the countryside, seeing the sights, while I was stuck with a bunch of officers at headquarters.

During that time, one of the guys who was Airborne qualified put in a 1049 (request for reassignment) for an Airborne unit. His request was turned down, and he was hot as a June bug on a BBQ grill. Then I happened across a bunch of guys who were also Airborne qualified and were bitching about the direction in which the company was heading. The company had been originally formed from all volunteers, both Airborne and leg. The unit had quickly transformed itself into a fine outfit, and its morale had been among the highest. But now, with all the Mickey Mouse bullshit, the unit was quickly falling apart. Before long, we drafted a letter requesting transfer to an Airborne unit. Most of the Airborne personnel signed it.

The letter was sent to MACV headquarters in Saigon to the

grand wizard himself, Gen. William Westmoreland. Not a week later, our CO called a company formation and informed us that a letter from Saigon ordered that any request for transfer to Airborne unit be honored for those qualified to go.

In May 1967, the 218th MP Company lost about 20 percent of its strength. Jeep and I were among those who decided to transfer out. I felt a lot of guilt over leaving the outfit I had been with for a year and a half, but I could be part of the Mickey Mouse Club no longer.

CHAPTER 11

Jeep and I went to Duc Pho, Republic of Vietnam, and the 1st Brigade, 101st Airborne Division. We were excited about being with such a distinguished unit, and we were ready to do battle with the elusive Viet Cong. I was elated at being a member of the Screaming Eagles. I couldn't wait to write home and tell my folks the good news. Of course, what I thought was good for me would not necessarily be good for my mother, who believed I was safe and sound and out of harm's way at bustling Cam Ranh Bay. There was no way I could explain to her the importance of being back among paratroopers again, since she thought I was nuts for going Airborne to begin with—and that was before Vietnam started up. The only thing I could tell her was that I was in the rear policing unruly troopers when they came in from the field. There was no way I could make her understand how weary I was growing of all the legs at Cam Ranh Bay, who were bitching and moaning about what a rough time they were having.

We reported in at the provost marshal's office and were met by a short, stubby major named Weinstein. I wasn't too impressed with the unimposing little field-grade (majors, lieutenant colonels, and colonels) officer, but by the way he was looking at us, I don't think he was too impressed either. So I guess that left us on even ground.

It wasn't too long before I found myself looking at the front of my pants to check my fly to see if it was open. The major sure liked checking out crotches. He was continually looking up, then down, unable to maintain eye contact for more than a few seconds at a time. He reminded me of the English cartoon character Noddy. Noddy, of course, was a bloody ass! I was soon to discover that Major Weinstein was as well.

The good major informed us that we were members of the United States Army, and as such there were some things that he as provost marshal demanded from us. We would maintain our personal appearance above that of the people we policed. We would keep our boots highly brush-shined and change our uniforms daily—twice a day if they became soiled. We would also keep our hair cut, no more than an inch on top, with whitewalls on the sides. On and on he went.

I had to look around to make sure I was in Vietnam; Stateside lifer bullshit was beginning to depress me. I tried to consider the source, but the West Point graduate had never heard a shot fired in anger, and he clearly didn't have a clue on how to keep troops motivated in a combat zone. He tried to make us believe that he felt keeping his MPs strac would keep us alive and safe; we knew he was only bucking for a promotion. Well, I'd spent enough time as an REMF to deal with him. Or so I thought.

Before releasing us to the tender mercies of the detachment commanding officer, Major Weinstein reminded us that military courtesy would be strictly adhered to at all times. Officers would be saluted and addressed as "sir," and NCOs would be addressed as "Sergeant." That said, we were dismissed with a salute and a wave of his hand.

All the lifer bullshit didn't really mean a thing. I'd lost interest in it in the first few minutes, paying more attention to my surroundings than to Major Weinstein. While I was checking out his office, I realized that the furnishings in the room wouldn't have been out of place anywhere back in the States.

Nice big desk, oversized fan, extra pair of shined boots sitting against the wall, and what appeared to be starched fatigues hanging from coat hangers in the rear of the room. The guy was totally unaware of where he was. In his mind he was still back in the States, and if you were really in Vietnam, that was a dangerous place to be. I decided then and there to ignore this guy, or at least take him with a grain of salt. Jeep was on the same page as me, but others appeared to be buying this lifer bullshit.

Glad to be out of the major's tent, I gave a sigh of relief. Even the hot, muggy air of Vietnam outdoors was preferable to the stuffy atmosphere of the provost marshal's office. I'd already figured the clown out: he led by intimidation and not by example, which meant that he didn't lead at all.

The REMF bullshit continued as we reported to the detachment commander, Lieutenant Shields, a tall, slender young officer who, seen alongside Weinstein, made you believe that Laurel and Hardy were commanding the MPs. That was just a first impression, but it was an accurate one.

While the lieutenant rattled off the same line of intimidating bullshit that we had just received from Weinstein, once more I found myself daydreaming. The two provost officers were two peas from the same pod. My mind began to wander, and soon I was thinking about cold beer and getting laid.

"Specialist Walker, are you paying attention?" Lieutenant Shields demanded.

"Yes, sir," I stuttered, ashamed of myself for giving the skinny pip-squeak a free shot at me.

"Well, why are you still standing there?" he stammered. "I said 'dismissed.' " He and I were already on the wrong foot.

Outside, I asked Jeep his impressions of the major and was not surprised to learn that they were in line with my own. We knew then that we had screwed up leaving Cam Ranh Bay. We agreed to begin researching ways to get out of this chickenshit outfit. We had been 1/101st MPs for less than an hour.

We were shown to our new home by Sergeant Crawford, one of the detachment NCOs. We would be staying in squad-size tents with wooden-pallet flooring.

Crawford told us to store our equipment and report for

orientation in fifteen minutes. We looked at each other and
shook our heads—our third orientation in less than two hours.
What a way to spend the war!

I must admit that I was eager to find out what our duties would
be, so I stuck my gear under my cot and reported to Sergeant
Crawford for orientation. As soon as he opened his mouth, I
knew that we were dealing with another Weinstein/Shields
clone. These jerks must have gotten their lobotomies at the same
clinic. It wasn't Laurel and Hardy in command, but the Three
Stooges! These clowns wanted total conformity; Jeep and I were
card-carrying nonconformists. Only Whitey seemed to waver in
his resolve to beat these guys at their own game, but I figured
that Whitey would come around once the newness wore off.

Sergeant Crawford was another lifer who seemed to be
unaware that the brigade was in Vietnam, not Fort Campbell,
Kentucky. Bored to tears by his brief speech, I was elated when
he finally put a cap on it and dismissed us for the rest of the day.
Of course, he warned us that we would be assigned duties first
thing the next day.

It was going to be one hell of a war if we were going to have
to fight our officers and NCOs before we got to fight the
enemy. This particular brand of "professional" soldier was a
menace to the military. They strutted around rear areas barking
orders, bullying soldiers, and generally being a pain in the ass.
Talking was out, screaming was in. They were so incompetent,
they were pathetic. I watched as they made life miserable for
everyone concerned. Then it finally dawned on me—they were
the guys who'd been picked on by schoolyard bullies. Now it
was their turn. Through patience and conformity, they had
acquired high enough rank to become bullies themselves. They
were officers and NCOs who were so unaware of their own
inadequacies that they had to bully everyone around them to
keep the attention off themselves. They flunked their own self-
analysis, so they spent all their time desperately searching for
petty faults in others. Lacking the ability and the intestinal fortitude to be combat leaders themselves, they sought the safety
of rear areas and made sure those around them were too busy

to notice. I had seen that in other rear-echelon units, and had sworn that I would not get caught up in the same dilemma.

We spent most of the first day avoiding these petty tyrants and introducing ourselves to the other worker bees. We soon realized that the 218th MP Company would have outperformed the 1/101st MP detachment hands down. I experienced a certain amount of shame being assigned to the unit. Airborne, my ass! These people acted more like legs than legs did. There was no esprit de corps.

I soon found myself wandering down a dirt road that led up to a hill. At the base of the hill, I saw a sign that read, THE EYES OF THE EAGLE. On it were two 101st Airborne Division patches and a scroll that read LONG RANGE RECON! When I moved a little closer, I noticed that there was a drawing of a soldier holding up the head of a VC with the words MATHESON'S MARAUDERS emblazoned under it.

Now, I must admit that I was intrigued by this. Whoever those people were, they were likely some bad dudes. Patched tents were scattered around in no particular order, and the area around the tents was choked with brush and thorns. It looked as if a bunch of convicts lived there, and everyone was afraid to tell them to clean up their neighborhood.

Afraid that I would pick up some deadly organism if I remained there too long, I started to back away, then I heard someone yelling my name. Turning around, I recognized the first friendly face I had seen since coming to the 101st, my old platoon sergeant from the 82d, S. Sgt. Larry Beauchamp.

I hadn't seen him since September 1965, when we had served together at Fort Bragg and the Dominican Republic. A flood of great memories washed over me as I stood looking at him. Beauchamp and Sergeants Tyrone Adderly and John Jakovenko were the three outstanding Airborne NCOs who had had the greatest impact on my career in the military. Adderly and Jakovenko would later take part in the famous Special Forces Son Tay prison camp raid, deep inside North Vietnam. All three were warriors the United States should have been damned proud of. I know that I sure am.

Beauchamp and I were so happy to see each other that we

stood there shaking hands for what seemed like ten minutes, before he finally let go and invited me to come up LRRP Hill for a beer, my first since arriving at Duc Pho. We sat talking about all the good times at Bragg and DomRep, never touching on any of the bad things that had happened. Beauchamp soon had me feeling like a human again. He might have been a lifer, but he didn't have the lifer mentality that characterized soldiers like Weinstein, Shields, and Crawford. Like any good soldier, he followed orders, but I never saw him once take advantage of his rank. He earned your respect by his actions and demeanor, not by what he wore on his sleeve.

When I told him that I was in the MPs, he said that it was common knowledge in the brigade that most of the NCOs in my unit were rejects. After a couple more beers, I left with the promise that I would be back soon for another visit.

As I walked back down LRRP Hill, the germ of a plan began to formulate deep in the recesses of my mind: if things didn't work out with the MPs, I might just try a lateral move to brigade LRRP. Beauchamp had told me that a transfer to the LRRPs was a priority transfer, i.e., no unit commander could disapprove of a request for transfer to the LRRPs. Besides, I had the necessary "in"—my friend Staff Sergeant Beauchamp was a LRRP team leader.

I was anxious to tell Jeep of my recent good fortune. If I decided to jump ship, I wanted him to come with me. When I finally ran him down and apprised him of my emergency escape plan, Jeep listened patiently until I was finished. Then he dropped a bomb of his own on me. He had also been preparing an escape plan, except his entailed a transfer to Tiger Force, the nail-eating recon platoon of the 1/327th Infantry.

I was shocked when I heard this bit of news. A battalion recon platoon was out of the question for me. It was "hazardous duty" times ten! We'd only been in Duc Pho less than a day and had already heard about Tiger Force. They were one hell of a short-range recon platoon, but they never got it through their heads that they were only a platoon, and not a battalion. They suffered horrendous casualties taking on enemy units five to ten times their size.

We discussed the pros and cons of LRRPs and Tiger Force without really coming to agreement. I felt that six-man teams were a great concept, while Jeep thought they were on par with Japanese kamikaze pilots.

On the other hand, I thought the idea of a platoon-size recon element was a walking piece of meat looking for a hungry predator. The two of us were at a philosophical impasse that most likely would lead to our going separate ways in the near future.

The second day at the 1/101st MP detachment was much like the first. The NCOs were up early, shouting orders and harassing the troops. It would have been comical had I been on the sidelines watching. But I wasn't, and I soon grew tired of participating in the lifer posturing that seemed to dominate the unit's everyday activities.

The only break I got from the routine was when I got assigned to garbage patrol with Sergeant Franklin, known as "Rock." He was the only decent NCO I met in the 1/101st MPs. He performed his job with minimal bullshit, but had to spread a little around just so the other NCOs wouldn't think he had betrayed them. I began to suspect that most of the other NCOs had a healthy fear of the Rock. He refused to play lifer games or conform to the deviant mentality typical of the One Oh Worst MPs. I don't know about all the rest of the guys, but it surely impressed me. I guess the Rock's main problem was that he possessed a great sense of humor, and he was far, far too well educated for his peers. Or could it have possibly been that the Rock was black? Whatever the reason, the Rock had a handle on the situation, and I was more than happy to be on duty with him.

We spent the day observing GIs at the garbage dump and doing the best we could to keep the Vietnamese away from the trucks. I felt a deep sense of shame chasing the locals away from the dump. All they wanted was the garbage that we were throwing away. It wasn't like we were discarding ammunition or weapons. To survive, they would simply recycle our garbage for food, and rebuild their homes and furniture from our castoffs. I could easily have let myself become depressed, but

I shook the feeling off and told myself that I was only doing my job. I had witnessed poverty in DomRep, but nothing like what I saw in Vietnam. I would be especially thankful when the day finally came to an end. This was one duty that I would be sure to beg off of in the future.

Finally, the garbage detail came to an end, and we reported to CID. They were interested in any GI who had contact with the Vietnamese. Their main focus was on GIs who were buying and selling illegal drugs or who had sexual contact with Vietnamese.

During the time we were being interviewed by the CID, they were passing around cans of beer. They kept it in an honest-to-God Stateside refrigerator. I found the whole affair distasteful and avoided giving them any information. I didn't see anything wrong with smoking a little dope or enjoying a little boom-boom. Many lifers were doing a lot more damage dealing in the black market, not to mention all the "leaders" who were killing and maiming American boys out of sheer incompetence. To me, those were greater crimes than sins of the flesh or passing around a joint. CID was about as popular with soldiers as internal affairs is with street cops. In the animal world, those who feed on their own are called cannibals.

It was dark by the time I got back to my tent. I found a poker game in progress. The stakes were nickel-dime-quarter, but the pile of MPC in the center of the table could have easily led anyone unfamiliar with military scrip into believing there were some major players in the game.

Jeep was winning, and winning big. Good, I thought, he could buy the beer tonight. I was short on cash, as I had picked up the tab for the drinks the night before. I still had not been able to talk him out of the idea of going to Tiger Force.

The game broke up early, and a bunch of us headed down to the HHC (Headquarters & Headquarters Company) bar for the rest of the evening. On the way, I tried again to talk Jeep into coming with me to the Lurps. It was the same discussion, the same pros and cons—an uphill battle all the way. When we reached the club, I was as determined as ever to join the Lurps as soon as it became necessary to do so, and Jeep was still determined to go to Tiger Force. I would hate to leave my friend, but my mind was made up. Given the first reasonable excuse, I would submit my request for a transfer from the unit.

The third day in the 1/101st MPs was much like the others. The NCOs were still passing out ridiculous orders, Lieutenant Shields was still strutting around like the cock of the roost, getting ready to assign bad details to some idle people. It was already old. Just as I was hoping for some duty away from the detachment area, I was assigned to guard detainees in our temporary POW compound.

I sat there in the hot sun and watched the POWs as they sat there in the hot sun and watched me. It was really exciting duty, and ended up with me watching them while they watched me, without blinking. I came in a distant second place. Hell, I never could stare anybody down.

Throughout the day, I was reminded by more than one NCO that my boots needed shining or that my haircut was not up to standard. I felt like a goldfish in a bowl, with them on the outside looking in. Everybody in the pay grade of E-5 or above came in to scowl at the POWs and their handlers. I sat there nursing a growing rage and rapidly coming to the conclusion that I had to get out of the unit.

When I was finally relieved of duty, I rushed back to the poker game and tried to cool down by beating some of my fellow MPs out of their cash. Afterward, I made the nightly junket down to the HHC bar. There had to be more to the war than what I was engaged in. I was already developing a routine, and in Vietnam, routines made time pass very slowly.

As bad as things were, I still hadn't decided to take the big plunge and volunteer for a combat unit, but I was being pushed farther and farther in that direction every minute.

I went back to LRRP Hill to rekindle my friendship with Staff Sergeant Beauchamp, hoping that over a few cold beers I could get some friendly advice and a much-needed attitude adjustment. Knowing a Lurp team leader made it possible for me to sit in on some of their powwows as long as I didn't interfere with the direction of the conversations. I watched as these guys joked with each other and cut each other down as if ball-busting was nothing but a unit sport. They told an abundance of war stories, but I didn't feel they were doing it for my benefit. There was little doubt that these men had a lot of affection for each other and that they had seen their share of combat. That was what it was all about. They were men who had reputations as misfits, malcontents, and discipline problems. They were soldiers who thumbed their noses at authority but got the job done anyhow. In spite of an occasional character flaw here or there, these men had put aside petty jealousy, racial prejudice, and individualism for the mission and the good of the team. The *team* was everything. For the first time in my military career, I saw everything that I had been searching for: respect, camaraderie, loyalty, dedication, and courage.

As I was leaving later in the evening, I was approached by a Lurp who introduced himself as Rudy Lopez, a smiling Arizona native who carried his five feet six inches, 160 pounds, with authority but without intimidation. He got right to the point, telling me that by the questions I was asking he could tell that I wanted to join the LRRP.

"Look, man," he said, "I left a cushy job as a clerk typist to do what I'm doing and don't regret it a bit, but it's not for everyone. They dump your ass out in the middle of nowhere with five more Lurps, and the hunt is on. You have to find the enemy first, or he will find you and shit on your parade." He paused to let that sink in, then continued, "If you feel comfortable in a small-unit environment, come and join us. If not, stay where you are or go to a line unit."

I thanked him for the advice, then made my way down LRRP Hill. I had a lot of things to think about.

By the time I got to my tent, I knew that I had just left some very special people. I couldn't wait to talk with Jeep. I had to convince him to go to the LRRPs with me if I finally decided to do it. Finding him was no problem, but trying to talk him out of going to Tiger Force was futile.

My fourth day in this magnificent unit proved to be more of the same old bullshit. Once again, I was assigned to watch prisoners, but my main concern was to find a place to hide so that I could stay out of sight of marauding lifers. I was already tired of watching a number of passive Vietnamese detainees moping around, waiting to be interrogated. It was boring and tedious work, totally devoid of any sense of challenge or accomplishment. I wasn't fighting the enemy; I was battling boredom and the harassment of lifers who had nothing to do.

Our day guarding prisoners came to an early end; Jeep, Whitey, and I were relieved of duty from the guard detail and driven to the dirt road that connected the 1st Brigade, 101st, with the 25th Infantry Division. At our end was a large, heavily sandbagged bunker, which overlooked a checkpoint on the road. It would be our home for the next twenty-four hours. During daylight it was our job to stop and check all vehicles passing through on their way to the 25th Infantry Division. It wasn't very exciting work, but it beat the hell out of baby-sitting Vietnamese detainees.

I started off on the wrong foot with the NCOIC at the checkpoint by bragging that now I would have a chance to show what I could do in combat.

"I'm glad you think so, Walker," he said, "because you just drew another twenty-four hours on duty here." When Jeep started laughing, the sergeant quickly added, "I don't know what you're laughing at, Jepperson, the three of you will be keeping each other company."

We jumped down from the truck, and as the previous detail climbed aboard, we stood around, taking stock of our situation. There was a case of C rats in the bunker, plenty of water, an M-60 machine gun with twenty-five hundred rounds of ammo, an M-79 with fifty rounds of HE (high explosive), over two dozen fragmentation grenades, and a case of hand flares. This was in addition to our personal M-16s and each man's basic load of ammunition. We were loaded for bear and ready to kill something. But what? None of us had the slightest idea whom we were supposed to be fighting against or what he even looked like. We were pretty sure the enemy didn't run around with the letters VC or NVA painted on their shirts, but there just had to be some way to tell.

So there we were, along the dirt road that separated two U.S. Army units, eating dust all day long while we waved traffic through and generally felt pretty damn foolish. We soon began to see ourselves as the REMFs we really were, not the warriors we had envisioned ourselves—and the truth hurt. Occasionally, passing grunts took some pretty foul shots at us, and we deserved every one. None of us could really blame them for their remarks—a bunch of MPs sitting around screwing with everybody for no apparent reason.

As night approached, the sergeant of the guard came by to give us some instructions, to tell us what to expect, what we were supposed to do. Our mission at night was almost as pointless as that during the day. He told us that the VC laid land mines and booby traps in and along the highway under the cover of night, so we were supposed to keep alert to prevent him from conducting these activities.

I was dumbfounded by those instructions. During the day, we could see no more than four hundred meters down the road before it dipped and curved to the side out of view. At night the seeing was worse. I could only imagine that our counterparts in the 25th Infantry Division, securing the other end of the road, were suffering the same visual impairments. It didn't take a genius to figure out that there was a large chunk of land between our two checkpoints that no one could observe.

"You know, Sarge, this is a pretty stupid idea of securing the road this way," I announced offhandedly.

His look told me that I had definitely struck a chord. "Well, Walker, you three clowns are gonna get plenty of practice looking down this fucking road, because you've got another twenty-four hours to do it in!" he shouted back over his shoulder as he returned to his vehicle and drove off. Jeep and I looked at each other and started laughing. I wondered if I would ever learn to keep my mouth shut in front of lifers.

As darkness settled over us and our field of vision contracted until we could see out only twenty-five meters, I began to doubt that we would be able to protect our bunker—let alone the road—if the enemy decided to shut us down. I was beginning to experience new respect for the title of Cornelius Ryan's book *The Longest Day*.

I tried to keep a positive attitude during the night, and took turns with Jeep and Whitey, rotating our guard detail so that we could get a little shut-eye between us and still make sure that we didn't get our throats slit by enemy sappers before dawn.

As first light began to approach, I knew that we had not only accomplished our mission, but we had survived. On the other hand, I knew that we had survived only by the grace of God. If Chuck had wanted our bunker and the entire mile-long stretch of roadway, we would be dead, and VC flags would be flying all over the place.

I was propped up against the front wall of the bunker, enjoying the early-morning chill and eating a gourmet meal of chopped ham and eggs, when a truckload of troops from the 326th Engineers pulled up to begin their daily sweep for mines. I watched with minor interest as they dismounted and began to assemble across the road. Before beginning the sweep, they tested their mine-detecting equipment, then a young lieutenant and his driver drove up in a jeep and ordered them to move out. I watched them begin their long walk down the road where they would eventually link up with an engineer team from the 25th. Something distracted me for a few minutes, and when I looked back up I was impressed to see that, in less than twenty minutes, they were already three hundred meters down the road. I continued watching as the jeep with the lieutenant aboard tried to turn around in the middle of the road. As it did so, the right front wheel hit the shoulder and a gigantic column of smoke and dirt erupted, followed seconds later by the sound of a devastating blast. I watched in horror as the jeep tumbled high into the air and the two occupants were thrown out to the side. Mesmerized by the scene of the tragedy, I continued to watch as the dust began to settle. It was then that I saw more bodies lying in the road and a number of dazed and injured engineers standing around in apparent shock.

I grabbed my M-16 and leaped from the bunker in a full sprint down the road toward the scene of the carnage, hoping that I could be of some assistance to the wounded survivors. I hadn't gone more than a hundred meters when Lieutenant Shields passed me in his jeep, yelling for me to get back to the bunker. Reluctantly, I turned and walked slowly back to where

Jeep and Whitey stood waiting. I kept looking back over my shoulder as the first of the medevac choppers began to arrive to evacuate the dead and wounded. That was my first look at the real war in Vietnam. I was shocked at how quickly death and destruction could come.

When I reached the bunker, I moved inside and sat down to light up a cigarette. I was too shook up to make a lot of sense out of what I had just witnessed. Soon, Jeep dropped down next to me, and the two of us sat quietly side by side as Whitey gave us a running commentary on what was going on down the road. Finally I turned to Jeep and said, "I'm getting the fuck out of this unit."

After a few minutes Jeep answered, "Me, too." We had made up our minds; as soon as we could file our requests for transfer, the MPs would be history.

We were interrupted by the arrival of Lieutenant Shields and Sergeant Crawford. I sat there numb as the bumbling officer proceeded to chew me out for leaving my post. Finally, I could no longer take any more of his bullshit. I looked up at him and said, "Sir, I want the fuck out of this sorry outfit as soon as possible."

The gangly junior officer recoiled in horror, then gathered himself and informed me that I could talk to the provost marshal after my detail was over and not before.

I didn't have a problem being stuck out on the bunker detail for another twenty-four hours, and Jeep stated that he didn't mind either. However, Whitey expressed some open and hostile sentiments and accused us of being a few points left of center. Jeep and I both blew it off. We were getting out of the clusterfuck unit as soon as we could, and nothing was going to change our minds.

We took some more razzing from the grunts the next day, but, knowing that we would soon be joining them in the field, it was easier to take. Highly visible during the day, when it was safe, the lifers stopped by every couple of hours or so; they were nowhere around at night when Chuck came out to play.

Night fell once again, and the three of us, all born in merry old England, once more prepared to sell ourselves dearly to any VC battalion brave enough to take on the queen's finest. Once again, they avoided us like the plague.

Finally, the sun broke over the horizon, signaling the day I would go down to the provost marshal's office and put in my 1049 for brigade LRRPs. I knew that I would have to remain calm and professional when I reported to Major Weinstein to tell him I wanted to transfer. I also suspected that "I want out" wouldn't cut it with Major Weinstein.

We were finally relieved at midmorning by three lucky souls who would give their all to protect the pile of sandbags and the dirt strip in front of it. We returned to our platoon area just in time to participate in Major Weinstein's pep rally.

"Men," he began, "according to the Geneva Convention we are required to provide adequate housing to Vietnamese prisoners of war, and as we are taking more prisoners each and every day, the facilities we now have are not in accordance with the law." Exuding a look of self-importance that turned the stomachs of everyone in the formation, he stopped talking for a moment, then continued, "I'll make it short. As of today, we will begin a new program of upgrading our facilities, so let's roll up our sleeves and let's get going."

Finished with that rousing piece of motivational genius, the major stepped back and turned the rest of the program over to Lieutenant Shields, who added his three cents and then dismissed the formation.

I turned to Jeep and asked him to tell me if I was going deaf or had I really heard what I thought I had heard.

He responded, "No, Jim, you're not deaf. The goofy motherfucker actually said we would be building the housing."

The two of us stood there making no effort to hide our obvious discontent at this latest bit of news.

"What are you two waiting for—an invitation?" Lieutenant Shields demanded.

"No disrespect intended, sir, but we're waiting for the plane tickets," I responded, trying to keep the contempt out of my voice.

"What the hell are you talking about, Walker?" Lieutenant Shields said.

"The plane tickets to Geneva, sir, because the only way I'm going to build hootches for the VC is if I'm in Geneva," I said, this time letting the contempt show through. Jeep bit his lip to keep from laughing, and the rest of the MPs moved quickly out of the area to avoid getting caught in the cross fire.

"You two report to the provost marshal, right now," Lieutenant Shields screamed, losing any semblance of self-control.

We waited outside the provost marshal's office as Lieutenant Shields ranted and raved inside. We could hear him harping about our total lack of respect or concern for military discipline. We were beginning to see the humor in the situation and were having difficulty keeping serious. We both had smiles on our faces as we entered the antiseptic office of Major Weinstein. The brigade provost marshal gave us no opportunity to defend ourselves but immediately tore into us, telling us that we had been nothing but trouble ever since we had been assigned to his unit. He finished by saying that our lack of military discipline had rocked the morale of the entire unit even more so than the four misfits he had disposed of two days earlier.

I knew immediately that he was talking about Sandy "Boss" Weisberger, Mike "Sweet Pea" Kinnan, Tom "The Greek" Dokos, and Harvey "The Beaver" Beiber. They were all damn fine soldiers who had also tired of the silly game-playing that went on daily in the 1/101st MPs. They had taken it—and him—as long as they could, and had finally 1049d to brigade LRRPs. Now the Long Range Recon detachment would have one more recruit if it would take me.

We left the provost marshal's hootch with him still screaming in the background, but we were at least unofficially out of the MPs. Over the next few months, little changed at the 101st MP Detachment except the names on the weekly roster, as troopers kept transferring out at an astounding rate. By the time I left brigade LRRPs, nearly 40 percent of our unit strength was made up of former MPs.

CHAPTER 12

Depending on one's perspective, I either volunteered for the Lurps or I had been kicked out of the MPs. I didn't mind which way it went down in the history books; I was out of a Mickey Mouse outfit that had me destined for an early court-martial, and I was in a long-range recon patrol detachment where men were men and properly valued for it. No more Laurel and Hardy, no more Three Stooges, only the pride of being with a group of professional warriors who worked hard when it was time to work and played hard when it was time to play.

I gathered what I could carry, said a few hasty good-byes, and beat feet in the direction of Lurp Hill. Every thirty steps or so, I turned around to look back at the MP compound just to make sure I was gaining ground in the opposite direction. I had this awful sensation that I was walking east on a westbound escalator. The closer I got to the LRRP detachment, the more ecstatic I got. I was one happy trooper.

When I reported in to First Sergeant Smith, it was as a cherry Lurp ready for training. I knew I had a lot to learn, but I was committed to being as good as I could be. Top Smith's approach to me was exactly the opposite of what I had witnessed at the brigade MPs. He welcomed me to the unit and told me to go find a hootch or build one. Sounded fine to me! Since I had no shelter half, I bummed around the area until I spotted a tent with a vacancy. Part of the tent was occupied, and one of the guys living there was someone I already knew—Boss Weisberger. Before I could ask him if he wanted a hootchmate, Boss looked up and invited me to take the left-flap area. He and

Sweet Pea Kinnan had the main tent, while The Beaver Beiber occupied the right-flap area. We were all ex–military cops from the 101st MP detachment.

I dropped my gear and sat down to get a briefing from Boss on the current state of affairs in the LRRPs. I couldn't help but notice that Boss kept playing with a straw sticking through his ear. When he saw me looking he grinned and told me all about the LRRP rule about getting your ear pierced. Of course, that was against army and Airborne regulations, but Boss made it clear that we had our own regulations, which superseded all the official bullshit that slid down the information pipeline.

Well, why not? I thought. I should do my bit for the unit's morale. I asked where I could go to get my ear pierced, and Boss directed me to the brigade aid station. "See Lurch," he said as I headed off. I was thirty feet away before I realized I didn't know who Lurch was. When I turned around and asked Boss, he only smirked and said, "You'll know him when you see him."

Boss was right on the money. I spotted Lurch as soon as I entered the aid station. He was a big mother, six feet, four inches and weighing in at somewhere between a Brahma bull and a saltwater crocodile; the only fat on that army medic was a tiny piece of ass left over from the last guy to cross him. Not wanting to be the "next" guy to cross him, I decided to try the cool approach, telling him who I was and what I wanted.

"Sit down, bucko," he said.

I was still playing it cool, like getting my ear pierced was just a day in the life of Limey, when Lurch reached up and shoved a hot needle through my earlobe. Just in time, I swallowed the scream that raced from deep within the pit of my stomach all the way up to the downhill side of my larynx, at the same time managing to blow-dry the tears welling up at the anterior corners of my eyes. *Jesus,* that stung! But I couldn't let on that I felt any pain.

I kept talking a mile a minute, rattling off a bunch of bullshit about how glad I was to be a Lurp and what a bunch of shit-heads MPs were. Finally, Lurch looked up and said, "Shut the fuck up."

I was trying to pop the seal where my sphincter had slammed shut when he added, "Where the hell did you get that fucking accent, bucko?"

Summoning up some courage I bought on credit, I replied, "England. You got a problem with that?"

"Nope," he said, grinning, "I just didn't know we had a fucking Limey in the outfit." With that he invited me to have a cold beer with him over at the 176th Assault Helicopter Company bar. Realizing that my death sentence had been commuted, I told him I'd have to take him up on it later. I had to get the rest of my equipment from the MP area before it got ripped off.

Walking back down the road to the MP compound, I passed Lurp Hill and yelled up to Boss that I'd be right back. He looked down, saw me twisting the straw piercing my ear, and laughed.

At the MP compound, I quickly gathered the rest of my gear. I was still somewhat dejected that Jeep had decided to go to Tiger Force. I would miss him.

When I got back to the LRRP compound with the rest of my equipment, I was met by S. Sgt. Ronnie Weems. He called me over and introduced himself, using his first name and not mentioning his rank. He then told me of the LRRP creed that I must live up to if I was to be one of them. "Never do you snitch out another Lurp," he said. "Never do you take family problems out of the area. This is our family, and no one has any business knowing our affairs. We don't talk about Lurps to people who are not Lurps."

I nodded silently.

"And most important of all," he added, "Lurps don't leave Lurps behind."

I thought about that for a minute, not sure exactly what he meant. Then I realized that he was deadly serious, and suddenly I understood that was the secret that made us special.

He went on to explain that when a Lurp was down—either KIA or WIA—the other five members of his team would never leave him behind even if it meant that they would lose their own lives. On insertion, if one Lurp went in, then the whole team went in—no matter if the LZ was hot or cold. That was the way it was! I knew then that I had found a home.

Sergeant Weems looked at me and smiled. He knew without a response from me that I had just signed on for the duration. With that, he turned and went into his hootch.

I was just turning to go when I heard a bloodcurdling *"Motherfucker!"* come from Weems's tent. I jerked my head around just as a tiny object flew past my head and landed on the ground behind me. I looked down and saw a scorpion flipping over on its legs, tail raised high.

Weems stormed out of his hootch and stomped the angry scorpion into mush, cursing every creature with more than two legs and a tail.

I couldn't help but laugh. He was really comical standing there over the dead insect raging like a maddened bull.

"What the fuck are you laughing at, Limey?" Weems growled threateningly, waiting for me to say the wrong thing.

Oh no! I thought. He's pissed now!

Before I could respond, he said, "Gimme your knife, Limey." I handed him my K-bar and was getting ready to warn him to be careful, the knife was razor sharp, when he cut his hand open. Letting the blood flow freely, he disappeared into his tent only to resurface moments later with a couple of beers in his other hand. Tossing me a brew, he bitched, "The motherfucker stung me and had to pay the price."

I found out later that the scorpion had been Weems's unofficial pet. As long as it didn't bother him, he didn't bother it. He had tolerated the dangerous critter in his hootch for weeks. They had always given each other plenty of space, until the fatal sting—fatal to the scorpion.

I had been in the LRRPs less than a day and already felt at home. Several of the guys came over and introduced themselves, while others just looked me over without saying a word. Clay Wentworth sauntered over and asked me how much time in grade I had. When I told him I had fourteen months as an SP4, he told me that he had just made E-5 with ten months' time in grade as an E-4, and that as the senior E-4 in the unit I would be next in line for E-5 stripes. That made me feel pretty good about myself. In the unit only one day, and I was already in line for a promotion. Only time would tell!

The night was fast approaching. As I looked around the detachment area, I saw a number of Lurps disappear into one of the larger tents. Curious, I walked over and went inside. Looking around, I spotted eight or nine guys passing around a huge pipe. Not wanting to be left out, I moved in and found a spot in their circle. I took a toke when it was offered and passed the pipe on to the next Lurp. Next, I was handed a beer. I nodded my thanks and took a couple of hits off the cold brew, then sat it between my legs. This is great! I thought.

Then an elbow in the ribs and harsh whispers informed me that I had committed the unpardonable sin. Embarrassed, I quickly passed the beer to the next guy. Well, how was I supposed to know?

So that's the way the evening went—a toke on the pipe, followed by a swig from the community can of beer. It wasn't long before I found myself getting high. Not quite an out-of-body experience, but the next best thing.

Lurch suddenly blurted out, "Hey, Limey, what's the difference between an elephant and a loaf of bread?"

"Hell, I give up. I dunno," I answered good-naturedly.

"Remind me not to send you to the store for a loaf of bread," countered the big medic. Everybody started laughing and pointing at me. I didn't think it was particularly funny, but I found myself laughing harder than the rest of them.

"Hey, Limey," Lurch said again, "where does an elephant sit?" I looked at Lurch through squinting eyes and shook my head in mock ignorance.

"Anywhere he wants" was Lurch's quick response.

Strange, that wasn't very funny either, I thought to myself. So why was I rolling on the ground in a fit of hysterical laughter?

The next hour was spent sharing in ridiculous banter, everybody teasing and joking around without the slightest provocation. I could sense the feeling of camaraderie and fraternity among these guys.

Suddenly things got real quiet. I sensed that someone was

about to make a speech; it was that reverent moment of silence that always preceded something profound.

Weems broke the spell. "Remember, Limey," he said, "what we do stays within the unit. We work hard, and we play hard, but under no circumstances do we drink or smoke pot before a mission or during a mission. Pot and booze are taboo in the bush. They will get you killed."

I nodded my understanding. That made good sense to me. Then the reverent moment was broken when somebody said, "They will get you killed in the bush, but in the rear they will only get you fuuuuccccckkkkked up." So much for lessons learned!

As the party continued, I stepped outside for a breath of fresh air. I hadn't seen Rudy Lopez or Jim Cody at the party, Lurps I had met before I joined the unit. When I spotted Rey Martinez standing nearby, I asked him if he knew where they were. Rey looked up and pointed to a mountain about two klicks away, then said that Rudy, Jim, and Ron Gartner had been seriously wounded a couple of days earlier, pulling security for a team of engineers when one of them detonated a mine.

I was stunned. Only a week earlier the LRRP detachment had suffered its worse loss to date. An entire team had been made nonoperational as the result of being ambushed at first light in their NDP. Fireball Dixon had been killed, Kolarik, Tolson, Cruz, and Derby Jones had been wounded; the only Lurp not hurt was Larry Christian. Because of Jones and Christian's tenacity in battle, the remainder of the team survived. Somehow two men held back an estimated enemy platoon.

Derby Jones was put in for the nation's second highest award for heroism, the Distinguished Service Cross. Jones and Christian ended up with the Silver Star. I guess it would have helped if Derby Jones had connections in the higher ranks.

Shaking off this bit of bad news, I went back into the tent to join the rest of the guys. For the first time I understood why they partied so hard and so often—the next day could always be their last.

When I woke up, it was already daylight. I had no idea what

had happened to the remainder of the evening. I didn't even know how I had managed to get back to my hootch. All I knew was that someone had inflated my head with a high-pressure hose—at least that was the way it felt. By the expression on Boss's face, my head must have looked as bad as it felt. I hoped that I had not upset any of my hootchmates when I came in during the night. When nothing was said, I made a beeline for the "water buffalo" to wash off the party crud and rinse the sleep from my eyes. On the way back, I ran into Larry Beauchamp, who informed me that I had slept through morning formation. In no uncertain terms, he told me that I had better get my shit together or I would be back writing parking tickets and shining handcuffs with the MPs. The LRRP detachment had one formation each day, and I was expected to make it.

I made a mental note to myself that I would never miss another morning formation, even if I had to crawl to it on all fours.

Back at the hootch, Boss already had hot water boiling for coffee. The four of us—Boss, Sweet Pea, The Beaver, and I—sat around drinking coffee and bullshitting as we cleaned our weapons. Out in the compound, no one was screaming and yelling. Everything was peaceful. It was relaxed and quietly professional, unlike most military areas I had experienced before.

I was inside looking out, and enjoying every minute of it. I liked the idea of being different from everyone else. I didn't even mind if everyone on the outside thought I was nuts for being a Lurp. They didn't know the truth.

During the second day, I was introduced to our detachment commander, Lt. Dan McIsaac. Once again, there were no demands, no yelling, no bullshit. Just a welcome and a short statement about what would be expected of me. I found myself skeptical that he was really an officer or just one of the guys playing make-believe. Lieutenant McIsaac sure wasn't trying to impress anyone with his rank or his status; he was friendly and helpful with the few questions I had. So there it was—

different type of soldiers, different type of NCOs, and a different type of officer.

I was uncontrollably excited. I went back to my hootch and cleaned my weapon again, not because it was dirty, but because staying busy kept me from doing cartwheels across the compound. I was anxious to be assigned to a team, and looking forward to the training that would make me one of these guys. I couldn't wait to get a mission under my belt, so I could prove myself worthy to the rest of the Lurps. In the back of my mind, I wanted to avenge the casualties recently sustained by the Lurps and the engineers. Witnessing the destruction of those engineers out on the road had affected me deeply. I would never forget the swift horror of those deaths.

My thoughts were interrupted by Boss Weisberger, entering the tent to tell me it was time for chow. He quickly emptied a case of C rats on the ground, labels down. He mixed them around several times before telling me to dig in. With my normal run of luck I ended up with a box of chopped ham and eggs, the breakfast of choice on death row. Hell, even the dreaded ham and lima beans was preferred over chopped ham and eggs. Properly heated and liberally coated with Tabasco sauce, the sordid mess would be edible if not enjoyable. Things could have been worse. They could have forced me to eat at the mess hall.

Early that afternoon, George "Rommel" Murphy pulled up in the unit's single three-quarter-ton truck, affectionately known as the Lurpmobile. Rommel yelled at me to get in, he was going to take me down to brigade supply to pick up my rucksack and the equipment that I would need as a Lurp. The first thing I noticed as I climbed into the truck was that the usual vinyl bench seat had been replaced with bucket seats. Before I could make a comment, Rommel gave me the standard Lurp grin—which I had already discovered meant "ask no questions"—and began to explain LRRP requisition procedures. He told me that we were part of the U.S. Army—sort of—therefore we were "government issue." All of the equipment around us and in neighboring supply dumps was also "government issue." By extrapolation, and a healthy dose of

Lurp logic, it belonged to us. To confuse the issue even more, the brigade LRRP Detachment was a provisional unit, which meant we didn't exist on paper. As a provisional unit, we had no way to acquire necessary supplies and equipment through normal channels. We were forced to beg for handouts through the units we were attached to. Unfortunately, those units only infrequently thought enough of us to cooperate fully. So we simply requisitioned and liberated various items of equipment under the auspices of (1) the LRRP Laws and (2) the Rule of Mine. It worked for us! The three-quarter-ton Lurpmobile I was riding in had found a new home in the unit under LRRP Law 3-101, the Law of Nocturnal Confiscation. Our water buffalo had turned up in the area under LRRP Law 3-245, the Law of Kleptomania. After we had painted over the old unit designations, replacing them with our own, no one would ever be the wiser.

The story of the blue bucket seats was a different matter. Rommel and Sergeant Bacek had been sitting in the Lurpmobile on the tarmac at the Phan Rang Air Base. A not-too-bright airman had driven up a short time later and inadvertently parked his jeep next to Rommel. Sergeant Bacek struck up a friendly conversation with the young airman, and shortly thereafter offered to buy him a beer. While Bacek and the driver were toasting the "wild blue yonder" boys, Rommel discovered that blue air force jeep bucket seats come under the category of LRRP Law 1-444—Interservice Copulation. He soon had the bucket seats unbolted from the floor of the jeep, drove around to the air force EM club to pick up Bacek, and was on his way back to the LRRP compound with the air force driver none the wiser.

Rommel cautioned me to keep my eyes open for anything the Lurps could use, and a certain refrigerator came immediately to mind. Since Bacek and Rommel were the official unit interpreters of the LRRP Law and the Rule of Mine, I told Rommel about the available refrigerator.

We arrived at the brigade supply tent a short time later, and I picked up my basic equipment. I was told that other items of minor importance such as rucksack, rope, D-ring, OD tape, camouflage sticks, insect repellent, etc., I would have to beg, borrow, or steal. I was learning real quick that we got all the leftovers and used equipment. But that was okay: I knew where I could get my hands on some M-79s and M-60s if it became necessary; the MPs sure didn't need them.

We arrived back at our area just as it was getting dark. When we passed some guy down on all fours baying up at the sky just behind my tent, I asked Rommel, "Who the hell is that?"

"Oh, that's Doc Kraft. He likes to howl at the moon." Hell, even a blind man could see that the moon hadn't even come out yet.

When Rommel saw me looking up in the sky, he added, "The Wolfman knows the moon is there, he doesn't need to see it."

One of our medics thought he was a werewolf! We were in some deep, deep trouble! The longer I watched him, the funnier it became. No one else seemed to pay any attention to him. Even Lieutenant McIsaac and Top Smith paid him no heed. Rommel told me that howling was the Wolfman's "thing," and since he was one of the best medics in the detachment, they didn't let it bother them. Well, if that was the case, I sure wasn't going to let it bother me. I just thought it was a little strange. I stowed my equipment in my hootch and ate my evening C rats.

The second night was no different from the night before. It was party time at the LRRP compound. But this time, I kept my drinking and smoking to a minimum. I was determined to make at least one formation on time.

The same old elephant jokes started making the rounds, but for some reason they were still funny. During the party, someone told the story of a long-range patrol that had become a legend in brigade LRRPs. One of the teams had been patrolling through the jungle when it suddenly broke out into a clearing where a dozen or so VC were sitting in front of a large blackboard while a VC instructor was busily engaged in teaching a lesson. Apparently, he was too absorbed in the joys of teaching to notice that the six-man LRRP team had crashed his class. Until they opened fire. Before the surviving VC could get their act together, the Lurps had grabbed the blackboard and hauled ass for the hills, leaving behind a number of dead and wounded enemy soldiers. The Lurps made it to a clearing a short distance away and were extracted.

After the team reached the rear, the blackboard was given to an interpreter to decipher. He soon reported that the VC instructor was teaching a class called "Beware of American Long-Range Reconnaissance Patrols." It was at that time, I was told, that the VC/NVA placed a bounty on the head of any Lurp captured or killed. Rumor also had it that Soviet *Spetsnaz* (special operations units) were training NVA soldiers in special counter-LRRP patrolling techniques in an attempt to combat U.S. long-range patrols. We had become a thorn in the side of the enemy.

The party finally died down, and I made my way back to my hootch, nearly sober and only a little high. I soon drifted off to sleep.

CHAPTER 13

Brigade Lurps showed up for morning formation in the uniform of the day—the uniform of the day being an assortment of green boxer shorts, towel wraparounds, and even a few pair of fatigue pants. The only thing that was standard in the gathering were the hangovers that we nursed from the previous night's party.

After the brief, sixty-second formation, called more to meet military standard operating procedures than to accomplish anything constructive, we staggered slowly back to our tents. Boss Weisberger, one of my hootchmates, had decided to skip formation and get a little more of his beauty sleep. God knows he needed it! But I decided to wake him up so I wouldn't have to suffer my category-ten hangover alone.

When I entered the hootch, I found him sitting on the side of his cot, head in his hands. I had almost forgotten the previous night's elephant jokes that had us rolling on the ground. Of course after several warm beers, a few hits off his old pipe, and a couple of hours of war stories, everything seemed hilarious. Lurps not only worked hard, they played hard, too. I was beginning to appreciate that subtle sense of satirical humor that characterized them. It was at times a sick, sordid type of humor, but it was humor nonetheless.

We eulogized fellow Lurps who had been killed or seriously wounded, but made fun of the ones who had received only minor wounds. We laughed at the near misses. We joked about the screwups: "Yeah, and the dumb fucker fell out of the chopper at fifteen feet. He thought he was a fucking bird." On and on the stories continued until exhaustion set in. Only then would the party wind down as the Lurps staggered away, alone or in pairs, to crash as close to their bunks as possible. There were only twenty-four hours in a day, and it seemed as if everybody wanted to get as much out of it as they could. The next day could be the day that you ran out of hours too early. There was no future after death. We all knew it, so we partied hard.

The first hint that something was in the wind came when I saw the old-timers cleaning their weapons. The second was when Top Smith quietly gathered a group of us newbies and told us to draw extra magazines and clean our personal weapons. The third and final hint occurred when Lieutenant McIsaac and Top Smith were spotted heading down LRRP Hill toward S-2 (intelligence).

At that point, I was feeling pretty damn good about my observation and intelligence skills, so I sauntered over to where Sergeants Weems, Martinez, and Beauchamp were sitting around cleaning their weapons.

"Hey, Rey, figure something's up?"

Martinez gave me a look that had "dumb cherry motherfucker" written all over it. "No, Limey, Smitty just wants you rookies to get some practice loading magazines."

The three of them laughed. Feeling pretty stupid, I turned to slither under the door on my way out of the hootch, when Beauchamp asked, "Do you have a Purple Heart yet?"

Hell, Beauchamp had known me for over three years; he knew I didn't have one. I waited for the punch line.

"Well, you just might get one tomorrow. Betcha we're going back into the Song Ve Valley for a repeat performance of last week's raid."

I went back to my hootch and ran into Boss. I asked him for the lowdown on the Song Ve Valley. He told me that the valley was a nasty place. Full of VC, NVA, rice paddies, jungles, and a damned lot of unfriendly villages. If you managed to get away from all the people who wanted a piece of your ass, you usually ran right smack into a pissed-off snake, a bunch of blood-sucking leeches, or an oversize tiger with a hankering for Occidental food.

A large sluggish river meandered across the floor of the valley. Villages dotted the countryside, and the occupants made little effort to hide the fact that they weren't enthusiastic supporters of the South Vietnamese government or its foreign allies. The place sounded like a hell of a nice place to visit—from about five thousand feet above.

The Lurps had pulled a prisoner snatch in the valley just a few days before I had joined the unit. They were in and out, with their prisoners in tow, in eight minutes. The only return fire they had received had been just before the extraction. No one got hit. The mission had been a total success. Only later, during the interrogation of the prisoners, did they realize how much of a success it had been. The Lurps of the 1st Brigade, 101st Airborne Division, had captured the highest-ranking enemy soldier of the war up to that point: a somewhat dejected NVA colonel suddenly found himself in SVN control.

Top Smith and Lieutenant McIsaac returned to the detachment area and called us together for a premission briefing. Beauchamp had been right, we were going back into the Song Ve Valley for a brief R & R. The previous raid had been so successful that S-2 felt that a second visit was in order. The information obtained from the captured NVA officer had been priceless, and S-2 had gotten some intel that he had already been replaced. Since the enemy undoubtedly believed that lightning never struck twice in the same place, they were probably sitting out there without a clue once more, not expecting the same thing to happen again. That conclusion made me wonder where in the hell S-2 was getting its information.

The briefing took place at 1300 hours. Top Smith produced an aerial photo showing the village that we were to raid, about thirty thatched huts and a communal building. Each team was assigned a separate sector to search. We were to spend no more than ten minutes on the ground. We would have to be quick but thorough. Danger points were discussed. Our major concern was a hedgerow of tall brush that we would have to move through before we actually reached the edge of the village.

If we could catch Mr. Charles with his pants down, then there would be no problem until we started to withdraw. On the other hand, if he was waiting for us in the cover of the hedgerow, we would be up to our asses in deep doo-doo. My thoughts ran to the latter. I just couldn't imagine the VC falling for the same thing twice in less than a week—especially in the same area. Most of the Lurps shared my opinion. Chuck wasn't as stupid as S-2 believed. Lieutenant McIsaac and Top Smith also agreed, and they didn't hesitate to add that we had every reason to be extra cautious. They recommended that we stay flexible, expect the worst, and act accordingly.

The operation orders had been given, and we had to follow through with the program. I loved it! It reminded me of that renowned quote, Theirs not to reason why, theirs but to do and die.

We were assigned to helicopters, four Lurps to each ship, leaving room for three prisoners on each aircraft on the extraction. Somebody had a lot more ambition than we did.

We were told that there would be another short briefing in the morning, just before the CA (combat assault). At that time, we would be notified of any changes or new intel. Top dismissed us and told us to go and pack the necessary ammunition and equipment.

I returned to my hootch and continued loading extra mags. I

decided to carry at least thirty magazines with eighteen rounds in each, which gave me a grand total of 540 rounds. The cyclic rate of fire of an M-16 was eight hundred rounds per minute. Even adding three seconds to change magazines, it was obvious to me that I had less than two minutes of sustained firepower on rock 'n' roll. I would have to hump a lot more ammo or learn how to avoid sustained fire.

I was fumbling around, trying to attach the seven grenades—five frags, a willy pete (white phosphorus), and a smoke—to my LBE when I looked up and saw Rey Martinez grinning at me. I could sense what he was thinking. Dumb fucking cherry! I didn't know if he was going to screw with me or help me, so I gave him my best I'm-so-totally-fucking-confused look and waited for his assistance. After a few awkward moments, he got up and walked over to give me a brief but intense lesson on how to pack for a recon mission.

"Look, Limey, the first thing you do is get rid of some of these canteens. You're going out on a raid, not to a house fire." Rey took out one of the canteens and tossed it aside. I watched as he stowed five fragmentation grenades in the empty canteen pouch, then strapped a willy pete to one side of my LBE and a smoke grenade to the other side. He filled two ammo pouches with M-16 magazines, reached back and handed me a couple of seven-mag bandoliers, and said, "Pack one of these in your ruck and wear the other one across your chest. Now, if you find your ass in the middle of a firefight you won't be trying to bum some extra frags or a magazine or two from the Lurp next to you."

I nodded my appreciation as Martinez got up and rejoined the group of vets he had been sitting with. So that was all there was to it! I was now ready for my first mission. Not exactly what I had envisioned, but ready nonetheless. It's funny, knowing you finally had all your shit together still didn't make you feel any more prepared. There was that lingering doubt about your ability to perform. I had known Rey for only a few days, but he had already earned my respect. My only problem was that I was not used to seeing someone who was in a good mood all the time. Martinez was always laughing or smiling.

It didn't take me long to realize that not only did Lurps conduct six-man long-range recon patrols behind enemy lines, but we were also expected to tackle just about any other mission that came down the pipeline. When the army got its hands on a group of volunteers, it made sure that it got its money's worth.

By 1800 hours, all preparation for the coming mission was complete. Each team leader had defined the role of his teammates during the raid, and had then coordinated his plans with the overall mission plan to eliminate any confusion once we were on the ground. There would be no time to correct mistakes once the movie started. There would be only one take.

Clay Wentworth had assigned me the task of collecting the prisoners who were taken from the ville. I was to bind them, blindfold them, then hand them over to other team members for extraction. I assumed that he felt my MP training qualified me for the job. He told me not to go past the hedgerow unless an emergency arose. In other words, I was to keep my cherry ass out of the way and try not to get killed. I wasn't overly pleased with my role, but I was just savvy enough to appreciate my potential. I knew that I would have to be quick and decisive in fulfilling my assignment. Timing would be everything. If I caused a bottleneck in the operation, I could throw everything off schedule. People could die if I screwed up. Beads of cold perspiration rushed down my spine. I wasn't sure if I was ready for that kind of responsibility.

There was a lot of excitement in the air as I joined the group of Lurps milling around outside the hootches. Most of them were just standing around bullshitting and reliving old war stories. I felt left out. What could I contribute? "Well, guys, when I was with the MPs I found myself out on a perilous convoy escort, when this killer water buffalo . . ." or "There I was in the back room with mamma-san, with just a thin veneer of panties between total ecstasy and me, when this goddamned South Vietnamese cop . . ." No, I wasn't one of them yet. I hadn't paid my dues for membership in their club. I was still a pledge, waiting to undergo the ritual that would qualify me for full membership in the fraternity of warriors.

Lurch came over and invited me to go with him and a few of

the guys over to the 176th AHC club to down a few cold beers and engage in a general bullshit session with the chopper crews who would be supporting us on the next day's mission. It never hurt to enhance relationships with those who would be called on to bail your ass out of a tight one. When we reached the club, it was already crowded with chopper crewmen, busily engaged in marinating themselves in Budweiser. They were quick to forgive our intrusion and waved us over to share their brew. It didn't take long before Lurch was tossing out elephant jokes. He soon had the entire club rolling on the floor. The amazing thing was that everyone had heard him tell the same damn jokes a hundred times before. The big medic had missed his calling. He should have been a comedian, not the bag man on a long-range recon team. Then again, maybe being six four and 225 pounds just made old jokes funnier on the retelling.

By the time the evening drew to a close, I was feeling a hell of a lot better about myself. I was beginning to feel like a part of a team. I knew that I still had to prove myself in the bush, but it was obvious that I'd been granted a kind of conditional approval on the part of my comrades that would remain in effect only until I met the final test of combat.

We returned to our hootches around 2200 hours. Most of us crashed on our cots to sleep off the effects of the beer and dream of home or the glory of tomorrow's battle. That may sound a little melodramatic, but most of us were still only kids. I awoke several times during the night. Boss, Sweet Pea, and The Beaver appeared to have gone right to sleep. Worried about my performance on the coming mission, I was able to do little more than toss and turn. I was having a major run of self-doubt and remorse over my decision to volunteer for Lurps. LRRP had sounded so heroic at the time that I had volunteered without even weighing the consequences of my actions. I could see myself riding high on the backseat of a big, black convertible, covered with confetti and ticker tape, while thousands of people cheered my return to the World. I waved to them, bravely ignoring the cramping in my arms from all the medals hanging from my chest. The reality of it all was just sinking in. I knew that I was now part of a group of very special people, but could I really live up to the requirements?

At 0300, I was up, scavenging through my meager personal belongings for packets of coffee, cream, and sugar. There was no way that I was going to get any sleep. I was just too damned excited. I dropped a fingertip-size ball of C-4 into the C-ration-can stove on my footlocker and soon had a canteen cup of water boiling. I fired up a cigarette and sat back to let the caffeine and nicotine drive away the monsters that were tearing at my guts.

My activities soon awakened my hootchmates, but I let their grumbling roll off my back. I had become Americanized enough to accept that particular profanity for what it was—a GI's favorite term of endearment. No insult was intended; none was taken. These Americans had sure bastardized the king's good English!

I slipped out the door, easing it shut to avoid waking any more of my comrades. Flipping the cigarette butt out into the detachment street, I leaned against the sandbags to enjoy the steaming cup of coffee. It was even better than usual in the coolness of that final hour of darkness before first light. I heard a sound in the next hootch where the glow of a candle lit the narrow crack between the floor and the base of the door. Letting my curiosity get the best of me, I strolled over to see what was going on and found that Weems, Lurch, Martinez, and Top Smith were sitting in the lifer's hootch downing coffee and chain-smoking Winstons. They invited me to join them. The five of us sat around discussing everything from cars to women to the Land of the Magic Twenty-Four-Hour Generator. No one spoke of the coming mission. It was going to happen, so why talk about it. It wouldn't change a thing.

By 0530 hours, the rest of the detachment was up. There was a sense of tension in the air. You couldn't see it, but the atmosphere was charged with an invisible energy that fed on the anxiety and excitement generated by the mission, which was only an hour away. Everyone hurried to police up their areas and carry out a last-minute check of their equipment.

Someone snapped a profile shot of Martinez, Weems, and

me. Martinez was up front, smiling that ever-present, almost cocky, self-confident grin that had become his trademark. Weems stood to Rey's right, hamming it up as only he could. I stood to the rear, trying to broadcast a big, shit-eating grin, hoping that it would give me the air of invincibility that my two comrades displayed. It didn't!

Ten minutes later, we were being shuttled out to the chopper pad in the Lurpmobile. We arrived to find the choppers ready, engines idling, rotors stirring the early-morning air. The aircrews looked anxious to get the show on the road. I wondered if they were being fed fortified Wheaties for breakfast.

Smiles of overconfidence flashed back and forth. Mine was bogus. I tried to draw strength from the others, but sensed that there really wasn't any extra to go around. Then we were onloading into our designated ships. All the anxiety disappeared, replaced by excitement. I was ready to kick ass and take dog tags. Then the choppers lifted away from the pad.

We were flying in formation at twenty-five hundred feet. I looked out at the Vietnamese countryside and felt the exhilaration of covering all of that impassable jungle with the ease of a soaring eagle.

I found myself wondering why Charlie didn't clear the fuck out of Dodge or just give it up. How could he have a snowball's chance in Vietnam to achieve victory against so powerful a foe as the United States? You had to give the little bastards credit for guts.

I looked around the open cabin. The camouflaged faces of Pizza Joe and Clay Wentworth were set with a look of fierce determination. All the lingering doubts I had about my own performance dissolved in the face of their self-confidence, which somehow instilled in me an overwhelming inner peace. At that very moment, I knew that I would do okay. I was ready.

The Song Ve Valley swept into view. At this altitude it was beautiful. I looked at the door gunner. He smiled, nodded his head, said something into his headset mike, then he held up two fingers—just two minutes until touching down. Bile was rising from my stomach.

Coming in at a high speed, we lost altitude fast. I shifted my feet outside the chopper and started reaching for the tubular metal skid running a foot below my jungle boots. In a burst of uncontrolled excitement, I unassed the slick when it was still several feet from touching down, but when I looked up, the rest of my teammates were already running toward the hedgerow, a hundred meters from our LZ.

Sporadic rifle fire greeted us as we reached the cover of the hedgerow. I didn't realize the motherfuckers were onto us until I heard the distinct clatter of the AK-47 rounds popping overhead. These were not warning shots informing the villagers of our arrival.

The small-arms fire began to increase in volume. All of us understood that the second raid was not going to be a cakewalk. Looking to my flanks for the first time, I realized that I wasn't alone. A group of Lurps to my right was close to entering the hamlet. They were advancing in a crouch, laying down a heavy volume of suppressive fire in an attempt to keep the enemy's heads down. There was a lot of movement within the confines of the hamlet. Dinks in black pajamas and khaki uniforms were running back and forth among the fleeing villagers. They were carrying an assortment of weapons and seemed to be trying to set up some type of defense. We had taken them by surprise, but there were still enough NVA/VC in the hamlet to make things awfully hot for us.

I was having a difficult time picking out military targets; a lot of women and children were milling around, trying to avoid the heavy cross fire that was making life in the hamlet a poor bet.

On my right, Rommel moved in behind some cover. Then he stood and fired into a haystack. I thought it was rather strange until I saw the pile of dry straw catch fire from his tracers. Seconds later, a single Viet Cong stormed out the back of the blazing haystack, then crumpled to the ground as several bursts of M-16 fire canceled his escape-and-evasion plans.

Three armed VC on my left were trying to withdraw from their defensive position into the safety of the ville. Along with three or four other Lurps moving up on my left, I opened fire and watched in satisfaction as the three enemy soldiers crumpled to the ground.

I dropped to one knee and reloaded my weapon, totally unaware of how many magazines I had already gone through. My first burst had been on rock 'n' roll, but I remembered switching to semiautomatic sometime during the firefight. I just couldn't remember how many mags I had fed into my weapon. All that I was sure of was that our surprise party had turned into a nightmare.

I seemed out of control, yet under the direct influence of some type of pure survival instinct. My mind kept telling me to continue dishing out punishment or I would find myself on the receiving end of it. I became enraged, then tried to justify that rage by destroying the assholes defending the hamlet who had screwed up my day. It was all totally insane! I didn't know what I was doing or why, yet I was vaguely aware that I was doing what I had been trained to do—to terminate anything that was in front of me. Gone was any of the fear and apprehension that had terrorized me earlier. The adrenaline rush had taken over, and I was having one hell of a good time.

Suddenly the "good times" came to a screeching halt. Lieutenant McIsaac was screaming that we were taking .51-caliber antiaircraft machine-gun fire from the mountains above us. He yelled for us to abort the mission and return to the LZ. In the back of my mind, I recalled the overhead limbs and branches showering down around us. I had ignored it at the time, but now I realized that the enemy soldiers had learned a lesson from the first raid and had set up a 12.7mm gun emplacement on the side of the mountain to cover the open approaches to the village. Thank God the gunner was a lousy shot! The heavy rounds were pulverizing the overhead vegetation but, so far, had left us unscathed. Possibly the VC had mistakenly situated the machine gun in a position where the barrel couldn't depress enough to reach us. Whatever the case, we needed to vacate the premises quickly before they discovered the cure to their problem.

As we sprinted for the rear, someone behind me was yelling, "Back out, we're compromised."

"No shit, Sherlock!" I shouted. "What was your first fucking clue?" Then I was laughing like some high-school kid who had just gotten away with a prank. I looked around, embarrassed, only to discover that there wasn't a solemn face in the crowd. Everyone was laughing and shouting insults at the VC in the village. The momentary insanity of combat had taken over all of us as we rushed to get out of Dodge. So far, we had been very, very lucky—not one of us had been hit.

Rey Martinez reached the chopper ahead of me and dove headfirst into the open cargo bay. The momentum of his leap carried him all the way across the metal floor of the cabin and out into the rice paddy on the other side. He jumped back to his feet and, with a sheepish grin on his face, climbed back into the extraction ship.

The turbine on our chopper was pulling pitch to gain enough power to escape the LZ, when I saw Boss sprinting back toward the enemy-controlled ville. I stared in shocked disbelief as the VC gunners concentrated their fire on the running Lurp. The gods must have been with him as he made it unhit to a makeshift fence near the edge of the hamlet. Suddenly I saw him bend at the waist, and thinking that he had been hit, muttered, "Oh no!" But he had only stooped to retrieve something from the ground. He turned and dashed madly back toward the waiting chopper. The extraction ship was already lifting away from the LZ as Boss scrambled aboard. He was grinning from ear to ear. Sergeant Weems seemed to be giving him one hell of an ass-chewing, but, just as their chopper disappeared from my view, I could tell that they were all laughing hilariously.

The six slicks soon joined formation as they climbed away from the paddy while Charlie-model Huey gunships moved in to destroy the enemy village we had just left. I wondered if the gunships had been supporting us when we assaulted the hamlet. In the heat of the battle, I couldn't recall if they had been flying cover for us or not.

Suddenly the door gunner signaled that we were going down. I fought back a rush of panic as I looked around, expecting the ship to explode at any second. I had heard the sounds of enemy ground fire cracking past the helicopter, I had even seen tracers, but I couldn't recall any of the rounds actually hitting the chopper. I thought the show was over as I braced myself for the impact that I knew was coming.

Seconds later, the door gunner flashed a thumbs-up, signaling that everything was okay. We were still going down, but our descent was being controlled by the pilot. Just when I was wondering what in the hell was happening, I spotted the C & C ship sitting dead in the paddy below. A number of Lurps were already forming a defensive perimeter around the downed Huey. We were obviously going in to reinforce them. Our choppers set down as close as possible, and we all piled out and took up positions around the crippled ship. As our bird lifted out, Weems's chopper landed a few meters away and dropped off his Lurps. The crew of the downed C & C ship quickly climbed aboard and went out with the last chopper.

Spreading out along the closest paddy dike, we lay awaiting Charlie's next move. I had watched the same scene unfold in countless westerns at the movies. This was where the good guys and the bad guys sat back to see who would make the first move. I think they called it a Mexican standoff. If Martinez had been a little closer, I would have asked him.

Watching the ville not more than five hundred meters away, we lay in the paddy for over an hour. Gunships circled overhead, providing air support until help could arrive. Soon we began to draw small-arms fire from the direction of the ville. I kept my fingers crossed that the .51-caliber would stay out of commission. If it didn't, our Mexican standoff might become a Maryland duck shoot. They could see us, but we couldn't see them. The only thing that seemed to be in our favor was their lousy marksmanship.

I took stock of the situation. We were in the middle of an open field, guarding an expensive piece of "wreckage" that none of us owned. On the other side of the field were a large number of people with ideologies that differed somewhat from ours and on whose parade we had just gone to great lengths to rain. A lot of our ammo had been expended in the initial assault, and our air cover had pretty well exhausted its resources destroying the village. Our slicks had returned to base to refuel and drop off the aircrew of the downed C & C ship.

The sun was coming up, promising a scorcher of a day, and there wasn't an ounce of shade within a quarter of a klick. Except for the above, things were looking okay.

I leaned against the dike trying to relax. Pizza Joe and Clay Wentworth began to joke back and forth. The crazy sons of bitches thought the whole affair was funny. Hell, I guess I was too much of a cherry to see the humor in it! I looked over at Boss and noticed that this new turn of events didn't seem to be bothering him either. He lay with his back to the paddy dike, picking idly at his fingernails. The rest of the Lurps seemed to be taking the whole thing in stride. They must have known something that had never been passed on to me, but I'd be damned if I'd let them know that my asshole had fused shut. If they could be nonchalant, then so could I. At least on the outside!

We lay quietly in the hot sun another hour, waiting for one of the big CH-47s to arrive on the scene to pull out the downed Huey. I nursed the water in my single canteen in a vain attempt to conserve my supply while warding off the heatstroke I knew was only minutes away. I couldn't tell what was worse—the snipers in the ville or the sun beating down overhead. Either one would kill us, given time or opportunity.

After a while, I began to question my sanity. I had actually volunteered for this bullshit! I could have been back in Cam Ranh Bay or Phan Rang downing cold beers and enjoying life in the rear. But no, instead I was in the middle of a sunbaked rice paddy, getting my brains fried while a bunch of little people were sitting in the jungle shade, trying to shoot my balls off. Suddenly, being a Lurp didn't seem quite so glamorous.

As I watched the gunships go off station and head for the rear, an icy finger of fear began to creep from the crack of my ass and run up along my spine. A feeling of doom swept over me as I looked around the little perimeter and realized just how exposed we really were.

I heard the throbbing of helicopters just as I spotted the big Chinook and its two escorting gunships break over a distant tree line. The CH-47 orbited high overhead while the gunships made a rocket run on the ville. A second pass with miniguns blazing kept the VC pinned down as the Chinook came in and set down a few meters away from our perimeter. The rotor wash kicked up enough dust and debris to totally obscure the entire scene from the watching enemy soldiers. The ramp was lowered, and a couple of crewmen dashed out and affixed a steel cable to the downed Huey. They motioned for us to board the big cargo helicopter, then piled in behind us as the Chinook lifted off to hover directly over the C & C ship. We felt the sudden jerk as the slack came out of the cable and the Huey was snatched from the ground. But by the time we reached about fifteen hundred feet, the Huey was swinging back and forth, threatening to cause our pilot to lose control of the Chinook. He quickly signaled the crew chief to release the load. Free of the wrecked chopper, the Chinook immediately stabilized, and the pilot regained control. What had taken the U.S. Army hours to accomplish, we could have done in ten minutes with a single block of C-4 plastic explosive!

A group of smiling Lurps was waiting for us with cold beers when we arrived at the chopper pad. As we rode back to the detachment area, we laughed and joked about the experience we had just survived. If we could make light of the danger, it was almost as if it had never really existed. When we reached the compound, the rest of the unit came out to greet us. A lot of good-natured backslapping and jostling went on as the "VC for lunch bunch" was welcomed back from its adventures. We were quick to partake in the merriment but couldn't help but realize how close we had come to not being around to celebrate our good fortune.

After the beer began flowing, the party turned into a wild affair. I was really enjoying myself when I noticed Boss going from hootch to hootch asking, "Where is it?" I didn't understand what was going on until a little later when he rejoined the group. He was standing there, somewhat disgruntled and nursing a beer, when I walked up and asked him what he was looking for. I couldn't keep from smiling as he told me the story of what had happened back at the LZ. Just before the mission, one of the old-timers had loaned Boss his floppy hat with the stern warning that he could wear it on the raid but he had better not lose it. After the order for withdrawal was given, Boss had dashed for the chopper but had failed to remove his floppy hat beforehand. The rotor wash from the Huey blew the borrowed boonie hat from his head and sent it spinning back toward the enemy ville. Boss, more willing to face the enemy than the veteran Lurp who had loaned him the hat, took off across the rice paddy in pursuit of the borrowed headgear. After recovering it, he was on his way back to the waiting ship when he passed a VC garden and spotted a large, ripe melon in the middle of the patch. Not one to pass up the "fruits" of his labor, Boss again braved enemy fire as he stopped to snatch the large watermelon.

I could only admire his guts while questioning his sanity. He told me that in the confusion of going back in to secure the downed C & C ship, someone had made off with his booty. He wasn't going to give up the search until he discovered who had made off with his hard-earned watermelon. I waited until he had moved on in his futile search for the missing melon before I busted a gut laughing. I would never have believed that a day so fraught with danger could end up on such a humorous note.

CHAPTER 14

The raid was history, and it had been a token victory. We lost a chopper but had suffered no casualties. The enemy lost eight or nine men, confirmed by bodies left on the battlefield, although a final body count had not been possible.

Casualties during the month of May had been unusually high, and a steady stream of replacements had been reporting in to brigade LRRPs. Lieutenant McIsaac and Top Smith had a monumental task on their hands training the dozen or so newbies that had arrived. A week of classes running twelve hours a day would teach them the basics of LRRP tactics. Everyone would participate, either as an instructor or a student. The extra training would prove beneficial, and no one complained.

Doc "Wolfman" Kraft and Alan "Lurch" Cornett gave classes on first aid. During those classes, I discovered that Lurch knew a hell of a lot more about the human body than piercing ears. Wolfman surprised me by showing me that he was quite adept in the medical field. Both medics impressed me. Some line companies had lost out when those two soldiers volunteered for LRRPs.

Lieutenant McIsaac conducted classes on hand-to-hand training, but it was not the Mickey Mouse horseplay we had been through in basic and AIT. This was tough, realistic, slam-bang hand-to-hand, with human bodies thrown through the air and smashed into the ground. No punches were pulled. Take-downs were ferocious. Sprains, bruises, and bloody bodies were the price of not paying attention. Doc Neihuser, another detachment medic, stood by to treat the casualties and to pick up the pieces. The weak at heart among the new recruits quickly dropped out to return to their old units. With the anticipation of coming reconnaissance patrols, morale and interest were high. All of us realized that the ultimate test would come on our first mission.

We were taken out to a secure area where we practiced setting charges and booby traps with C-4 explosives. Nothing was safe from us as we practiced destroying trees, abandoned buildings, holes in the ground, anything that did not have U.S. Army stenciled on it. We held contests where we used enormous quantities of C-4 to see who could blow palm trees the highest. In the field, it was SOP for Lurps to carry a kilo of C-4 along with det cord and blasting caps. We were taught to feel comfortable with the explosives, as if they were our personal toys.

We learned how to call in and direct gunships. Each cherry Lurp was taught to communicate with the Huey gunships over a PRC-25 radio. We practiced until everyone could do it right. The gunships and slicks of the 176th Aviation Company were our single lifeline to survival. Without the ability to communicate our needs to them quickly and clearly, we were doomed. Map- and compass-reading classes were conducted by Sergeant Weems and a few of the other team leaders. My earlier exposure to the subject at Fort Bragg had been boring, and I had learned next to nothing. Well, maybe a little. I knew that most maps were green with some red, white, and blue on them. I also knew that coordinates would show my location. By the end of the day of training, I could plot my location, shoot and compute back azimuths, and use a variety of other map-reading techniques. I even found myself asking intelligent questions. The final test involved determining a back azimuth, then walking out to a location, predetermined by Weems.

We sat and laughed until our sides ached as we watched Vendetti on his map/compass exercise. He was the only Lurp I saw get lost within five hundred meters of our position. God, I thought, are we in trouble. Of course, I wasn't that much better! Vendetti was assigned to a team as a scout, but he was no Kit Carson, that was for sure. Of course, his initial difficulties wouldn't be that big a problem since all the senior scouts on the team were veteran reconners.

We were down to less than a dozen newbies when the training finally ended. Most had departed when they realized that they weren't up to the training and that going into the field was near at hand. It was becoming apparent to us all that there were no free rides in the LRRPs. Either you had what it took, or you were out. No hard feelings, just bye-bye!

When the training ended, new teams were formed. I was assigned as senior scout for Team 6. I was shocked! But my doubts were put to rest when I found out that Top Smith was to lead Team 6.

CHAPTER 15

In less than a week, a large number of volunteers had disappeared, but I had finally been accepted as a member of Team 6, and I felt pretty damned good about that. Top Smith never made a big deal out of cutting people from the brigade LRRPs. It wasn't his desire to embarrass anyone, but not everyone was cut out for long-range patrolling. In a way it was like trying out for the varsity football team. You knew only a few guys would make it, and you just hoped you could be one of them. It was the same way in LRRPs. Some guys looked good in training, some didn't. Top would call in those who were having a hard time passing muster, and he would sit them down for a private talk. Within a few days they were gone. None of us knew the reason why those who left were not selected, but we were all certain that Top Smith was the fairest NCO any of us had ever served with.

After I had made the LRRPs, I strutted around the detachment area and the bar over at the 176th AHC like a bantam rooster on the prowl. I had myself really believing I was something special. It was during this time I ran into a young paratrooper from the 501st Signal Battalion. I had noticed him always hanging around the LRRPs anytime we congregated at the bar to tell war stories—normally for a round of drinks. The wilder the story, the more drinks we received. For some reason, this kid got the impression that I carried some weight within my unit. He came up to me one day and said, "Hey, you guys are really something else! My name is Sullens, and I want in on the action. How about helping me get into LRRPs?"

Not really knowing what to say, I took a long swig from the

beer he had put in front of me, then came back with the only thing I could think of that made sense at the time. "Uh-huh, I'm Limey. Go over there and see Martinez and tell him I sent you. I'm kinda busy right now." I pointed to the table where Rey "Marty" Martinez sat with a couple of the old-timers. I turned back to my beer and continued my conversation with Boss and Kinnan, who were both pretty excited about their recent assignment to Sergeant Weems's team.

After a few minutes, I looked over at the old-timers' table. Martinez was giving me an icy stare as Sullens stood there pointing directly at me. I could only imagine what Marty must have been thinking.

During the remainder of the evening, I had pretty much forgotten about the Sullens kid, until Marty came over and told me that he was going to vouch for him to get into the unit and had already set up an interview with Top Smith for the next day. That was the same as saying Sullens was in—as long as he could hack the training.

The next afternoon, I was returning from the shower point, and I heard someone strumming a guitar. It sounded pretty good, so I walked over to see who it was. There was Sullens, sitting under a canvas cover alongside a small rise. He looked up at me and grinned as he sang, "Hey, Top, where's Limey going with that gun in his hand?" Sullens liked to customize the lyrics to fit the moment. I liked him right off. It was the start of a great but very short friendship.

CHAPTER 16

Team 6 consisted of Master Sergeant Smith, team leader; Specialist Fourth Class Brown, junior scout; Sergeant Gray, senior

RTO; Specialist Fourth Class Beiber, junior RTO; Specialist Fourth Class Kraft, medic; and me, senior scout. It was a really great team for my first mission. We had received a day's notice to get our equipment in order before our briefing. I packed and repacked my rucksack under the watchful eyes of some of the old-timers. They were quick to answer my questions and offer a number of helpful hints. They seemed as interested in my welfare as I was. When I had finished packing, I struggled into my ruck, then stood up and jumped up and down to see if anything was loose enough to rattle. The only noise I could detect came from outside of my ruck. A liberal dose of OD tape solved that problem in a hurry. It had taken me nearly two hours to get everything ready, but I was satisfied with the results.

Top Smith held an informal meeting with his new team in the early afternoon. He brought up several points that I had not yet considered. He pointed out that we were a LRRP team. This meant that our job was long-range reconnaissance patrolling, and he emphasized "reconnaissance." He told us that we were not in the field to earn medals but to locate the enemy. We would communicate by hand signals. Whispering would be a last resort. He went on to say that the only time we would initiate contact would be if we were spotted by the enemy or on the last day of the mission. If we sighted the enemy in our RZ on the last day of the patrol, we would lay an ambush close to our extraction point and hit any target of opportunity that came into range.

Top talked about the jungle, assuring us that it was not to be feared. The jungle was "neutral." It could be our friend, or it could be our foe. That was entirely up to us. He reminded us that the VC and the NVA were for the most part just like us, a bunch of city slickers and country boys. The only things born in the bush were snakes, lizards, monkeys, and other assorted creatures seen only on the pages of *National Geographic*.

He told us that we had the upper hand on Charlie. The enemy was there by necessity, and we were there because we wanted to be. The last thing the enemy expected was a six-man long-range patrol in his backyard. He warned us to keep our shit wired tight at all times, and not to treat any mission as a cakewalk until after the extraction. That was the only time we would ever let down our guard.

His final admonishment was to tell us that anyone who didn't have his shit together out on the patrol would be handed his walking papers upon our return. Fun time was over. The business of war was at hand.

With the words of wisdom completed, we walked back to our hootches to mentally prepare for the mission. I was as nervous as a fox in a henhouse. I checked my equipment over and over again. The next day would bring me the chance to finally prove myself.

It was getting dark, and I found myself once again cleaning my M-16. I looked up as the Wolfman mounted his favorite rock and bid the moon a sorrowful good-night. He was a character, but by God, he was our character.

I woke up before first light and began heating water for morning coffee. I had already learned to make sure ahead of time that all the necessary ingredients were close at hand. I risked a tongue-lashing if I awakened any of my hootchmates, but Beiber was already up and stirring about; like me, he was suffering from premission anxiety.

Sitting there in silence, drinking our coffee, we watched Top Smith and Sergeant Bacek head toward the 176th AHC for their overflights. We had two teams going into separate RZs, each five square klicks, late that afternoon. The following day, Weems's and Lynch's teams would also be inserted in RZs of five square klicks, giving us a saturation zone of about twenty square klicks.

By the time Top Smith and Sergeant Bacek returned from their overflights, the rest of the detachment was up and moving around camp. There would be no morning formation. Assisted by disgruntled Lurps who had not been drawn for a mission, teams were making last-minute preparations.

At 1000 hours, Top Smith formed up Team 6 for its first-ever mission briefing. It was short, sweet, and to the point. He told us that the overflight choppers had taken enemy fire so we had to assume that Charlie was present in both our recon zones.

Our team was going into virgin territory; to our knowledge, no other American troops had ever been in the area. Any signs of man having been there would have been left behind by the enemy. Until the overflights, intelligence had no information on enemy activity in the area, although it had been suspected that the NVA were infiltrating into this part of the Song Ve Valley.

Our insertion LZ was about five hundred meters from the nearest tree line, so we would have to hump through elephant grass and light bamboo before reaching the concealment of the jungle. After he finished with the briefing, Top Smith looked at our bright and shining faces and asked us if there were any questions. Not wanting to put my foot in my mouth nor show any signs of nervousness, I opted to be silent. I asked Top Smith for the map and went off to my hootch with The Beaver to look it over, not really knowing for sure what I was looking for.

The Beaver and I were scanning the map, checking elevations, terrain features, and any other landmark that would help me in my role as point man when Top Smith approached me with some bad news. Specialist Fourth Class Brown had called it quits, unvolunteered himself from the Lurps. I was shocked! He had been so gung ho during training, and all he had talked about was his chance to be a real Lurp. Top told me that Brown had suddenly decided that recon was not for him, and that the rest of us had some screws loose.

I started to laugh, but it died in my throat when Top said that I was getting Richards as my junior scout. Richards had gotten lost on a previous mission. It could have happened to anybody, but Richards was in sight of his perimeter. I hoped things would work out better this time. Richards was a good guy, but he was a little young and a bit too anxious to please. Top had given Richards a one-on-one briefing on the mission so his last-minute assignment wouldn't be a burden on the rest of us.

I found a shady spot and lay down to take a nap. It was 1100 hours, and the insertion wouldn't go in until 1600 hours. I awoke at 1300 hours with a tremendous thirst. The lukewarm water in my canteen didn't help slake my parched throat, so I made the short trip over to the 176th AHC club for a cold Coke and some decent conversation. When I walked in I found Richards sitting there drinking a beer. That he was drinking *a* beer was bad enough, but three empties were sitting in front of him. I asked him what he thought he was doing, drinking beer before a mission. He mumbled, gave me a go-to-hell look, then ordered another beer.

My first impulse was to snatch him off the chair and kick his ass up over his head. Instead, I shook off the urge, bought a Coke, and left. Walking back to the detachment area, I realized that I was in a hell of a predicament. "Lurps don't snitch other Lurps out!" That was part of our creed. Now I found myself in a situation where I would have to break that tenet or jeopardize the safety of the team.

I knew there was no way I could let Richards go on the mission. To permit him to pull my slack was asking for tragedy to occur. I felt a responsibility for my team's safety, and was not going to let Richards put us all at risk. The only thing I could do was to tell Top Smith and let him decide what to do. After all, he was the team leader, and it was his shot to call. I didn't really want to get involved in this kind of controversy, but Richards had left me little choice.

Pappy Lynch overheard me tell Top about the problem, and when Top left to go look for Richards, Lynch walked up and started chewing me out. His attitude angered me to the point that I told him to go screw himself, and if he felt so strongly about Richards, he could take him on his team. I stormed off to my hootch, disappointed at Lynch for not understanding the problem—Richards's breaking of the rule about no alcohol before a mission. At the time, I had no idea that Pappy Lynch would have taken care of the problem without involving our first sergeant.

Thirty minutes later, Top Smith introduced me to my new junior scout, Eddie Mounts. At least Eddie was sober! I was still upset with Pappy Lynch for busting my buns and hoped that the rest of the detachment would understand what I had done.

I was still mulling things over when it got to be time to paint on my camouflage. It was tedious work. To make it go on easier, I applied U.S. Army–issue insect repellent to soften the cammo stick and make the application simpler. Finally, I was cammo'd up and ready to go. Just before leaving for the helipad, I was approached by Bob McKinnon and told not to worry. He said that Pappy Lynch had been way out of line in dressing me down for turning in Richards. He told me that under the circumstances, I had done all that I could do. McKinnon will never know the gratitude I had for him at that moment.

Then Rommel arrived in the Lurpmobile. At the helipad the six of us did a final equipment check, then loaded onto the chopper in reverse order. Filled with excitement and anticipation of the coming mission, I sat in the open door, waiting for the pilots to make their final checks.

A short time later, we were airborne, and I was astounded by the beauty of the land passing beneath us. Soon we had ascended to three thousand feet and had picked up a couple of D-Model gunships, which put me at ease. Our door gunners checked their M-60 machine guns to make sure they were operational. The short bursts caught me daydreaming and briefly scared the hell out of me.

Our slick made two false insertions before letting us out on the third one. I hit the ground running, with the rest of the team right behind me. I led them away from the LZ, stopping after fifty meters to lie dog. This was the danger time, when we were most vulnerable. If the enemy didn't locate us in the next fifteen to thirty minutes, the chances were good that we had gotten in unnoticed. For a full half hour, we lay still and listened to a gentle breeze rustle through the elephant grass. No other sound interrupted the silence that encompassed us.

Top Smith finally gave us the signal to move out. I hadn't realized how heavy my pack was, but after thirty minutes, it was really digging into my back. Another thirty minutes of edging slowly through the elephant grass, fighting wait-a-minute vines with every step, was taking its toll on me. My hands were slashed by the razor-sharp edges of the grass. My back was aching, and the sweat was draining from pores I never knew existed. We were getting a hell of a workout.

Fifty meters from the tree line, I held the team up once again. I wanted to wait and listen before we broke out of the grass and into the dense jungle. If the enemy was waiting anywhere, it would be there in the edge of the trees. Finally, satisfied that no one was lying in wait ahead of us, we cautiously entered the jungle. The silence was deafening, and although the sun no longer beat down on us directly, the poor air circulation among the trees made the atmosphere almost suffocating.

I led the rest of the team a hundred meters back into the bush before halting again. I dropped my rucksack and did a short cloverleaf recon of the immediate area. It didn't take me long to discover that the area was crisscrossed with a maze of trails. It looked like the hub of a major airport. None of the trails appeared to have been freshly used, but we could take no chances. The enemy could always show up at any moment.

When I reported back to Top Smith and told him of my discovery, he decided that we would stay put for a while as our location would serve as an excellent NDP. We were only six hundred meters from the LZ, and there were a couple of trails less than thirty meters away.

After we set up our position, we made a thorough check of the immediate surroundings. An open tiger pit had been excavated less than twenty feet from our perimeter, but the trap was so old that the punji stakes had rotted and collapsed in the bottom of the pit.

We cleared our NDP of twigs and branches, then formed our wagon wheel for the night. I crawled out of my position about twenty feet, then turned around to view our perimeter. Even though I knew where it was, it was still almost invisible. When darkness fell, it would be impossible for Charlie to find us, even with the help of a full moon. Satisfied, I returned to the perimeter to eat my evening meal, cold C rats. In silence, we took turns eating. That was the first time I had ever seen Wolfman quiet for more than ten minutes.

Night was falling rapidly. We pulled guard duty in hour-and-a-half increments. That was my first night in the jungle, and I had no idea what sounds to expect. Only time and experience would alert me to the fact that certain noises were not made by native animals. We placed our discarded C-ration cans in the tiger pit and covered them with loose dirt. That done, we settled in for the night. I had the early-morning watch. Rolling up in my poncho liner, I had no problem dropping off to sleep. I was totally exhausted.

Clank . . . clank . . . clank! I was up in a second, my weapon pointed directly at the source of the noise. *Clank . . . clank . . . clank.* I looked over at Top Smith. Something was out there all right, and it didn't care if it was making noise or not. We woke the rest of the team. Motioning me to follow him, Top Smith low-crawled out of the perimeter toward the source of the noise. Anticipating an ambush, I followed him toward the racket.

Keeping Top in sight, I continued to slither forward on my stomach. Suddenly, the noise stopped. The loud silence was followed seconds later by the scurrying of tiny feet. Relieved, I had to stop myself from laughing. We had broken up a party of jungle animals that had jumped into the tiger pit to feast on the remnants of our unfinished C rats. I hoped that we had flushed them in time to save their lives. No wild animal could survive long after a dose of ham and lima beans.

I was too hyped up to sleep. I stayed awake while Mounts and Gray pulled their watches, then I did my own turn at guard duty. At first light, I was amazed to discover that I was still alert and not the least bit tired.

I woke the rest of the team, and without a command each man rolled over on his stomach and pointed his weapon to the outside of the wagon wheel. The period right at first light was another danger time. If the enemy had somehow discovered our location during the night, first light was the time he would launch his attack.

A full hour passed with no sign that we were being watched. Not wanting to take any chances so close to a trail network, Top Smith signaled that we were not to make any fires. So we sat back, two at a time, and ate our C rations cold.

After eating, we *buried* the cans, pulled in the claymores, sterilized our NDP, then moved out cautiously, paralleling the trail. We stopped every hundred meters or so just to look and listen. During the pauses, I dropped my pack and moved out to check the trail. It was cold and hadn't been used in months. We continued humping, the jungle still hot and stifling. I was dragging ass, but I couldn't let on that I was having trouble. All the easy time in the MPs had allowed me to grow soft. I was a long way from being in shape, and I was paying the price.

Top Smith halted the patrol late in the day and told Mounts and me to find a night defense position close to a secondary landing zone that we had spotted earlier. Heading out of the bush, we started through the elephant grass toward another section of the jungle. Entering it, I turned around and asked Mounts if he knew what Top Smith was looking for in an NDP.

"Hell, I don't know, Limey," he whispered. "This is my first mission, too."

Holy shit, I thought, my first mission, and three of the six team members are cherries! I knew right then and there we would have a real interesting time if we made contact.

We soon found a trail running parallel to the tree line, not more than a hundred meters from the secondary LZ. It would make a perfect place to observe the enemy and hit him if the opportunity presented itself. Moving back to the tree line, I motioned for the rest of the team to join us. Top Smith seemed to be pleased, smiling and nodding his approval. That was enough to put me on cloud nine for the rest of the day.

We spent the next three days searching for Viet Cong but found no activity or recent signs that the enemy was still using the area.

Extracted on the morning of our fifth day, I missed the jungle as soon as we were lifted out of it. The sunlight casting narrow rays through the leafy shield of broken vegetation, dappling the forest floor in shadow and light, was a thing of beauty that could never be duplicated by man. The light morning mist, the sweet, pungent aroma of decaying plant life, and the peace and quiet were unique to the jungle, and I would never forget any of them.

Our mission turned out to be little more than a peaceful walk in the woods. But you never knew that going in. The intensity, the stress, the anxiety had all been real. Each of us left a little piece of ourselves out there in the Southeast Asian jungle on every mission we ran. It was the price we paid for the passage; we didn't know then that the stress would shorten our lives over the long haul. When you're young and full of piss and vinegar, you don't care about things like that.

CHAPTER 17

When we arrived back at the helipad, we were greeted by a smiling Rommel and the Lurpmobile. Rommel had brought a full cooler of beer along with our transportation.

On the way back to the compound, the anger and frustration came out. Everyone was pissed off. We had done our best to locate the enemy, but we had been inserted into a cold recon zone. Top Smith tried to make things a little easier by telling us there may not have been any enemy soldiers in our RZ, but it was just as important to discover where he wasn't as it was to find out where he was. The way Top put it, it all made sense. We could find the enemy through the process of elimination, it would just take time. But two of our teams had struck out. Only Weems's and Lynch's teams were still in the bush. They had gone in a day after us, and neither team had yet reported anything positive.

When we got back to the compound, I stowed my gear and fieldstripped my M-16. I had just started to clean my weapon when I heard a commotion outside my hootch. Something was going on, as I could hear the Lurps assembling. Not wanting to be left out, I left the hootch to join them. Everyone was standing outside the TOC, trying to listen to traffic coming in over the radio. Weems's team was on the air. They had located a target. Things were sketchy at first, but we finally understood that the team had found the enemy. Weems was calling for air support. They were outside the artillery fan, so the only support available was air.

Initially there was a lot of static, but from what we could gather, Weems finally left the FAC frequency and jumped back down to the detachment freq, and he came in loud and clear, giving us a brief situation report.

From their position on a hilltop, the team had spotted the enemy in a village below them and were engaging them with supporting fire. They would continue the mission and observe the outcome of the air strikes. That was all, end of transmission.

We all looked at each other, then back at the radio. There had to be more than that. But nothing else came in.

There was no beer party for me that night. Sleep came easily. The mission had worn me out and left me totally exhausted.

Morning came too soon; I was still worn out. The ritual first cup of coffee was needed to get me back on my feet. I knew that it would still be quite a while before Weems's and Lynch's teams got back in. Two of my hootchmates, Boss and Sweet Pea, were out with Weems, and The Beaver was still crashed. I resisted the urge to roll him out of the sack to keep me company. Instead, I pulled out my rucksack and began to repack it for the next mission.

After I finished, I still had some time to kill, so I grabbed my weapon and headed down toward the Tiger Force compound to make sure Jeep was okay. But I could have saved myself the trip. When I got there, I discovered that the entire 1/327 was in the field, including Tiger Force. I left a note with the battalion clerk, telling Jeep I'd been by, then made the long trek back to LRRP Hill.

When I reached the detachment area, I discovered that Weems and Lynch were already back in. As a matter of fact, the two team leaders were engaged in an argument as I walked up. It appeared that Lynch was refusing to believe that Weems had brought in a tactical air strike the day before because he had not seen it with his eyes. I thought he was joking, but he was dead serious, and was really making an ass of himself.

This is where I stepped in and opened my big mouth. I told Pappy Lynch, "FAC spotted the target, most of the detachment listened to Weems call it in over the air, and the air force fighter-bombers verified it after their bomb runs. Now what is your fucking problem?" This stopped the argument, but it also sealed my fate with Pappy Lynch. He sneered as he told me to keep my mouth shut in the future, and he was quick to remind me that I was a cherry with nothing to say in the unit. Although I had made an enemy of Lynch, my friendship with Weems was sealed, and that was fine by me.

Realizing that it was a good time to vacate the area, I went back to my hootch, where Boss and Sweet Pea were unpacking their gear. Boss said that they had spotted a dozen armed VC in the village, about a half a klick below their OP. Weems had called in the FAC and had him mark the village with a smoke rocket, then direct the fast movers to destroy the target. The team had watched the ville the rest of the day without detecting any movement. The following morning before their extraction they continued to watch the target area, noting that none of the bodies had been moved from the day before. The destruction of the target had been complete. An accurate body count was impossible, so Weems and his team would not officially be credited with any kills. Four teams had scoured the AO, and one had located the enemy. But that single team had given the enemy something to think about.

A few days later, two pallets of LRRP rations arrived at the compound. We were like a bunch of kids at Christmas. These were the new-style LRRP rations. Like everyone else, I fought my way into the crowd around the pallets and grabbed up an armful, taking them back to the security of my hootch to sort through them. The meal selections looked tantalizing. I put aside all my favorites. Soon the place resembled an Oriental market. The bargaining didn't stop until everyone had fulfilled his needs. Only then did we take the time to stash our rations.

An hour later, one very pissed off Lieutenant McIsaac stormed into our area. He had gone to the pallets to draw his supply of LRRP rations only to discover that the only ones remaining were those that no one wanted. It was time to pull rank. "Okay, you guys, I'll turn my back," the Lieutenant announced, "and when I turn around again, I want all the LRRP rations in a pile right here."

Nobody moved. El Tee was a great guy, but fuck it—you snooze, you lose, man! It wasn't our fault he was out of the area when the pallets arrived.

Resigning himself to the fact that he was shit out of luck, El Tee bent over and picked up the cast-off rations and walked back to his hootch. With newfound respect for the man, we watched him go. Of course, none of us saw the silly grin on his face. He would have the last laugh. Lieutenant McIsaac was a mustang. He had come up through the enlisted ranks to the grade of staff sergeant E-6 before attending OCS to earn his commission.

The next day, my team got a warning order for a mission. Once again, we would be operating outside the artillery fan. The new RZ was in the Song Ve Valley, about ten klicks from our last RZ. Reports from enemy defectors said that North Vietnamese Army regulars had been infiltrating the area and taking control from the local VC. Brigade wanted us to verify the information.

Our team would be pretty much the same as the last mission: Top Smith—team leader, Eddie Mounts, Beaver, Gray, and myself, with Cornett subbing for Kraft. By the time Top Smith returned from the overflight, we had already checked and rechecked our equipment and were ready to go. Insertion was set for 1600 hours.

The Huey made two false insertions before we leaped out on the third one and headed for the nearest tree line, 150 meters away. The LZ was wide open, offering no cover or concealment at all, but twenty-five meters into the jungle, we dropped into a dense thicket and lay dog. A half hour passed before we were satisfied that we had gotten in without being spotted. Top signaled me to move out. I did so cautiously, scanning the area to my front for anything out of place. The jungle was quiet, and before long I was relaxed, yet still fully alert. The jungle was no longer a thing to be feared; it had become my friend, and I felt safe within its grasp. Dense underbrush ahead caused me to decrease our already deliberate pace to avoid making noise that could announce our presence to the enemy. Evening shadows were beginning to lengthen, and I found myself looking for a likely night defense position.

Top Smith finally halted the patrol in a spot that I thought would make an excellent NDP. We crawled into some deep underbrush and set up our usual wagon-wheel perimeter for the night.

I was assigned the first security shift, so I got myself as comfortable as I could as the darkness settled in over us. I was startled at first by the nearby call of the Asian reptile that mimicked American soldiers: Fuck you. Fuck you. I smiled at the thought of how many cherries had shit their pants hearing that lizard for the first time.

The night passed without any problems, and the first illumination of the false dawn began to make the jungle discernible around us. This was the time that the enemy usually attacked. We were all awake and alert for that critical period of the mission, but nothing happened. Top indicated that we were to chow down in shifts, two men eating while four remained alert.

When we had finished and had policed up the NDP, we moved out in a new direction. Within an hour, I heard a faint metallic *clink* and stopped the patrol. I couldn't get an exact bearing on the sound because of the diffusing effect of the thick jungle, but it was coming from somewhere to our front. Suddenly the noise faded away. I looked back at Mounts, who nodded. He, too, had heard the noise. Somewhere, not far away, enemy soldiers were about.

Slowly I dropped my ruck and crawled forward through the underbrush. Eddie was right behind me. We hadn't traveled more than twenty-five meters when we hit a heavily used trail. I signaled Mounts to cover me while I went forward to investigate it. It didn't take much effort to deduce that the trail had been used very recently: clear and detailed sandal and boot prints had been made on the damp earth. We backtracked cautiously to where we had left the rest of my teammates. This is what it was all about. I could see the excitement in the expressions of Top and the others. The hunt was on. We moved up slowly and, about fifteen yards into the jungle, began to parallel the trail. Every fifty meters or so, we stopped and listened for a few minutes to make sure that no one was moving out on the trail or after us. During the halts, Mounts and I dropped our rucks and moved up to observe the high-speed trail. Our nerve-racking pace continued for the rest of the day. We knew Charlie was out there, but where? Two hours before dark, we located a dense stand of cover, twenty meters off the trail, and set up our NDP.

We followed the same routine for the next two days but still couldn't sight the enemy we knew was around us. Occasionally we heard noises, and at times we could even smell the aroma of wood fires and *nuoc mam* sauce, but we never once got sight of the enemy. We considered the possibility of requesting that our mission be extended, but we were running short of water and could not chance a resupply. On the fifth day, disappointed, we turned away from the trail and headed for the PZ. The mission turned out to be another walk in the woods. The area was hot, but without our making a visual, another team would have to go in to confirm the enemy's presence. We probably could have accomplished this with another day or two, but no one can patrol in the jungles of Vietnam without adequate water.

Back in the rear, we once again cleaned our weapons and repacked our rucks, hoping that we would get the nod to go back out in the same RZ. Unfortunately, it never happened.

I decided to make another trip down to Tiger Force to see Jeep. This time, luck was with me, as Tiger Force had just come back in from the bush. Jeep looked bad, real bad, as if he had not slept for a week or more. His weight was down, too, perhaps ten to fifteen pounds. We sat and drank a few beers and swapped war stories for a while. Jeep had changed somehow. Less than a month in the Tigers, he was no longer the funny, happy-go-lucky individual I had known in the States. He had become downcast and extremely cynical. When I asked him how he was holding up, he refused to answer, then kind of blew it off when I pushed a little harder. I wondered what he was holding back. What had he seen or done that he couldn't bring himself to tell me about?

A little later, we said our good-byes. There was a pain in my heart and sorrow that I couldn't come to grips with. I tried to forget it, but without much success.

Later, in my hootch, sharing a beer with Boss, I told him about the visit to see Jeep. Boss advised me to shake it off, to go back and see Jeep the next morning. Chances were that Jeep and I just weren't running on the same track. It happened. That said, we both quieted so that we could listen to Wolfman howling at the moon. It was no longer a novel event, but something he had taken to doing with more and more frequency. The army plays "Taps" at night; the LRRPs had Wolfman.

The next morning started on a negative note. Sergeant Weems had to take our detachment mascot down the hill and destroy it. Although the scout dog handlers had given him all his shots, he had still developed distemper. It was a blow to those of us who had come to appreciate him.

The remainder of the day went no better. I walked to the Tiger Force compound for another talk with Jeep, but they had already returned to the field. They had been in the rear for only forty-eight hours before their services were demanded once again. I was devastated; I felt that if I had taken the opportunity last time, I could have talked Jeep into coming to the LRRPs. I returned to the compound to drown my sorrow in beer. I needed some way to shake the bad vibes I was experiencing.

CHAPTER 18

We had another mission to prepare for, and it wasn't much of a surprise to any of us that it was not going to be a Lurp mission. We would be going back into the Song Ve Valley in detachment strength—another misuse of our talent by higher command. Our detachment and elements of a nearby ARVN Ranger battalion were to conduct sweeps of the valley floor and to evacuate all civilian inhabitants along with their personal possessions, including livestock. I wanted to ask Lieutenant McIsaac if the operation would qualify us as cowboys, but sensing his mood after being told of the operation, I decided to keep my mouth shut.

Our unit was about to participate in what was being called the largest single civil-affairs project to date. With the rest of the brigade roaming the mountains and jungles around us as flankers, we didn't really expect to have a lot of trouble from Charlie, who had only three options: He could take us on in the open; he could go after the rest of the brigade in the bush; he could shag ass before his escape routes were shut down, then come back to fight on a better day.

At the briefing, we were told that the Vietnamese civilians occupying the south end of the valley would be waiting for us outside a ville, ready for evacuation. Anything north of that point was in the designated free-fire zone. Free-fire meant just what it said—we didn't have to wait until something declared itself a danger to us, but could blow it away without provocation. Nothing was safe in the free-fire zone. Dogs, cats, chickens, ducks, people, trees that moved in the wind.

I went back to rearrange my rucksack so I could hump a few

hundred more rounds of ammo (free-fire zones often proved hazardous to one's basic load), and discovered that while I was at the briefing, some no-good son of a bitch had raided my grub. The best of my new LRRP rations had mysteriously disappeared and been replaced by garbage rations that no one would eat. Pork and scalloped potatoes and chili con carne had been substituted for the wonderful beef and chicken meals that I was so fond of. Pork and scalloped were the only LRRP ration that was better mixed with cold water (for the reason that plaster of paris sets up faster if made with warm water). Chili con carne, on the other hand, if not mixed with hot water and set aside for the duration of the war, simply refused to rehydrate at all. Except for the slight flavor of cumin, eating one of these rations reminded one of dining on an inexpensive, dry dog food.

As I scanned the hootch, scarcely controlling my rage, I spotted Boss, Sweet Pea, and The Beaver looking at me in bewilderment, as if they had also been raided. And like me, they knew that if they spoke up about the heist, they, too, would soon become the brunt of everyone's teasing about not being able to secure their immediate areas. Someone had ripped us off, and I immediately suspected that it was our CO, Lieutenant McIsaac. While we were slumming around in the rear, he had pulled a raid on our rucks. Undaunted, I went to my hidden stash, only to discover that it, too, had been raided. I couldn't prove it was Mac, nor did I really want to. We had been had by one of the best. Why, Ole Mac had more time in a T-10 parachute than I had in a T-shirt.

So, reluctantly, I returned to the task at hand, knowing that a couple of days of trash rations might play havoc with my diet, but they surely wouldn't kill me. At least the LRRP rats were better than C rats. On the day of the mission, the detachment was transported, team by team, to the helipad. After a brief wait, we found ourselves airborne. Secretly, I hoped that this trip would go off a little better than the last one.

We touched down just outside the ville and spread out across the paddies, then we sat down propped against the paddy dikes, waiting to move out. Two hours later, we were still waiting. It was the army way.

As a precaution, Sergeant McKinnon had gone in the day before with a recon team and had lain dog in the jungle outside the ville, observing the Vietnamese who were to be evacuated, just in case the enemy decided to hide a few of their people among them. Nobody wanted to walk into an ambush with a bunch of civilians caught in the middle.

McKinnon had a newbie on his team who had been running his mouth a lot about how much ass he was going to kick, and Mac had to threaten the guy to get him to back off. When McKinnon saw that we had inserted, he ordered his team to move out and link up with the rest of the detachment. They had not gone a hundred meters before this FNG started complaining that he couldn't take the heat and the hump. McKinnon immediately stopped the patrol and gave the stud a verbal ass-whipping that came up just short of qualifying him for a disability discharge. Another one hundred meters, and our hero started crying that he couldn't make it without help. McKinnon had no choice but to split the man's load with the rest of the team, even taking away his weapon. Lieutenant McIsaac shipped his sorry ass out to the detachment on the first available slick.

I watched as the Vietnamese civilians to our rear jabbered their heads off. Behind them, over a thousand head of cattle trudged along, probably every bit as tired and hot as we were. Where was Rowdy Yates when you really needed him? "Head 'em up, move 'em out, Rawhiiiiiiiiiide."

Finally, nearly three hours into the mission, the ARVN Rangers showed up. They came in by Chinook helicopters as we stood watching. It was a real comfort to see them stumbling around, bumping into each other, chattering, and holding hands. The Keystone Kops couldn't have been any more hilarious. If they had been our support, we would have been in deep shit, yet they were supposed to be the cream of the Vietnamese Army! I turned to Boss for a little support and understanding and saw him nodding toward a hootch perhaps a hundred meters away. "Limey," he said, "I've been watching that hootch for over two hours and nobody has come out." Before I could respond, automatic fire broke out to our rear. Expecting to have to open up on an assaulting wave of enemy troops, I grabbed my weapon and spun around. Instead I was met with a sight that I will never forget: the ARVNs were shooting at the cattle. The Vietnamese civilians looked on stoically as their own military, their protectors, systematically destroyed their wealth. Winning the hearts and minds of the people! Yeah.

I was shamed by what I saw. We all were. We self-consciously shied away from the South Vietnamese Rangers, not wanting any part of the slaughter nor to be seen to share in their guilt. In the background, Lieutenant McIsaac was screaming at the ARVNs to stop. *"Limey, move out! Take point!"* he shouted. *"Beaver, left flank. Boss, right flank!"*

We moved quickly; he meant business. Boss was still eyeing that lone hootch. What the hell, I thought. Joined by a couple of the other guys, we headed in the general direction of the hootch.

We all reached it. I stepped nonchalantly through the door, only to have the hair on the back of my neck stand up as the disgusting odor of death hit me. I brought my weapon up, alert. Someone or something was definitely dead in there. The stench was horrible, and the close air and high humidity in the small building magnified the aroma. Weapon at the ready, I stepped through an open doorway into an adjoining room. More dead than alive, an enemy soldier lay on a mat on the bamboo bed. He stared at me with cold, lifeless eyes. I covered him while Boss and Bill Scanlon moved up to search him. The VC had been there for a while. His upper arm had been badly shattered. Pieces of bone showed in the mangled flesh of the wound. It didn't take a medic to realize that the wound had never been treated. Gangrene had set in, and maggots were eating the ruined flesh around the wound.

The VC never uttered a word. He would not even give us the satisfaction of witnessing his pain. Just that cold, blank stare. He was either the bravest man I had ever met or the biggest fool. But we had a mission to accomplish and didn't have the time or the inclination to screw with an enemy prisoner.

Reluctantly, we gave him over to the ARVNs with a warning that he wasn't a cow. Then, alert for any sign of activity, we walked through the first of a series of abandoned villes. Some of the guys searched the place and ended up putting their Zippos to use. Since the area had been declared a free-fire zone and all the civilians were moving out, leaving the buildings behind would only benefit the enemy.

Suddenly, less than a hundred feet away, a hootch disintegrated with a roar and a blinding explosion. I dived to the ground. Obviously, the enemy had hidden explosives in at least one of the buildings. It was the only proof we needed. Not having the time to conduct a more thorough search, we started to set fire to the entire village.

It wasn't long before we received a call from a C & C chopper to stop the torching. A few minutes later, the call came in again for us to cease and desist. What a bunch of shit! We were furious. I guess the order of the day had been changed during our absence, and that "clear the valley, but don't mess it up any" superseded the original orders. Well, none of us bought that line of thinking. The Zippos stayed busy and so did the guys. And other secondary explosions detonated around us, confirming our suspicions. With half the ville ablaze, a Huey helicopter hovered about four hundred feet overhead. I could see the unhappy officer in the open cabin talking on the radio, his arms flailing madly. We all prayed the moron would lose his balance and join us on the ground. Eventually, Lieutenant McIsaac, tired of getting his ass chewed on, told us to knock it off and move out. Two or three klicks to our right, out across a series of paddies, I saw a squad of VC running into the bush. But with them out of range, all I could do was to point and grunt. If the motormouth in the C & C ship had been doing his job, those enemy soldiers would have been lying dead in the paddies instead of disappearing into the jungle. We were disgusted.

Already miserable, I kept moving forward, the hot sun blazing down on us. If this was the life of the line companies, I wanted no part of it.

We continued humping. When my mind began to drift, I

stopped the detachment to take a break. I never got an argument from Lieutenant McIsaac, nor the rest of the guys; we were all exhausted. I sat back against my ruck and took a long drink of water. Minutes later, I stood to get a better idea of our surroundings before we moved out. A river meandered to our left, with dense jungle just beyond it. On our right was more jungle. We were an inviting target. I prayed that Charlie didn't have mortars or artillery and a spotter nearby. If he did, we were goners. The grunts could have these paddies. There just wasn't enough cover for a full-fledged Lurp.

I couldn't speak or understand Vietnamese, but I knew what "VC" meant. Four or five ARVN Rangers came running up the line toward us in a panic. "VC—VC!" they yelled and pointed toward our front. With an M-16 in one hand and a sawed-off M-79 in the other, I took off in the direction the ARVNs were pointing. Boss and The Beaver were keeping pace with me all the way. We ran forward about a hundred meters, finally stopping when we failed to spot anyone. We carefully searched for tunnels, spider holes, and bunkers through the brush around the paddies but found nothing. Then we spotted a hootch back in the brush across the river. A path led to the front door. More out of frustration than anything else, I fired an M-79 round at the hootch, nearly four hundred meters away. The HE round landed a little short. I made a mental adjustment and popped another round downrange with the same results. Something must be wrong with this damn thing, I thought. Or maybe I'm just out of range. Boss and The Beaver moved up and joined me in the target practice, edging closer to the target. After we fired ten rounds at the hootch (and found it with four), Top Smith arrived on the scene and said, "Okay, you guys had your fun, now go over there and check it out."

Our first sergeant stood with his hands on his hips as the three of us made the long walk out to the hootch. We crossed the river and climbed up the narrow path. I looked back just before we got there. Top Smith hadn't moved from his spot. I hoped that we would find a body to justify using all those HE rounds we had put out. I was feeling about as low as a dumb cherry. Never before had I heard Top Smith raise his voice; he was pissed.

We made a thorough search of the hootch and the surrounding underbrush but found nothing. There was no body anywhere. We did, however, find a good-sized snake in its final death throes. When Top saw us all standing together, looking down at a spot on the ground, he hollered from across the river, "Well, Limey, what have you got?"

"One real dead VC snake, Top."

I could see him mulling that over in his head. He wouldn't laugh, but I could sense that he wanted to. We had really made asses of ourselves. "Move it out, you three" was all he said when we got back across the river.

We started forward on our trek once again. No enemy, just more paddies, brush, and hot sun. What we all needed was a cold beer or, the next best thing, cold water. The water in our canteens was nearly boiling from exposure to the sun. The river water was cool. I knew that for a fact since I had already crossed the damn thing twice. I promised myself that I would fill at least one of my canteens from the river at the next break.

A couple of hours later, the column came to a halt, giving me the opportunity to refill my canteens from the river. I dropped a halazone tablet into my canteen, shook it, and set it aside. I decided to treat myself to a hatful of cool water over my overcooked head. Big mistake! The cool water met the boiling flesh on my "hat rest" and immediately caused a raging headache. The cool water had seemed ice cold against my boiling head, and I had to sit down before I passed out.

It took me a little while to recover, but the word eventually came up the line to get up and get moving. I felt a little better and was more alert than I had been. But an hour later, I was dragging again. This time I felt sick and found myself hallucinating. I tried just putting one foot in front of the other for the rest of the day, wishing that someone would turn off the sun. On a Lurp mission I was always wired tight for four or five days, alert to the slightest noise. But out there on the valley floor, I was loosely bailed, and about half the time was oblivious to my surroundings. It was not a very comfortable feeling.

It was late afternoon when we finally stopped for the day. We formed a perimeter out on a large sandbar covered with vegetation. We put out claymore mines and settled in for the night. No one had brought entrenching tools, so digging foxholes was out of the question. We would spend the night exposed, in the cover of the brush. I was lucky enough to pull the last guard duty. I had no trouble falling asleep; closing my eyes seemed to be the only prompting I needed. I couldn't even tell you if I dreamed. But at 0400 hours, I was awakened for my turn at watch with a solid seven hours of much-needed sleep under my belt, just about the most since I had been in-country. Uncle Ho's entire army could have walked past me that night, and I would never have known. I was a little shook up that I had let my guard down so far, and promised myself that it would never happen again. I had trained myself to waken at the slightest sound or change in the atmosphere. I had let myself down.

An hour after first light, we moved outside the perimeter and retrieved the claymore. The worst chore of the day was about to begin. I had to eat some of those horrible pork and scalloped potatoes Lieutenant McIsaac had stuck me with. Even boiling water, salt, and pepper failed to help, but I forced myself to eat, promising someday to get even with El Tee.

Moving out again, I felt much better than I had during the day before. I filled a couple of canteens when we crossed the river, waiting for the last of the detachment to do the same. Then we humped, moving, always moving. We were watchful and alert, and a slight breeze helped to keep us cool. Then that same stench as the day before hit me.

I caught Boss's eye. He nodded. We signaled to stop the patrol. Dropping our packs, Boss, The Beaver, and I slowly moved forward. A dead VC was floating facedown in the river, and man, was he ripe! Small fish were swarming over the body, nibbling and tugging at the flesh.

I looked up to tell the rest of the guys what we had seen, but spotted Lieutenant McIsaac filling his canteen not more than one hundred meters downstream from the body. I decided to keep my big mouth shut. Well, for the time being. Out of pure cussedness, I smiled, returned to my rucksack, and fired up a cigarette, trying the whole time to keep a straight face as I watched El Tee filling the rest of his canteens with cool, delicious water. It looked as if we would be getting even with El Tee much quicker than I had hoped.

Soon, it was time to saddle up and move out again. We recrossed the river, stopping once to watch our illustrious CO throw up. What an ungentlemanly thing to do! All of my missing LRRP-rat spaghetti was being deposited in the river right before my eyes. El Tee vomited until only dry heaves came from his stomach. Lucky for us, we had filled our canteens about a klick downstream, or we would have all been standing beside our leader in the river.

Five minutes later, after he had recovered some of his composure, Lieutenant McIsaac came up to me and asked why I hadn't warned them about the body in the river. I smiled and said, "Hell, El Tee, I thought with the water flowing so quickly over all that sand and rock, by the time it got to you it would almost be purified. Besides, the fish were eating all the loose flesh."

I waited for him to vomit once again, but he managed to retain some composure. He raised an eyebrow toward me and snarled, "Move the fuck out, Limey." Revenge was such a very sweet thing.

We spent the rest of the day humping across the rice paddies and through the brush, always expecting the attack that never came. No VC, no gunfire, nothing but the lousy sun beating us into the ground. Day two had been better than the first. I felt stronger, better able to tolerate the harsh conditions.

The third day proved to be the same as the second. Humping, watching, and waiting. By the time we approached another abandoned ville, I was almost hoping for contact.

A sudden burst of M-16 fire snapped me back to reality. It had come from my right flank, over where Boss and Weems were. They were in contact!

I dropped my ruck and ran toward their position, with The

My mother, Marguerite Patricia Walker née Chiasson, while in the British army. Notice the country-of-origin tab on her right shoulder. Hull, England, February 1943 (Author's collection)

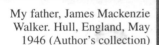

My father, James Mackenzie Walker. Hull, England, May 1946 (Author's collection)

Author at the steps where he watched the neighborhood manure fights. 28 Marshall Street, Hull, England, 1947 (Author's collection)

Tom "The Greek" Dokos and Mike "Sweet Pea" Kinnan in front of the POW compound. Duc Pho, May 1967 (Tom Dokos collection)

LRRP Hill, Duc Pho. Hill in the background is where Lopez, Gartner, and Cody were wounded. May 1967 (Danny Neihuser collection)

Remains of a house after demolition training. Duc Pho, June 1967 (Danny Neihuser collection)

Our LRRP sign. Wherever we went, it went. (Brian Kraft collection)

Bob McKinnon, one of the author's team leaders, with a Swedish K. Duc Pho, June 1967 (Bob McKinnon collection)

Larry Christian profiling his maroon beret. Duc Pho, June 1967 (Bill Scanlon collection)

Dead VC during the cattle drive mission in the Song Ve Valley, June 1967. Lieutenant McIsaac did not appreciate the author's explanation of water purification. (Danny Neihuser collection)

Brian "Wolfman" Kraft taking a break during the cattle drive. Song Ve Valley, 1967 (Brian Kraft collection)

1/101st Airborne ammunition dump exploding. Duc Pho, 1967 (Bill Scanlon collection)

Virgil Paulk and Bill Scanlon in front of a wrecked Huey helicopter. Tam Ky Corridor, July 1967 (Bill Scanlon collection)

Left to right: author, Braun, Sinclair, and Beiber getting ready for an overnight ambush. Duc Pho, August 1967 (Bob McKinnon collection)

Standing, left to right: Larry Christian, John Hines, Brian "Wolfman" Kraft, Sandy "Boss" Weisberger, Lt. Dan McIsaac. *Kneeling:* unknown pilots. Duc Pho, August 1967 (Dan McIsaac collection)

Left to right: Ernie Winston, Danny Neihuser, Thomas, Lester "Super Spade" Hite, John Chadwick, Ronnie Weems. Chu Lai, October 1967 (Danny Neihuser collection)

Left to right: Paul Dufresne, Clay Wentworth, Brian "Wolfman" Kraft, Joseph "Pizza Joe" Remiro, Harvey "The Beaver" Beiber. Chu Lai, October 1967 (Brian Kraft collection)

After Lieutenant McIsaac's award ceremony in Chu Lai, November 1967. *Front row, left to right:* Thompson, Clay Wentworth, unknown, Danny Neihuser, unknown, Frank Shanley. *Middle row:* Thomas, "Jaybird" Magill, Harvey "The Beaver" Beiber, author. *Standing:* Lt. Dan McIsaac, Lester "Super Spade" Hite, Derby Jones, unknown, George Peppers, Lloyd "Top" Smith. (Dan McIsaac collection)

Eddie Cecena while in Phan Rang running LRRP missions for the 3/506th Infantry, December 1967 (Brian Kraft collection)

Sandy "Boss" Weisberger ditto

Front row, left to right: Tom "The Greek" Dokos, Bob McKinnon, Lloyd "Top" Smith. *Back row:* author, Sandy "Boss" Weisberger, Ralph Church, Rudy Lopez, Larry Christian, Gary Fandell. Phan Rang, December 1967 (Bob McKinnon collection)

Team leader extraordinaire Walter Bacek. Phan Rang, December 1967 (Tom Dokos collection)

Kneeling, left to right: Peppy Wenglarz, author, Rudy Lopez, Kenn Miller, Larry Forrest. *Standing:* George "Rommel" Murphy, Sandy "Boss" Weisberger, Alan "Lurch" Cornett, John Chadwick, Rey Martinez, "Jaybird" Magill, Gene Ackerson. Taken at the 1992 Ranger Rendezvous, Fort Benning, Georgia, June 1992 (Author's collection)

Beaver right on my tail. I was wired tight and anxious to fire something up. By the time I reached Boss and Weems, they were already on their second bunker. The entire right side of the ville was full of bunkers. Boss and Weems had already killed three dinks in the first bunker and were fragging the rest, one by one. Weems tossed a willy pete into one bunker, and I followed behind it with a frag. The white phosphorus went off just as a VC tried to get out. The frag went off a second later. The dink slipped back into the raging fire in the bunker, and no further activity was heard from it. All around me now, Lurps were blasting bunkers—WPs followed by frags, detonation after detonation. Bunkers were hit, then hit again, as the Lurps methodically destroyed the encampment. The VC had been waiting for us to move by before they attacked. But they had underestimated us. Boss and Weems had screwed up their day. No rice and fish heads for those boys that night!

We searched the jungle parallel to the bunker line. Nothing. Those VC had simply committed suicide. Without any supporting fire, they had left themselves wide open, and they had paid for their mistake. Even if they had been able to initiate their ambush, they would have likely paid a heavy price while trying to break contact and get back into the bush, unless they had tunnels or trenches running back into the jungle. We searched but found nothing.

We decided to remain in the shade and to eat before moving on. The second chile con carne wasn't actually so bad, maybe even as palatable as some of the mess hall chow. As I sat propped up against a tree, just beginning to eat, I looked up and saw Eddie Mounts staring at me. Ignoring him, I continued to eat. When I looked up a second time, he was still staring. I finally tired of it and demanded to know just what the fuck he was staring at.

He gulped and said, "That's the biggest fucking snake I've ever seen."

I am petrified of snakes. Not wanting to betray my fear, I continued eating. "Where?" I asked, almost too nonchalantly.

"It just went behind you," he said.

Still trying to maintain some semblance of cool, I continued to eat, but the blood in my veins began turning to ice from my feet up. I knew that if the guys became aware of how afraid of snakes I was, they would never lighten up. I would be finding snakes everywhere. My rucksack, hootch, boots, bunk—even the shithouse. Nowhere would be safe.

We spent three more uneventful days crisscrossing the Song Ve Valley, humping through the paddies and brush, looking for the enemy without success. Apparently, they had decided to avoid contact this time around. We were finally extracted from that godforsaken valley and returned to our base camp to clean up and tend to our scrapes and bruises.

According to the after-action report, the 1/101st Airborne had relocated 6,256 villagers and 1,341 head of cattle; 470 enemy soldiers had been killed, by actual body count.

The rest of the brigade must have been having a jolly ole time in the bush killing dinks while we Lurps were sweltering in the paddies! But I guess we killed our fair share.

We were filthy; a quick trip to the shower point was in order. Stripping off our rotting clothes, we threw them on the ground and stepped into the shower. Two dozen bare asses washed off the crud and filth accumulated over the past week. All I needed to complete the ecstasy I felt was a thorough massage, preferably one with all the trimmings. Exhausted, at first it was all I could do to soap down; I let the lukewarm water carry away the filth. The longer I remained under the shower, the better I felt. After fifteen minutes, I was totally refreshed. It was party time!

Before dark, the party started in earnest. Wolfman sat on his rock and howled loudly to the heavens. A group of us stood by the dusty road drinking beer while we watched our favorite son. The family was home again. The Wolfman continued to howl as we drank. As luck would have it, a lifer captain walked by and took exception to our behavior, especially the Wolfman's.

"Who the hell is that?" the captain asked, pointing at Wolfman.

"That's the Wolfman, sir," I replied.

"Well, get him off that rock and have him shut up," the captain ordered.

I looked at the rest of the guys and then at Wolfman, expecting someone to say something, then finally made eyeball contact with the good captain and in my most sarcastic tone replied, "Sorry, I can't do that, that's the Wolfman's fucking rock." The captain clenched his fists, gritted his teeth, and stomped off—but not before I threw him my best salute and proudly blared out "Airborne Lurp, sir!" The captain continued down the hill, followed by our laughter. Fuck it, I thought, what's he going to do? Send me to Vietnam?

The road party started to break up as we were half expecting the captain to return with the brigade sergeant major. Personally, I went to the cooler for another beer, having every intention of going back to the hootch and to bed. But my plans for an early evening came to a halt when I bumped into Mark "Wolverine" Thompson, who asked me to follow him to his tent for a surprise. I wondered what the the surprise was and told him I'd be there after I took a piss break. By the time I arrived, Wolverine had a dozen Lurps packed into a tent built for four. Just another pot party, I thought. Then the big surprise came. Mark had just received a new reel-to-reel tape from his hometown radio station. The music was set to its highest volume, and for the first time I listened to a new generation of music. The Doors screamed about fire. Country Joe and the Fish counted to four and wanted to know what the hell we were fighting for. The Beatles were now on some kind of Magical Mystery Tour. The more I smoked and drank, the better the music sounded. I went outside and lay down on our bunker, watching Puff the Magic Dragon work death and destruction not more than three or four klicks outside the perimeter; I was oblivious to my surroundings; I was on my own Magical Mystery Tour. Relaxed and at peace with myself, I slowly went to sleep. The breeze, the hum of the mosquitoes disappeared. They would have to find their meal somewhere else. The South China Sea breeze was on my side for once. I drifted off to never-never land.

I woke the following morning, nervous and restless. Picking up my weapon, I left the detachment area and took a walk to the scout dog detachment area. After a few minutes of bullshitting, I left and wandered around. Nowhere in particular, just walking to shake a bad feeling I was having. Not being able to get a handle on it, I walked back to the LRRP detachment area. Arriving, I spotted Jay "Jaybird" Magill, an MP who would join our ranks within a few days, talking with Lurch, Wolfman, and Beaver.

I had a strange feeling something was up. Walking over to their group, I received no eye contact at all. They started to nervously mill around, eyes focused on the ground. Finally Jaybird broke the silence. "Limey, I have some bad news for you."

"What, we're busted for smoking bad pot?" Nobody laughed at my poor sense of humor.

"Limey," Jaybird continued, "Jeep was hit yesterday." Stunned, I sat down on the ground. Jay crouched down beside me and continued, "When the Tigers were being extracted after the cattle drive, the chopper they were on was blown up. Tigers are not releasing any info on the casualties, but it was supposed to be pretty bad." Jaybird then got up, mumbled an "I'm sorry," and left the detachment area. So much for funny feelings!

I wanted to go to the 25th Evac Hospital, but I knew that the road between the 1/101st Airborne and the 25th Division was closed so I decided to go to the horse's mouth for information on Jeep's demise—Tiger Force.

On the walk down to the 1/327 Infantry's Tiger Force, I swore to myself repeatedly that I would never again allow myself to get close to another person. I looked for and found a reliable source for the story, Sam "Chief" Ybarra. Sam said that it had been a real screwup. Simple as that. After the cattle drive, the Tigers had gotten into their respective choppers for extraction. Someone in Jeep's chopper was not paying attention, and the safety pin in a fragmentation grenade was inadvertently pulled. When the grenade exploded, it detonated other grenades in the chopper. Everyone in the slick had become a casualty. Some dead, but all wounded. Even Chief had no idea who had been killed, just that the Tigers were six troopers short.

Back at the unit, no amount of Lurch's jokes or jesting from the guys could help me. I drank in uncommon silence, moody and brooding. Feeling sorry for myself, I sat alone, saying nothing to anyone.

CHAPTER 19

In war, you learned to put grief behind you as quickly as you could. Dwelling on thoughts of lost comrades was the fastest way to meet up with them again. So I got myself under control and swore that I wouldn't let myself make close friends in the future—an oath that I would not keep.

I needed to go out in the field at the earliest opportunity, so when Staff Sergeant Beauchamp's team came up one member short, I jumped at the chance to get out into the bush. I was pretty excited about a mission with Beauchamp's Team 4, especially since, compared to the rest of the team, I was a cherry. The only thing that bothered me about the mission was that Larry had designated me to carry the PRC-25. It was one heavy, cumbersome addition to a standard load, and usually a burden pawned off on some newbie, like me. But commo was often the only thing that kept Lurps off the casualty lists, so I wasn't about to bitch.

My ruck was packed, M-16 cleaned, and magazines emptied then reloaded with fresh ammo—I had remembered to load only eighteen rounds per mag. The old guys told me that it was okay to load a mag with twenty rounds, but after a while that tended to weaken the spring, which might result in your automatic weapon going single-shot on you right in the middle of a firefight.

As evening gave way to night, all of us from Team 4 sat around, discussing the warning order we had been given earlier in the day. With a mission the next day, beer was out. Coffee and hot chocolate were the drinks of the evening.

I felt a twinge of envy as I looked around the detachment area and saw some of the other guys drinking and joking around. But there would be plenty of time for that after the mission.

I had the good fortune to be part of a group of pros. Staff Sergeant Beauchamp was our team leader, and Sgt. Pat Kinser was senior scout and ATL. Specialist 4 Sullivan was the junior scout, Specialist 4 Redmar the senior RTO, Specialist 4 Neihuser the team medic, and me humping the artillery radio.

I had gone through my SOI, memorizing the frequencies that were most important, especially those for TOC and the primary artillery nets. Redmar's radio would be set to the TOC frequency; mine would be kept on the redleg (artillery) band in case we needed to call in a fire mission quickly. But I had also memorized the TOC frequency just in case we got separated; I wanted to make sure that I could reach base camp so I could get an extraction without having to go through another party. God forbid that I would have to depend on someone I didn't even know to save our asses in an emergency. It was bad enough just to think that the duds of the Security Platoon made up our reaction force.

When the topic of discussion finally moved to girls and fast cars, I retreated to my hootch to get some beauty rest.

Sleep didn't come easy for me that night, and only after I convinced myself that I wouldn't screw up on the patrol did I finally doze off. A couple of hours later, I was up again, doing what I thought was normal at that time of the morning— hunting for an elusive packet of hot chocolate or coffee, and getting an ass-chewing from my sleeping hootchmates for being such a noisy son of a bitch. Since it was still dark outside, I decided to go for a stroll.

With a cup of hot coffee in one hand and a cigarette in the other, I meandered down the hill toward brigade headquarters and the MP detachment. I hadn't gone more than halfway down the hill when an MP jeep pulled up next to me. I immediately recognized the numero uno jerk of the MP detachment, Lieutenant Shields, and thought to myself, Aw c'mon, what did I do now?

"What are you doing out roving around the area this time of the morning, Walker?" the kindhearted asshole asked in his normally surly manner.

"Oh, just walking and thinking, sir," I replied, trying to be as cool and under control as I could be.

The lieutenant had never won any trophies for excess IQ, so I waited a good two minutes while he searched for an appropriate response. When he finally spoke again, I was stunned by his statement. "You Lurps aren't allowed out after dark. All you do is create problems, steal, and fight. Now get back to your area; that's an order."

I was deeply hurt. But since he was an officer, of sorts, I nodded and turned to walk away. But before I had taken a full step, I looked back over my shoulder and added, "Sir, you forgot to mention killing, plundering, and raping."

I didn't wait for a response. None came. Lieutenant Shields had obviously overreacted a bit. We might have been guilty of a number of violations of the rules and regulations, but who didn't let off a little steam once in a while? It was more than that. It was the LRRP mystique that made the asshole dislike us. Of course, it might have been some of the other stuff, too. Maybe it was the fact that we were an all-volunteer unit, with a lot of unit pride and a reputation for being good at what we did. All I knew was that, like the lieutenant, I used to be an MP, but I felt a lot better about being a Lurp.

I was still awake when the rest of the detachment began to stir. I watched as Ernie Winston returned from one of his nightly one-man patrols. He washed off his cammo and came over to share a cup of coffee. I knew better than to ask him what he had done that night because it wouldn't have been cool, but I was certain that sometime during the day, S-2 would be confounded by another discovery of a dead VC in the paddy but wouldn't be able to match up the body with a contact report.

Time sure flies when you want it to run slow. We soon

reported to the 176th Assault Helicopter Company and boarded the slick that would take us out to our RZ, northwest of Duc Pho. As usual, my mind was in overdrive as I mentally checked and rechecked the list of frequencies. I reminded myself to make sure I got a commo check with arty as soon as we inserted.

The chopper dropped rapidly as we approached our LZ, but we were still a couple hundred feet above the jungle when Beauchamp tapped the aircraft commander on the helmet and yelled something in his ear. Then he turned to us and mouthed, "No fucking way!"

It was at this point that I first really looked at our LZ and realized that we were not going in. Beauchamp hadn't been given the opportunity to go out on an overflight of our AO to select an LZ. This one looked like something a greenskeeper at a golf course would have been proud of. It was brown instead of green, but the grass had that same freshly manicured look to it. Whatever had happened down there had destroyed all the vegetation. Lurps need cover and concealment to do their work, and there was neither cover nor concealment below us. Beauchamp aborted the mission.

When we got back to base camp, we were told that the area around our LZ had been sprayed with a defoliant to kill the vegetation. Brigade immediately gave us another mission in the same AO, but this time let the team leader do an overflight before we went in.

The next morning was the same routine as before: drink a lot of coffee and show up at the 176th AHC on time. Once again, we loaded on the chopper and headed out to take the war to the enemy. Shit, but this was exciting!

This time the LZ was perfect, with more than enough elephant grass to hide in after inserting, and dense bush no more than fifty meters away. Yes, it was the ideal LZ. Unfortunately, we weren't the only ones who thought so. Charlie realized the same thing, and we discovered very quickly that he didn't want us in his neighborhood.

The chopper had just flared to drop us off when the enemy opened up from the tree line. The first indication that we were going in hot was when we heard rounds smacking against the side of the aircraft. Tracers passed through the open cabin door, making cracking sounds that we could hear over the roar of the helicopter's motor. I knew that there were most likely four invisible nontracers escorting each of the tracers passing over our heads. We were dead men unless a miracle occurred.

The pilot did a quick pedal turn and dropped his nose to pick up forward speed. The maneuver seemed to throw off the enemy's aim. We climbed up and away from the LZ, trailing smoke behind us. One of the door gunners had caught a round in the leg. It didn't look life-threatening, but he was bleeding pretty badly. The rotor wash was throwing his blood around inside the cabin, making it look like we had all been hit. But, amazingly, no one else had been wounded.

We made it back to the 176th's helipad, still smoking but under our own power. Rommel Murphy was there in minutes with the Lurpmobile. He was shaking his head. Evidently, we had ruined his plans for the day.

"Are you guys ever gonna insert, Limey?" he asked nonchalantly as I threw my gear into the back of the truck.

"Hey, fuck you, Murphy," I sneered, feigning hostility. "Where's the cold beer?"

Rommel jerked a thumb over his shoulder, indicating a cooler on the front seat passenger side of the three-quarter-ton truck. Good old Murphy! It was his way of getting our minds off what we had just been through. It worked!

I grabbed a cold one, opened it with my trusty church key, and was just starting to let the cold liquid run down the back of my parched throat when I heard, "What the hell do you think you're doing, Limey? We might be going back out again." It was Beauchamp, and he was pissed. I didn't say a word, and just handed the beer to Rommel. My team leader was right. I never should have assumed that we were done for the day.

By the time we reached LRRP Hill, the word had already gotten out that Team 4 had struck out for the second time in two days. Word was soon passed down that we would be going back out the next morning into a different LZ in the same AO.

The next morning we were unloading the truck at the 176th

AHC's compound, and I noticed that we had drawn a small crowd. Most likely the flyboys had some kind of pool going to see how long we would stay on the ground. The way our luck was going, whoever drew ten seconds was probably going to win the pot. As I was walking toward the helicopter, one of the door gunners who partied with us a lot remarked, "Don't you guys know when enough is enough, Limey?"

"Guess not, my good chap. I'm here, aren't I?" I replied, putting emphasis on the "chap" as he always got a cheap thrill out of my English accent.

For the third time in three days, our chopper flared over an LZ as we prepared to insert. The Minutemen pilots were good, and we leaped from the skids without there being a noticeable change in pitch.

We lay dog in the elephant grass as the sounds of the chopper faded into the distance. The only noise I could hear was the light breeze brushing across the top of the grass. I called for and got a good commo check with the artillery battery designated to support us. For the first time everything was good. We were finally on the ground, and no one had shot at us yet.

We waited a few minutes, then carefully headed for the cover of the jungle a short distance away. When we reached it, we dropped into a tight wagon-wheel perimeter and lay dog again, calling in another commo check. It appeared that we were "in" this time, and with a little luck, we would accomplish our mission.

We moved out soon afterward, making our way through the thick underbrush until we came to a spot that would make a suitable night defensive position. There was no point trying to continue moving in the tangle of trees and wait-a-minute vines with night coming on.

One by one, we put out our claymore mines, and the guys who were hungry opened a LRRP ration and ate their evening meal. I wasn't hungry, and as nervous as I was, if I'd eaten anything, it would have gone right through me. I didn't want to say anything to my teammates, but I had the feeling that this mission was jinxed.

We rose before first light and were awake, listening, when the day critters began their early-morning symphony. Thirty minutes later, we had gathered the claymores, sterilized the NDP, and prepared to move out. Before leaving, we made a final commo check just to make sure we could get help if we needed it.

During the first hour of our patrol, we realized that it was going to be impossible to move through the dense underbrush without sounding like a herd of elephants. Beauchamp stopped the patrol and sent Kinser and Sullivan ahead to try to locate a trail. We never liked walking a trail, but under the circumstances, breaking brush was a lousy alternative. Fifteen minutes later, our scouts were back with the disturbing news that we had been paralleling a trail since right after we pulled out of the NDP.

We moved forward, slowly, three to five meters apart until we finally broke out of the cover onto the trail. Even more cautiously than before, we tiptoed down the high-speed trail, carefully monitoring the vegetation on both sides.

Suddenly, an RPD opened up on us from the front of the patrol, the sound of its chatter almost deafening after the dead silence it had broken. I dove to the side of the trail, screaming into my mike for a fire mission. I looked up to see 7.62mm rounds splattering down the trail and heard the rest of the team beginning to return fire. Just as I was beginning to think that we were going to die where we lay, the redlegs acknowledged my transmission.

"Gimme some arty, Limey," Beauchamp screamed from up the trail as rounds smashed through trees. My pucker factor was already redlined.

"Damn it, Beauchamp, gimme some fucking coordinates," I yelled back at him, holding the headset against my chest.

When he shouted back the map coordinates, I passed the information to the artillery fire direction control officer who was standing by. When he asked me if I wanted a smoke round to mark the impact, I shouted, "Hell no, gimme HE on the deck. Got no time for smoke. We're up to our asses in dinks."

It seemed like an eternity before the heavy rounds were

crashing through the trees and detonating out in front of us. The enemy fire immediately dropped off enough for me to look around and see that Redmar was on the radio calling for an extraction. The last thing I wanted to do was stick around waiting for a reaction force from brigade security platoon.

I kept adjusting the artillery around us as Beauchamp got things under control. He turned Kinser around and instructed him to lead the rest of the team back toward the LZ, then he stayed behind to cover me as I adjusted fire on the run. Trying to keep up with the rest of the team, we would sprint fifty meters, stop, order the redlegs to "drop five zero," then turn and sprint fifty more meters. We kept that up all the way to the LZ. When we finally pulled up in the cover at the edge of the clearing, we found the rest of the team setting up security. Everything around us was dead quiet. Was it the calm before the storm?

We secured our PZ, hoping all the time that the artillery fire had disorganized Charlie's pursuit. Our luck held: the chopper arrived ten minutes later, slammed down into the grass, then flew us out to safety less than ten seconds later.

Rommel was there in the Lurpmobile to pick us up when we got in. But this time Limey got in the first word. "Shut the fuck up, Murphy," I said as I reached for the cooler. Beauchamp and the rest of my teammates had each grabbed a beer of their own. Rommel smiled at us and shook his head, glad to see us back in one piece.

CHAPTER 20

We had a number of newbies in the unit who still had to be trained, so we set up practice patrols just outside the perimeter wire. One of the new men, Staff Sergeant Federov, whom we quickly dubbed "The Russian," was a challenge in the making. At five feet, eight inches tall and six feet, four inches wide, he gave one the impression of a human bowling ball. I had my doubts that he would be able to carry *himself* out on patrol, let alone the seventy or more pounds of gear we routinely wore in the field. But I was soon to discover that The Russian was one strong son of a bitch. Unfortunately, he was as clumsy as he was strong.

We formed up in six-man training teams, consisting of three experienced Lurps and three cherries. Carrying full rucks, we moved outside the wire and began teaching the newbies the tricks of the trade. My team consisted of Ron Weems as team leader, Wolfman Kraft at drag, and me at point. We patrolled slowly around the perimeter, demonstrating patrolling techniques to the highly attentive FNGs. It's easy to train bright, motivated students who truly want to learn. We made sure we kept it interesting and explained the reasoning for each point we made. We demonstrated observation techniques—point looking forward and to the sides, slack straight ahead and high, the next three alternating the flanks, and drag covering the back trail.

Everything was going fine, and the new men were catching on quickly. Coming up to an opening in a hedgerow, I stopped the patrol and checked it out to make sure it wasn't booby-trapped. After ascertaining that it was clear, I signaled the team to move on. We took a break a short while later in an abandoned ville, nearly a klick outside the perimeter. When everyone was rested, we moved out again, heading back the same way we had come. It was something we would never have done in the field, but that close to the base, no one dreamed we had anything to worry about. To make matters worse, we weren't as alert as we normally were. I noticed that The Russian wasn't even breaking a sweat. Clearly, I had been wrong about his stamina.

When I reached the break in the hedgerow, I moved right through without checking and was a full twenty feet beyond it when I heard a loud and distinct click. I froze immediately, knowing instantly what it was. Someone had tripped a booby trap. Looking back slowly over my right shoulder, I saw that four of the five remaining members of the patrol were also standing motionless. But twenty meters down the hedgerow, The Russian was making his own path through the dense brush. Amazingly, he had tripped the arming device of a booby trap but it had failed to go off.

Weems ran over to him and chewed massive chunks from Federov's ass. The kindest thing I heard him say was ". . . you're an ignorant son of a bitch for trying to take a shortcut." After Weems finished feeding on the now thoroughly shamed FNG, I moved out in the direction of our detachment area. Wolfman had moved up to pull my slack. Every twenty or thirty paces, I heard him mutter under his breath, "I'll kill that stupid motherfucker." The closer we got to the base camp, the madder he got. By the time we reached the wire, I knew he meant what he said. If I didn't find some way to calm him down, he would soon be doing a number on The Russian. Back at our hootches, I stowed my equipment and conned Wolfman into joining me for a beer at the 176th Aviation Club to get him out of the area before Weems gave a critique on the patrol.

Walking uphill to the club, I tried my best to put Wolfman's mind at ease. "We were all cherries once," I explained. Wolfman was not impressed with my line of reasoning, and still wanted a piece of The Russian's ass. To his way of thinking, what The Russian did was stupid and unforgivable.

We entered the club and started drinking. After consuming half a six-pack, Wolfman began to see The Russian's misadventure as somewhat funny. Three more cans, and it was downright hysterical. By the time Wolfman finally decided to forget the matter, other Lurps were joining us. Soon we had a party in progress. Within an hour, we had one of the three long tables filled with Lurps. Our storytelling soon drew an audience of REMFs. That wouldn't have been a problem except the drunker we got the wilder the war stories grew, and the wilder the war stories, the more REMFs we attracted.

The only problem I had with drinking—besides hangovers—was that if I downed three beers, I would soon urinate six. I know that's physically impossible, but I once measured it and it was a fact. I wasn't a deeply religious person, so I didn't believe that it was a miracle of some sort. The only conclusion I could draw that made a lick of sense was that when I drank, the alcohol was dehydrating me.

After one of numerous trips out to relieve my bladder, I returned to the party to find that some outsider was occupying my seat. Then I noticed my floppy hat lying on the floor. Not only had the mannerless REMF taken over my seat, but the fool had tossed an important piece of my war kit in the dirt. It was more than I could tolerate.

Lurch Cornett had been in the middle of one of his hilarious comedy routines when I walked up to the table. When he saw me staring at the turd head in my seat, he stopped to see what I was going to do. Then he looked down at my hat on the floor, looked back up, and shrugged his shoulders before going back to entertaining the troops. My friend had just acknowledged to me that he had seen the REMF in my seat discard my hat. That was the only verification I needed.

I stood there weighing my alternatives. The REMF was about six feet tall and stocky, and for all I knew he might have been a Golden Glove champion. And taking him on might get the living shit knocked out of me. So I could swallow my pride, bend over and retrieve my hat, and slink out of the club. Or I could spring an ambush, beat his ass, and make him retrieve my hat. I picked the second option. It had become a matter of honor. I moved in quickly and snatched him out of my chair. As I proceeded to beat his ass unmercifully, he began to whimper and cry. I couldn't believe that the big dodo had intentionally provoked me, and was now acting like a little sissy. Limey might have a bad temper at times, but Limey doesn't fight crybabies! I stopped the fight and told him to go home to his mommy. He left the club with his head down and still whimpering.

I reclaimed my chair and rejoined the party. It was great to be with a group of guys who couldn't be intimidated. The party proceeded in good order, until some joker stomped in ranting and raving about how some sorry-assed Lurp had just attacked his buddy. This guy was *big*, and looked like he could acquit himself in a fight much better than his prima donna buddy, so, very innocently, I stood up and decked him. It was a classic LRRP ambush—he should have been more observant. That's why we were known as the Foul Dudes.

It was getting late, and some of the guys were already retreating to their hootches. But a few of us, determined to drink the club dry, decided to stay behind. By 2200 hours, we were totally shit-faced, and the club was still in no danger of going dry. I purchased a case of beer to go, then Jacobs and I started to leave the club. Suddenly Jacobs turned and punched me in the chest. Ordinarily, a good-natured punch from a buddy failed to get a rise out of me, but for some reason this time it made a lot of sense to return the favor. I carefully put the beer down on the ground and punched him back, making sure that I hit him just a little bit harder than he had popped me. Soon we were trading blows, then we were on the ground wrestling. It wasn't anything serious, just our way of letting off a little steam. Neither of us was angry, and we were just having a little fun when one of the newbies that had been in the club earlier walks up and screams, "I want you next, Limey." I couldn't believe my ears! The dude hadn't been around long enough to have his clothes washed, and he wanted a part of *moi*? I was surprised he knew my name!

Never one to turn down a challenge, I broke off my fun with Jacobs and snatched the FNG by the throat. I threw him to the ground and leaped on top of him, determined to take off his head. No damned cherry was going to interfere with our R & R—at least not without paying his dues and then some.

But I quickly discovered that this wanna-be was cut from the same cloth as the REMF who had taken over my seat. He begged and pleaded with me to stop before I had even touched him. Feeling magnanimous, I decided to let him up. After all, he hadn't really been guilty of anything more than bad judgment. I walked back over to pick up my case of beer and was just bending over to retrieve it when Jacobs yelled, "Watch out!"

I spun around expecting to get coldcocked, but instead found myself looking down the wrong end of an M-16. I was in shock! The damned cherry had me cold. I could do nothing but stand there looking stupid. What the hell, he had me, and he knew it! Suddenly, I turned my back on him, retrieved my rifle, grabbed my case of beer, and walked out of the area with Jacobs right beside me. If the SOB had the balls to shoot me in the back, let him have at it.

I awoke sometime the next morning to the concussive vibrations of an Arc Light impacting nearby, only to discover seconds later that hangovers could be just as damaging as B-52s, even without the telltale craters. An ultrabright sun shining directly in my face only exacerbated my misery. Fleeting memories of the night before flashed through my befuddled mind, but I couldn't recall if it had all really happened or my memories were just bits and pieces of fallout from some bad dream. I slowly got dressed and went over to Jacobs's tent for some confirmation.

When I found Jacobs, I almost didn't recognize him at first. The creature that was sitting spread-legged on his bunk had horribly swollen eyes, bruises on his face, and dried blood matted in his hair.

"Jesus Christ, Jacobs, you look like shit!" I offered as I sat down next to him on his cot.

He looked up at me and flashed a painful grin, then told me to go find a mirror and take a look at myself. Grabbing the signal mirror lying on his footlocker, I stared hard for a moment at the reflection looking back at me. It wasn't Limey. It looked like some alien that must have been standing right next to Jacobs when the train hit them both. So my hangover wasn't the least of my souvenirs from the night before. Had I only imagined that I'd won all those pugilistic encounters?

The two of us struggled down to the shower point to clean up and make ourselves presentable before Top Smith spotted us. But there was little doubt in my mind that Top had already gotten a full report on our nocturnal escapades.

Returning from the shower point a short time later, I was met by a very grim-looking detachment first sergeant. "What the hell is your problem, Limey? This is the fourth fight between Lurps in less than two days," Top said. He wasn't really angry, but only concerned over these friendly altercations we were getting into.

"Well, Top, I guess we're getting bored. There ain't shit going on," I said. "Hell, we haven't had a team out in five days."

Top stood there for a few seconds, reflecting on what I said, then nodded and walked away. Greatly relieved that he had spared me an ass-chewing, I headed over to visit a group of guys who were brewing some coffee.

I was offered a canteen cup of steaming brew, and nodded my head in appreciation. The Lurps were planning some kind of raid, but I had only come in on the tail end of it. They were complaining about not being able to get ice to keep their beer cold. I happened to mention seeing a refrigerator over at the CID compound that was looking for a new home. Weems glanced over at Bacek and winked, then turned around and shot down the idea. I realized that liberating the CID's fridge was what they had been planning when I showed up. I only hoped that they would include me on the actual mission.

All discussion ceased when Top Smith approached us with a new NCO at his side. Top introduced him as Staff Sergeant Johnson, who'd just transferred into the detachment from Hawk Recon Platoon, 2/327th. He was being assigned as a new team leader. Top Smith had been ordered to give up his own status as a team leader to spend more time in the rear doing whatever first sergeants do. Not one to disobey orders, Top reluctantly agreed to comply, but not before going off to find a suitable replacement for his team. Staff Sergeant Johnson had some damned big boots to fill.

Naturally, there would be some reorganizing of teams to even out the experience level. While I was happy to see an experienced NCO like Staff Sergeant Johnson join the detachment, I was still disappointed over losing Top Smith as my team leader. He had taught me nearly everything I knew about being a LRRP.

I returned to my hootch, wondering how badly our team would be broken apart. It didn't take long to find out. Staff Sergeant Johnson came to my tent a little later in the afternoon to introduce himself as my new team leader and to tell me that from then on I would be on Team 3. Team 6, my old team, no longer existed.

Team 3 would consist of Sergeants Johnson and McKinnon, Sinclair, Eddie Mounts, me, and Lurch Cornett as the team medic. It was my first experience in how team integrity could change almost daily because of R & Rs, transfers, sick call, injuries, and school assignments.

CHAPTER 21

Top Smith called an early-morning formation and informed everyone that he had not been at all happy with our attitudes the past few days. So, believing that idle minds are the devil's workshop, he went to headquarters and got brigade's permission to begin overnight ambushes no farther than two klicks outside the perimeter. They weren't proper LRRP missions, but they would do until we got some. Team 3 and another team were awarded the first opportunity to go out and screw up the neighborhood.

Sergeant Johnson assembled Team 3 for a premission briefing and assignment of duties. Since McKinnon outranked me on the team, I was replaced as the senior scout. The only openings left on the team were junior scout and junior RTO. Since Eddie Mounts had served before as my junior scout and was a fine slack man, I opted for the junior RTO position. Besides, Eddie weighed in at about 140 pounds soaking wet, and I didn't feel right about making him hump the PRC-25.

Out beyond our perimeter were a pair of villages about five hundred meters apart. We were to set up our ambush about a hundred meters to the right of the south ville. Any VC traveling between the two villages would have an equal opportunity to walk into one of our ambushes.

Eddie and I each loaded one magazine with tracers, then applied camouflage grease paint under candlelight. We didn't relax and drink a final cup of coffee until we were totally satisfied with our appearance. Looking "cool" was important in the bush.

We moved out at 2300 hours in single file. McKinnon was at point, Eddie pulling slack. Checking with the perimeter bunker, we slid silently into the darkness. Moving through rice paddies, we stopped every fifty meters or so to listen, but all that we heard were the normal sounds of the night.

The lights of the north village came into view pretty quickly, and by 0100 hours, we were set up and in position. We had selected an ambush site on line, using a rice paddy dike for cover and concealment.

The night was still and quiet. The earlier cloud cover had moved away from the moon, improving visibility to fifty meters. We lay silently along the earthen dike and waited.

Our wait didn't last long. Someone or something suddenly disturbed the regular chirping of the crickets, and they went silent as if someone had turned them off. Lying flat on my stomach, I could just make out the outline of someone who was walking directly into our sector. My heart began to pound.

The lone Charlie was being extremely careful as he approached. He moved slowly, stopping every ten paces or so as he came toward us. No one made a sound. Then, as if on some unheard signal, six M-16s erupted as one. On full-auto the tracers lit up the night and tore through the body of the lone VC. I could plainly see his face as he went down, full of shock and terror. In slow motion, the enemy soldier toppled over backward.

In the ensuing silence, I quickly slammed home another magazine. My teammates were doing the same. The six of us waited . . . for something, we weren't sure what.

Then a low, awful moan came from the fallen VC. Incredibly, he was still alive. Johnson yelled, *"Grenade out!"*

I heard the spoon *ping* as it flew from the frag, the dull *thud* as it struck the ground, followed seconds later by the concussion of the blast. The moaning stopped.

We waited and listened in the darkness for what seemed like an hour but was probably no more than a couple of minutes, then Johnson and McKinnon crawled out toward the dead VC to search his body and gather up any weapons and equipment he had been carrying. While they were completing their search, automatic gunfire and tracers erupted from where the other team was sitting in ambush. It was proving to be a great night for hunting.

Johnson and McKinnon were still searching the VC. Johnson was becoming exasperated and yelled for Sinclair to call for a flare ship. Within ten minutes, the ship had arrived overhead, turning darkness into daylight as it dropped flares over our position. It soon became much easier for my teammates to make a thorough search of the body. The two Lurps rejoined us quickly, then we sat back waiting for our night vision to return as the flare ship flew away. Sinclair informed the other team that we were moving out. They acknowledged and said that they would give us a half-hour head start before they moved out. The last thing we needed was to light each other up on our way back into the perimeter.

As we moved back into friendly territory, we all got a little excited. It was our first mission as a new team, and we had scored a kill. The contact had been fast, furious, and exhilarating. The boredom of the past few days was forgotten, and we were hungry for more.

When we reached the TOC, we dropped our gear outside the door and began to go through the dead VC's equipment—the spoils of war. We opened a small pouch and were amazed to find stacks of Vietnamese piasters. Our kill had been a VC paymaster. What a bonus! The money would go into the detachment refreshment fund and would help pay for a few of our parties. I looked up to see Pizza Joe Remiro, the senior scout from the other team, coming over to compare notes on our ambushes. He carried his M-16 in one hand and an M-1 in the other. But what caught my eye was the bloody, brown floppy hat he was wearing. They, too, had killed a VC, and Pizza Joe had snatched the guy's hat. There was blood and gray brain matter all over it, but he didn't seem to care. I told him that I thought it improved his appearance.

After he left, I went back to searching the dead VC's gear and discovered a bloody pack of Lucky Strikes. I divided the rest of the cigarettes among my teammates and stuck the empty pack in my pocket. They were Lucky for us, not him.

When we finished searching the gear, the members of both teams mingled together and began relating the stories of our recent good fortune. Morale was high. The rest of the detachment, awakened by our noisy boasting, staggered out of their hootches to see what was going on. Soon, cold beer was flowing, and an impromptu party ensued.

An hour later, wiped out from the night's activities and one beer more than I needed, I called it quits and headed back to my hootch. On the way, I spotted a large, dark shape against the back of the TOC. When I stepped around the corner to get a better look at the object, I discovered that someone had left a perfectly good refrigerator there in the shadows. It looked a lot like the one the CID boys on the other side of the camp had in their hootch. Well, with a new paint job and a few scratches and dents, it would never be mistaken for theirs. All we needed now was a generator to run it.

The stifling heat woke me late the next morning. It was almost noon. Still filthy from last night's ambush, I decided to shower before lunch. I grabbed my towel and walked around the back of the hootch to see if the shower point was crowded. While I was standing there looking, something large and white was bobbing up and down in the river as it flowed past the compound toward the South China Sea. Whatever it was bobbed a final time and then sank from view. I had no idea what it was, at least not until I spotted a couple of guys from CID entering our compound. I looked around and realized that I was the only one in sight. Had all my buddies *di di mau*'d and left me to face the music alone? The two agents walked up to me and immediately began questioning me about their missing refrigerator.

"Walker, this is between you and me," one frowning agent said. "Do you have any idea where our refrigerator is?"

"What refrigerator?" I answered, trying to look as innocent as possible.

"You know what refrigerator I'm talking about, Walker. Now answer the fucking question," he screamed.

"Oh, that refrigerator! The last time I saw it, you were getting a beer out of it."

"Walker, you're nothing but a smart-ass," the other agent offered.

I admit that I was surprised that it took the military sleuths so long to uncover my shortcoming; everyone else already knew it. I wasn't going to take any more insults from the likes of these two, and they weren't going to waste any more time trying to extract a confession from me, so we parted company. At least one problem was solved: we wouldn't have to confiscate a generator.

When I returned from my shower, refreshed and fully invigorated, I was surprised to find that normal activity had returned to the compound. Weems was standing outside his tent, beer in hand, grinning broadly as I walked up. He knew that I knew why that stupid grin was plastered all over his handsome mug, so I passed him without a word, letting my raised index finger do all the talking for me. I went into my hootch, knowing for sure that it was Weems who had set me up. That was going to cost the bastard at least a six-pack.

A few seconds later, Weems sauntered in with a cold beer in his hand and held it out to me as a peace offering. Hell, I wasn't mad. I was only a little perturbed that I didn't have an audience to witness my performance with the CID creeps. The two of us were soon sitting on my cot, sipping beers and talking about the old days in our neighborhoods in the Tri-City area of Chicago. That's when Jaybird Magill interrupted us. He was excited because there was a five-dollar bet between Vendetti and Bacek that Bacek couldn't piss over a two-and-a-half-ton truck. Hell, I'd already seen Bacek eat live cockroaches, worms, and broken glass, so I wouldn't bet that he couldn't piss over the truck.

Intrigued, I got up and followed Vendetti and Bacek and seven or eight other Lurps down the hill in search of a deuce-and-a-half.

We located one at the brigade motor pool. Bacek told Vendetti to go around to the other side of the truck just to make sure he didn't cheat. Gino didn't have to be asked twice. He already suspected that Bacek would cheat to win the bet. Standing to the front of the truck, we watched as Bacek, with a mighty roar, cut loose a stream of urine that not only cleared the truck by a full two feet but managed to soak poor old Vendetti from stem to stern. The diminutive Lurp came sprinting around the truck dripping, cursing, and stomping his feet, ready to kick somebody's ass. The more he raised hell, the harder we laughed. But Bacek wasn't laughing; he only wanted his five dollars.

Not wanting to stay for the outcome, I hurried back up LRRP Hill to spread the word of Bacek's amazing feat. I couldn't wait to see Weems's face when I told him. But when I related the story, he didn't even seem surprised. He informed me that Vendetti wasn't the first trooper Bacek had pulled that stunt on. In the past, he had earned spending money pissing on a goodly number of nonbelievers. I guess you just had to be there, man.

CHAPTER 22

Every team in the detachment wanted in on the action. The short-range ambush patrols were proving very successful. Soon it would be our turn again for a short trip outside the perimeter wire.

Lieutenant McIsaac and Top Smith wanted to make sure

there were no foul-ups out there at night, so they only allowed two teams at a time outside the wire. My team, Team 3, would have to wait at least another day before its next hunt.

I decided to walk over to the scout dog detachment for my customary free beer and some good conversation. I had been thinking about extending my tour in December, and wanted to see how other special units operated. I was not really considering leaving the LRRPs, but it never hurt to be aware of one's options.

When I arrived at their compound, I was greeted by a few old acquaintances and offered a can of Carling Black Label. I accepted it without reservation. To do otherwise would have been rude. At least it was beer, which made it better than water. I was soon propped up against a tree, bullshitting with some of the scouts, when one of the handlers asked me to help him out. He was mixing a batch of dog food in a large container, and he needed me to retrieve the food bowl from his dog, Mister Buck Sir. Mister Buck Sir was the biggest, darkest, meanest German shepherd that ever existed . . . anywhere. When I first approached Mister Buck Sir's cage, I was met by a very calm, seemingly laid-back animal. As I entered, his ears perked up and his head cocked to one side, as if he was just noticing me for the first time. There was no snarl, no shifting of weight, no change of demeanor—nothing to indicate anything more than mild curiosity. Yet, he was obviously watching my every move. I didn't give much thought to what was about to play out—until I turned around and noticed that I had attracted a pretty large audience. Now, I was pretty sure that they hadn't gathered because of the novelty of a Lurp's performing manual labor, but whatever the reason for their sudden interest in my actions, I wasn't about to let it go untested. As I bent over and reached for Mister Buck Sir's dog dish, a low, threatening growl emanated from somewhere well behind his two pair of shining, well-exposed, three-inch canines. The well-muscled, hundred-and-fifty-pound German shepherd was poised well back on rippling haunches, tensing for an attack. He now had a look on his face that registered somewhere between "major feeding" and "mass destruction" on the AKC's chart of canine mood espression. If it was "major feeding," I was the meal. If it was "mass destruction," I was the destructee. Either way, Limey was going to be the loser.

I could always take a hint, and this was no different. In a world-record triple jump, I was at the fence—with Mister Buck Sir right on my heels. The fence stopped him. It didn't stop me. Safely on the south side of the DMZ, I bent over, trying to force air back into my lungs. The air had been there only seconds before, but I think it must have passed through me and out the back end as I cleared the fence. I had come within inches of being the main feature on Mister Buck Sir's menu.

Laughing hysterically, a good half dozen members of the scout dog detachment were standing nearby. Shaking my hand, Mister Buck Sir's handler presented me a cold beer and, grinning, said, "I knew the dog didn't like Vietnamese and Americans, but I had no idea he had such a hard-on for Limeys, too." The motherfucker had set me up, and I had almost lost my life over it. But then I had to join in the laughter. We all knew that paybacks were hell. My turn would come. With my heart rate back to where it could sustain life, we sat and talked about old Mister Buck Sir. His name had been Buck. His original handler had been killed, and the dog had been pretty badly wounded. When he was assigned a new handler, he became a little meaner and a little more ferocious, so he had been renamed Mister Buck. A short while later, the dog had been wounded once again, and his handler, hit in the same action, had to be evacuated back to the States. After Mister Buck recovered, my buddy became his handler, but by then the dog had become so moody and violent that they had renamed him Mister Buck Sir. He had asked me to retrieve the dog's bowl because it had become a major mission in the scout dog detachment to recover it after each feeding. Mister Buck Sir would just sit and dare anyone to come into his pen and get it. It was then that I noticed that a hole had been drilled into the side of the bowl. When I asked about it, he said that normally a rope was tied through the hole so that the bowl could be retrieved. Someway or another the rope had become detached, and some fool was needed to go in and fetch it. I happened to be that fool!

It was late afternoon when I started back to LRRP Hill. And I had every intention of setting up one of my teammates. I needed to get back at someone quickly, or there was a danger that I might lose my edge. Then a plan came to mind. I would invite Wolfman to go with me over to the scout dog detachment to meet my new friend, Mister Buck Sir.

When I arrived at the compound, I ran into Lurch, who immediately asked me if I wanted a dog biscuit. I was mortified! The tale of my near brush with death had beaten me back to the LRRP detachment. Gone were my plans to expose Wolfman Kraft to the ravages of Mister Buck Sir's humor. I was a man without honor, almost persona non grata in my own world.

Thinking to drown my sorrows in a warm beer, I dejectedly walked over to our large metal cooler and was pleasantly amazed to discover that it was fully stocked with four or five large blocks of ice. Someone had been busy. I quickly retrieved a cold beer and joined a group of guys watching a couple of teams preparing for overnight ambushes outside the wire. We wished them good hunting.

After returning to the cooler a number of times, I noticed that there was a lot of straw floating on the surface of the water. This puzzled me, but since the beer was cold, I didn't feel I needed to seek an answer. Finally, I left the group and joined Sergeant Weems, who was preparing our evening meal. There would be no C rats that night; Weems had received a care package at mail call. We would be dining on canned chitterlings. Hell, I figured if I could eat tripe soup, I could surely handle some soul food. Besides, I was always the adventurous type. If it was edible, I would eat it. With a liberal dose of Tabasco sauce, the chitterlings were actually pretty good. As a matter of fact, I quickly discovered that if I held my breath while taking a bite, they were excellent.

After we had eaten, I asked Weems if he knew why straw was floating around in the beer cooler. "Beats the shit out of me, Limey. Ask Jaybird, he's the one who swiped the ice," he said.

It wasn't hard finding Magill. He was with Martinez and Dokos, and very drunk. I had a feeling that it wasn't a good time to inquire about the straw, but my curiosity got the better of me; I should have paid more heed to my feelings. Jaybird and the Greek had staked out a reefer truck, then followed it to the road separating the 25th Infantry Division from our compound. When the truck pulled over at the MP bunker, they had approached the driver and demanded their fair share of his precious cargo. The driver got a little cocky, then finally got out to pull open the reefer doors, saying, "Go ahead, get all the ice you want."

When the doors opened, Jaybird and the Greek saw a truckload of large blocks of ice. The only problem was that the ice was being used to chill corpses prior to their clearing graves registration. Stunned, the two Lurps stared at the cargo, momentarily lost for words. Not one to miss this opportunity, the driver got even more arrogant and said, "Go ahead, you toughassed Lurps, take all the ice you want."

It was a challenge he shouldn't have made. Jaybird and the Greek were not about to pass up that opportunity; ice was a rare commodity in Vietnam. The two Lurps quickly loaded all the ice that would fit in the back of the jeep. They had quickly reached the conclusion that the dead didn't need the ice more than the living.

After hearing the details of the story, I was firmly convinced that I was serving with some really sick individuals. The problem was that I fit in so damn well. I could just see my next letter home. "Dear Mom, How are you? I'm fine. We managed to get some ice for our beer this morning. Your loving son, Jim." My mother had been a registered nurse most of her adult life. I don't think she would have understood or appreciated the values her son and his friends possessed. She was back in the World trying to save lives, while we were over in Nam trying to take them. Didn't make a lot of sense from a moral viewpoint.

Returning to the cooler, I grabbed a final beer and retreated to my tent. The story of the ice was something I wanted to share with my hootchmates. "Hey, Boss, do you know where the ice in the cooler came from?" I inquired.

"Sure," the Boss replied. "You didn't know?"

"Hell," I said, "I'm going to sleep. I'm always the last to hear anything in this fucking outfit!"

It wasn't long before I was asleep. Beer and good food had that effect on me. Soon, I was no longer in Vietnam. I was home in the arms of an adoring blonde, willing to do anything for her war hero.

She was just about ready to prove it when an explosion destroyed my inner peace. Snapping myself back to reality, I grabbed my weapon and unassed my bunk. The explosion was no dream; someone had made contact not more than five hundred meters outside the perimeter. Most of the detachment was already up and scanning the wire. I heard someone in the perimeter security bunker yell that one of the teams was coming back through the wire, and they had a casualty.

As the Lurps reentered the compound, I could see Dave Sloan holding his head. There was dried blood around his ears. The team was hustled off to the TOC to give an after-action report and to get some treatment for Sloan.

We got the full story later when Top Smith came out of the debriefing. Not more than five hundred meters from the perimeter, the team had set up an ambush outside the abandoned ville. They figured it would be a good spot for Charlie to set up an OP to observe our base camp from. They were right! The problem was that Charlie had gotten there first. The enemy had silently watched as the team set up its ambush. After the team situated for the night, Charlie slipped up behind the team and tossed a grenade in their midst. But luck had been on our side. The paddy dike the Lurps were hiding behind shielded them from the explosion. The grenade had landed less than five meters from Sloan, but the blast had only blown his eardrums. The wound was not major, but it was enough to cost us a comrade. Dave Sloan was evacuated early the next morning to Cam Ranh Bay for medical treatment.

Sloan was the first casualty we had taken since I had joined the detachment. It taught me that we were not invulnerable, and that we weren't safe even close to our own compound. The enemy was out there, watching.

I was sitting with Bacek the next day, cleaning weapons, when the word came down that Team 3 would be going out on ambush at 2300 hours. I was ecstatic. We were going to get the opportunity to even the score for Sloan. I looked at Bacek and asked him if I could borrow his weapon for the ambush.

"No problem, Limey. Just don't fuck it up," he said.

With that, we traded weapons. I gave him my M-16 and took his over-and-under (M-16 with a grenade launcher attached under the barrel). I went to my rucksack and retrieved a half dozen canister rounds for the 79, then headed for the brigade firing range. I was anxious to see what the shotgun rounds would do. Placing a couple of filled sandbags about twenty meters downrange, I stepped back and fired a single shot from the grenade launcher. There was nothing left of the sandbags but a few pieces of shredded fabric. I was very impressed.

Later, back at the hootch, I was enjoying a cup of coffee and watching Eddie writing a letter to his wife. It was part of his premission routine. Each of us had a ritual we went through before every mission. To divert from it was taboo.

At 2300 hours, we slipped through the wire and out into the pitch black. Only a few stars were shining through the gaps in the clouds that completely obstructed the moon. We were fully aware that Charlie knew we were in the area, so we moved only twenty or thirty meters at a time, stopping to wait, look, and listen. Finally, we reached the ambush site along the Song Ve. I thought to myself that if we would just keep going we would pass through the Tam Ky Corridor right into the Song Ve Valley, the detachment's hunting grounds. Ambushes were fine for a little action, but I was yearning for another long-range reconnaissance patrol.

At our ambush site, Johnson split us up into two-man teams, ten meters apart. I was with Sinclair, and Lurch moved in behind us to keep tabs on both our left and right flanks. We had to be very careful to avoid firing up each other. One man would sleep while his partner stood watch. We would pull one-hour shifts.

I whispered for Sinclair to sack out and took the first watch myself. Not wanting to miss any of the action, I stayed awake a full two hours before I felt myself getting a little groggy. I shook Sinclair awake and told him to take over, then propped myself against a paddy dike and started to doze off.

It seemed like only minutes had passed when I was shaken back to consciousness by one extremely nervous Lurp. Looking up along the dike, I could see the silhouette of a VC walking toward us not more than thirty meters away. I started to slowly raise my weapon as he approached. Suddenly, my night vision went to hell as tracers from Sinclair's weapon laced through the darkness. He fired a half dozen rounds, then yelled, "Shit!" As soon as he had opened up, I fired nearly a full magazine on rock 'n' roll. I could see my tracers flashing in front of my eyes, then nothing as my weapon jammed. I panicked! I quickly fired the M-79 and was greeted by a click. The damn thing had failed to go off. By then the enemy soldier had dropped from sight. I was certain that I'd hit him. Hell, he was almost on top of me when I fired his ass up!

Yelling for Johnson to call for a flare ship so I could go out and locate the body, I heard him answer, "Limey, the only thing you almost hit was your fucking feet!"

Bullshit, I thought as Johnson ordered us to get ready to move out. We slowly backed out of the ambush site and made our way back to the perimeter. When we reached LRRP Hill, Top Smith was waiting, anxious for a situation report.

"Situation all fucked up, Top. My weapon jammed," I reported.

Top looked at me and, without raising his voice, said, "Limey, the next time you go out make sure your weapon is clean." He couldn't have hurt me more if he had hit me with a baseball bat. I had pissed Top off, and I knew it. I wanted to tell him that the weapon was clean, but thought that it would only sound like an excuse. I swore to myself that I would never again carry an M-16 to the field.

Still hurting from Top's rebuke, I walked over to Johnson

and asked him what in the hell he meant by saying that I had almost shot my feet off. He told me that he had watched my tracers barely clear the tops of my boots. I was still propped up against the paddy dike when Sinclair had opened up on the dink. By reflex, I had fired on full automatic without raising my weapon high enough. I had nearly become a casualty of my own friendly fire.

Embarrassed by my stupidity, and knowing that I was going to be the subject of some major teasing about my close call, I stayed awake the rest of the night.

The next morning I went looking for a more dependable weapon. Johnson refused to cut loose his Swedish-K, and the only other weapon in the armory not being used by anyone was the World War II–era .45-caliber M-3 grease gun that belonged to Melton. No amount of begging or cajoling would talk him into selling me the weapon, but he agreed to let me borrow it until I could locate or confiscate one of my own. The only problem was that he had only three thirty-round magazines for the weapon. I would have to find some more, or run the risk of having to reload in the middle of a firefight.

The only places I could think of that might have some extra grease-gun magazines were over at the Hawk (2/327) and Tiger Force (1/327) compounds. So Ernie Winston and I departed on a spur-of-the-moment scavenger hunt. By that afternoon, we had managed to secure seven additional thirty-round magazines.

Now all I needed was for Lieutenant McIsaac and Top Smith to okay my carrying the ancient relic to the field.

Ernie and I were heading back to the compound, shuffling along, not paying much attention to anything around us, when some idiot yelled, "Don't you two know when to salute an officer?"

We looked up to see a butter-bar 2d lieutenant standing with his hands on his hips. I stared at him, uncertain how to respond to such a stupid question. I felt like telling him, "No, sir, I only salute cherry officers in the field when there's a threat of snipers," but I let the feeling slide. Instead, I just looked at him.

"Knock that silly grin off your face," he demanded.

Hell, I was kinda shocked. I hadn't even realized I'd been grinning.

"What unit are you two men from?" he asked.

"Brigade Lurps," I answered proudly.

"Oh, Headquarters Company," he replied snippily. By this time he was beginning to get my goat. The two of us gave him his silly-assed salute, and I yelled at the top of my lungs, "Airborne, Lurp, sir!"

We held our salutes, forcing the green second lieutenant to return it, then we moved out smartly, leaving the dumb ass to stew in his own self-importance. Where did the 101st Airborne get some of these sorry officers from, anyway?

When we reached our compound I told Lieutenant McIsaac about our run-in with one of his peers. He warned us to lie low for a while and he would take care of any flak that came down the tube. With that over with, I asked permission from him and Top to carry the grease gun on my next mission. They gave me their okay with the understanding that I would carry extra ammunition with me at all times because they would be unable to quickly resupply me with .45-caliber ammunition in case my team got into a major contact. With their approval, I went down to the firing range. I went through ten thirty-round magazines without a misfire or jam. I was more than satisfied with the weapon's performance but had some lingering doubts about my ability to handle the ten-pound weapon and the weight of the additional ammo and magazines, along with my radio. What the hell, I decided I could do it! I was convinced that was the right decision.

CHAPTER 23

We finally got the news that our dry spell was coming to an end. We were going to begin running LRRP missions once again. Team 3 was one of the lucky three teams that had drawn an assignment.

All three teams would be operating in the area between the Tam Ky Corridor and the Song Ve Valley. My team was given an area in the mountains overlooking the Song Ve Valley. I felt sorry for the team that drew the corridor recon zone. It was a difficult area to patrol, much too open and flat for my taste.

This was to be my first full mission as a radio operator. It was going to test my strength and endurance to the maximum. Hopefully, the previous couple of months in the detachment had hardened me enough to handle the extra weight of the radio.

After I had packed my rucksack with all the routine necessities of a long-range reconnaissance patrol, I added the radio and extra batteries and the extra ammo I always carried, then tried to pick it up. It was hernia material, without a doubt! I had to put my back against the ruck, stick my arms through the straps, then call McKinnon over to pull me to my feet. There was no doubt in my mind that in a firefight I would never be able to haul ass with my teammates. I decided that should we have to cut and run, I was going to drop my ruck, jerk out the radio, and let Charlie have anything that was left.

The mission briefing was not all wine and roses; we were going into an area that almost guaranteed contact with the enemy. Our intel seemed to be improving over previous missions. We would be looking for a Main Force VC regiment that was supposedly operating between Tam Ky and the Song Ve Valley. We knew they could be anywhere, but if I was in their sandals, I would be up in the mountains where I had plenty of cover and concealment and a back door out of Dodge.

Johnson and the other two team leaders made their over-flights and returned to brief us on our RZs. We were once again lucky. Each night that we went into our planned NDPs, we would have an LZ close by in case we needed an emergency extract during the night. There were numerous single-ship landing zones in our AO. Johnson marked his overlay to indicate our probable patrol route and our extraction LZ.

We arrived at the tarmac to find the insertion slick waiting for us. Since I was humping one of the radios, I was the first to load onto the ship. I felt a little claustrophobic sitting in the middle of the helicopter. I had been used to riding the bird with my feet dangling out over the skids.

As we flew out toward the recon zone, I watched in silence as the jungle passed beneath us and the wind blew in through the open cabin, dashing away my anxieties. I was ready now for whatever the next five days would bring.

The slick flared in over the LZ, and before the pitch of the rotors could even change, we were out and running through the elephant grass. Twenty-five meters away we were down and listening. The sound of the Huey was fading to nothingness in the distance as the insertion aircraft was already dipping down again to make another false insert. Finally, it was gone and the elephant grass grew silent around us. Now it was only us and whoever else was out there.

We moved out cautiously toward the tree line, stopping several times to look and listen some more. Haste only got you killed. We had drilled ourselves over and over in the art of patience. We were only twenty-five meters away from the cover of the jungle, our new home for the next five days.

Finally, Johnson gave the signal to move out. We covered the last twenty-five meters and entered the lush jungle with a rush of enthusiasm. The exotic aroma of the rotting vegetation told us we were home. This was the kind of cover we worked best in, and it felt good to be there.

McKinnon took point, and we moved out, gliding noise-lessly through the trees. Ten minutes later he gave the signal to halt. He had found the trail that ran along the flank of the mountain. He backed up slowly and passed the good news back down through the patrol that the trail was just ahead and that it had been recently used. So far, luck was with us. We had a trail to monitor and an LZ nearby in case we needed to get out in a hurry.

We pulled back ten meters from the high-speed trail and set up our OP. Once again we made sure that we were in a good position to observe the trail without being seen ourselves. This was going to be one of those patrols where no one would be allowed to use the tiny balls of C-4 to brew up a cup of coffee in the morning. It was a hot area, and we would run a cold patrol, observing extreme caution at all times.

As darkness settled in, each member of the patrol was assigned his guard shift for the night. Later, during my watch at 2300 hours, I swore I could see lights out in the jungle. I picked up the starlight scope and looked through it, and was immediately greeted by flashes of green light all across the screen. Startled, I put the scope down again, waited a second for my night vision to adjust, and looked again with my naked eye. The lights were gone. When I went back to the scope again, I was treated to another dazzling light display.

I shook Johnson awake and handed the starlight scope to him, whispering for him to look in the direction where I had seen the lights. After looking, he whispered, "Fuck me, we'll check it out in the morning." Then he rolled over and went back to sleep. When I woke Eddie Mounts up to relieve me, I told him to keep an eye on the lights, then went to sleep myself.

At 0430 hours, we were all awake and eager to discover the source of the light display. But we waited until nearly 0800 hours to move out. The trail showed no signs of activity during the night.

We crossed the high-speed, taking special care not to leave boot prints. We moved a little farther until we came to the edge of the jungle. A few hundred meters away were at least a dozen hootches. Retreating back into the underbrush, Johnson pulled out his map and looked it over carefully. Nowhere could he find a village indicated. He decided to move the team farther up the mountain to put some distance between us and the mysterious ville.

After humping uphill for a couple of hours, the team leader called for a halt. Johnson and McKinnon went to the edge of the jungle and looked down into the valley. Then McKinnon came back to the team and told me to move up and join Johnson. When I reached him, he gave me his field glasses and told me to look down in the valley in the direction of the hootches. The scene I beheld made me feel all warm and cuddly inside; more than a dozen Viet Cong were milling around in a group in what appeared to be a general bullshit session. I knew that Johnson was about to give them something they could talk about. As the team leader pulled out his map, I continued the surveillance. I couldn't believe our good luck. More Viet Cong were moving into the open outside the hootches. There were now about two dozen VC in the clearing. I handed the binoculars back to Johnson and established contact with the our artillery support battery. I could already feel the excitement building. When the redleg fire-control officer told me they had my signal four-by-four, I asked him to stand by for a possible fire mission, then turned to Johnson for instructions; he was mulling things over. I suggested, "Let's wait and see if any more dinks join the party."

He thought it over for a second, then made his decision, "No, Limey, we're going to hit the motherfuckers right now."

I contacted the FDC again and requested a fire mission. "Two-four, I repeat, two-four, Victor Charlie in the tree line." Then I gave the grid coordinates I had just received from Johnson. I called for WP—white phosphorus—and told the fire-control officer that I would adjust.

The FDC read back the coordinates and seconds later I heard, "Shot out!" I repeated, "Shot out," and stood by. We didn't have long to wait. We heard the round whistle overhead, saw it explode, then heard the sound of its impact.

"Drop one hundred and fire for effect. HE!" Johnson whispered to me as I passed it on to the artillery battery. After confirming the shots were on the way, I nodded to Johnson, who passed me the glasses. It was the first time I ever saw people vaporized in an artillery barrage.

The rounds were dead on target, hitting in the center of the massed Viet Cong. When the smoke cleared, I could see that, where seconds before there had been two dozen enemy soldiers trying to decide which direction to run, now there was nothing.

As the smoke and debris settled, no more than four or five bodies were revealed on the ground. All other evidence of the gathering had been cast to the four winds. Speechless, I handed the glasses back to Johnson.

Six rounds of heavy artillery fire had totally devastated an area of a hundred square meters and everything inside it. We had just snuffed out twenty-four lives in the blink of an eye, and these people still wanted to fight us! The feeling of sheer power and control was overwhelming.

My thoughts were suddenly interrupted by Johnson telling me to make another adjustment and ask for another round. I quickly repeated his command, "Add one hundred and fire for effect." Again the screaming shells passed overhead, and then came the explosions.

After the second volley, the FDC called for a sit rep. I could no longer remain calm as I came back with "You're kicking their fucking asses. Pile it on."

After a few seconds' hesitation, the FDC replied, "Please maintain proper radio procedure, Whiskey 3-4, over." Johnson must have thought I was nuts when I suddenly held the handset at arm's length and gave it the finger. The lifer at the other end should have been standing next to me at that moment. Maybe he would have understood my enthusiasm.

Gathering my wits, I called back, "A dozen VC vaporized, six bodies in view, and another three doing a new dance in the open, over."

Seconds later I received, "Roger that last transmission, battery standing by, out."

I had a feeling that my time as an RTO would be short-lived if I didn't learn to watch my mouth. Well, no problem! If Lieutenant McIsaac questioned me about my radio procedure, I would just claim insanity. Hell, he knew all his Lurps were half crazy anyway!

We knew we had to collect our wits and get our shit together in a hurry. It wouldn't take long for Charlie to realize that those artillery rounds were not H & I fire; someone had called it in and adjusted it. They would be looking for us as soon as they got reorganized.

Fading back into the jungle, we recrossed the trail and moved about fifteen meters beyond before we stopped and set up an NDP about a hundred meters from a suitable LZ.

One by one we slipped out of the perimeter to set claymore mines. We were bubbling over with self-confidence, and were more than ready to give them another ass-kicking. Even though none of us spoke a word, our happiness showed in our eyes. In three days, we would be able to talk to our hearts' content, but just then we were practicing total noise discipline. Our luck would hold. The night was uneventful.

The next morning we downed LRRP rations cold and set off, eager to find some more targets. By 0800 hours, we were pushing slowly and carefully up the mountain. By noon, we had moved back across the trail to the edge of the jungle again to monitor the valley below. Luck was still with us, and we soon located another target. It was not as rich as the last one, but it was a valid target nonetheless.

At a bend in the river, not more than six hundred meters below us, were five more suspicious-looking hootches. They stood out because there was no indication that the land around them had been cultivated. Either they were abandoned or they were occupied by Vietnamese engaged in an activity other than farming. In this part of the world, if you weren't farming, you were soldiering.

We took turns observing the thatched buildings but saw no signs of life around them. That didn't seem normal. Right below us, about five hundred meters, was a gully leading directly into the jungle.

Johnson gave me a grid coordinate and told me to contact the redlegs and request a smoke round. A few minutes later the single marker round hit right in the heart of the gully below us. I told the FDC to mark it. We now had the gully registered in case we had some inquisitive VC try to use it as an avenue of approach to sneak up on us.

We set our claymores and bedded down for the evening. Sometime during the night, I was awakened by Johnson, who told me the hootches down below had been occupied. I could see nothing with my naked eye, but the starlight scope revealed streaks of light flashing across the lens. He was right! Charlie was home again.

We avoided using the starlight scope to observe the hootches to prevent its being damaged by the bright light emanating from them, but we did use it to keep an eye on the gully. It was the only way the VC could have reached the hootches undetected. We maintained our vigilance throughout the night and into the early-morning hours.

All of us were up before daybreak. Except for the lights, no one had seen any activity inside the hootches. We knew they had to still be in there. It was too good to be true—we had a second target awaiting us.

By 0800 hours, most of the team had eaten. I had the field glasses on the huts, watching, when a single figure stepped out and stretched his arms over his head. I waited and continued watching. Within five minutes, three more black-clad figures moved into the open.

Calling Johnson over, I gave him the glasses and went to my radio to get a commo check from the FDC. I told him to stand by for a fire mission. I watched my team leader observing the enemy soldiers, waiting to get his final grid coordinates for a fire mission. Instead, Johnson gave me the map and field glasses and, smiling, said, "It's your baby, Limey."

He had given me an easy assignment. The bend in the river right in front of me was right there on the map. Computing the target coordinates was a piece of cake.

I took my time to make sure I was on the money, then called in the fire mission. Six more Viet Cong were now in the open and were about to get a nasty early-morning greeting.

I raised the redlegs on the radio and gave them the coordinates for my fire mission, calling for a single WP round. The round landed about two hundred meters short of the hootches. I made the quick adjustment and called for HE, fire for effect. The barrage smothered the area around the hootches without directly hitting any of them. Two VC were hit by shrapnel and lying in a heap near one of the doorways. I called the FDC and asked for another round, but was denied any more support at that time because they had a priority mission for a unit in contact. We understood the situation.

I would have to be satisfied with the damage already inflicted. Johnson gave the order to pack up and move out. He had no intention of keeping us in the area any longer; we had just set two fires on the same match.

We moved out and soon crossed the now familiar trail, making sure to erase any evidence of our presence. We moved cautiously as we headed for another section of our recon zone.

Johnson decided to search the area for trails and set up an ambush for the following day. Locating another trail turned out to be no problem at all. McKinnon found a good one two hours after we began looking. We set out claymores twenty feet back from the trail and settled in for the night.

No one used the trail during the hours of darkness. The next morning we discussed returning to our happy hunting ground on the other side of the mountain to have one more go at the enemy. But time was becoming critical, and because of the lack of a decent LZ on the other side of the mountain we decided to spend the remainder of our mission observing another section of the trail we had spent the night on.

After our morning meal of cold LRRP rations, we moved out parallel to the trial. By midafternoon, we again set out our mechanical ambush and waited for any unsuspecting Viet Cong to screw up and pay us a visit. With an LZ less than two hundred meters away, we were in a perfect location for any type of contact. We spent the rest of the afternoon and night without seeing or hearing anything. What had started out as one hell of a party was ending up on a dry note.

We extracted the following morning as scheduled. I was

quite content with our success. The brigade Lurps had once again left their calling card.

Propped up in the chopper, I felt a great amount of pride in what I was doing and in the people I was doing it with. Back at the Lurp compound, a shower and a cold beer would remove the stress that had built up in me during the past five days.

CHAPTER 24

It hadn't been a particularly demanding day. With nothing scheduled in the way of training, I passed the time cleaning my equipment and repacking my ruck. It paid to be prepared just in case an unexpected mission came along.

Going through the well-picked-over sundry packs, I was pleasantly surprised to discover an overlooked packet of cocoa. Normally, that was one of the first items claimed by scavenging LRRPs when rifling sundries. Delighted by my discovery, I quickly pinched off a small piece of C-4 from the block I kept stashed in the hootch, and rolled it into a marble-size ball between the tips of my thumb and my trigger finger. I dropped the ball into a C-rat-can stove, ignited it, and quickly had a canteen cup of boiling water ready for the cocoa. A couple packets of sugar and several envelopes of powdered cream, and I had a drink fit for a civilian. Just as I sat back to light up a cigarette and enjoy my first steaming cup of hot chocolate in weeks, Sweet Pea jumped up to go outside and kicked over my cocoa as he passed. I watched in utter horror as the creamy brown nectar slowly soaked into the parched earthen floor of our hootch. It was more than I could handle. Now, I realize that there are greater catastrophes in life than spilling a cup of cocoa, but at that particular moment I couldn't think of a single one. I leaped to my feet and screamed at the top of my lungs, *"What the fuck do you think you're doing, Sweet Pea?"*

Sweet Pea slowly turned on his heels and stared at me with hatred in his eyes, making it pretty clear that I was not the only one having a bad day. He glared at me and sneered, "Well, Limey, if you looked where in the hell you put your shit, accidents wouldn't happen."

Wrong response! There is a little fuse in the back of our brains that is supposed to kick in at times like this and keep our tempers from overheating. Well, mine shorted out just when I needed it the most. I puffed out my chest like a strutting bantam rooster and gave Sweat Pea a shove that should have pushed him into the next province. Unfortunately, it accomplished nothing more than to cause his circuit breaker to short out. He recovered quickly and repaid my shove with one of his own, along with some pretty heavy interest. The next thing I knew, we had squared off and were burying punches in each other's torso. A peaceful cup of cocoa was now the cause of a battle royal.

Fights between brother Lurps were not all that uncommon; we constantly tried to intimidate each other to establish a pecking order within the unit. In most cases, it was only harmless, good-natured fun between comrades, designed more to let off steam than to cause lasting damage. Our anger was normally reserved for military personnel outside our immediate detachment area, but lately we had found that other units were giving Lurps a wide berth.

After Sweet Pea and I had been mixing it up for several minutes and were down wrestling in the dirt, John Chadwick decided that we'd both had enough and stepped in between us and physically broke us apart. Chad was a quiet guy, but at six feet six inches and a muscular 220 pounds, his intimidation factor was right up there. He got our immediate attention. Neither Sweet Pea nor I was so far blinded by anger that we didn't realize the big guy was giving us a chance to end the fight before one or both of us got our asses stomped. Lurch, who was every bit as big as Chadwick, was already hovering a few feet away, ready to help Chad end the feud. The fight was over instantly, with the two of us shaking hands. A good fistfight had a way of breaking up the boredom engendered by too much time in the rear.

I had returned to my hootch and was licking my cuts and bruises when I decided to rifle through the sundries to see if I might have overlooked a *second* packet of cocoa. When I didn't find one, I decided to settle for a cup of coffee. I was beginning to feel pretty low about the way I had jumped Sweet Pea over something as trivial as a cup of cocoa, and was trying to think of some way I could apologize to him without making myself look like the world's biggest chump. Suddenly, Boss came in, looked down, and said, "Limey, if you want to fight your hootchmates, you're gonna have to do it in someone else's tent."

Before I could respond, he added, "One more time, and you can pack your shit and get out." Caught off guard, I thought hard for a few seconds before replying, and a second after I did, I wished that I had thought a little harder. "Look, Boss, it takes two to tango, and I sure wasn't dancing by myself!"

He shook his head at this weak attempt on my part to excuse my actions. "Yeah, is that right? Well, this is the second conversation I've had over your little battle, and I've already given the same ultimatum to Sweet Pea." Boss and Sweet Pea were teammates, so it was obvious that he wasn't playing any favorites.

The whole affair had me feeling about as low as snake shit. I had come to the LRRPs a shy, introverted kid, and now I found myself acting like a royal asshole to the very men who had accepted me as their brother. I had let the macho recondo image go to my head, and realized that if I didn't soon find some happy medium, I would be on the outside of the LRRPs looking in. The thought was devastating, but it was true. Lieutenant McIsaac and Top Smith would only put up with so much attitude before they pulled the plug on me. So I came to the conclusion that I had to get my act together and mend some fences pretty quickly, especially between Sweet Pea and myself. I chugged down the rest of my coffee and went out to try to locate my hootchmate, but he was nowhere to be found in the compound, and no one seemed to have any idea where he had gone. So I decided the best thing to do was to go back to the hootch, have a cold beer, and wait for Sweet Pea to return.

I grabbed a brew at Wolfman's tent and was returning to my own when I spotted Beaver holding a spool of commo wire. Normally that would not have attracted my attention, but he was grinning as he stood behind our tent, stripping wire off the spool, and he was with some other person I couldn't make out. I knew that we weren't having our own private phone line installed. Vietnam Bell hadn't gotten around to enlisted pukes yet, so I walked over to check out the situation.

"Hey, Beaver, mind telling me what you're doing there?" I asked, sipping my beer.

"No, I can't, Limey. It's a surprise," he replied, looking hurt that I had even asked.

I looked past him down the wire as it slowly uncoiled off the spool. "Well, could you at least tell me who's on the other end?"

"Sweet Pea!"

As badly as I wanted to apologize to Sweet Pea, I knew that following the wire over to him at that particular time would be extremely bad form, so I nodded to Beaver and turned and walked away. I hadn't gone very far before curiosity overcame me. Boss would know what was going on, so I went looking for him. I found him sitting in our hootch nursing a brew. When I asked him what Beaver and Sweet Pea were doing, he shook his head and told me that he was just as much in the dark as I was. Without anything else being said, we sat back on his cot and quietly sipped our beers. God only knew what was going on behind our hootch, but it was bound to be a dandy.

Boss and I knocked off a six-pack before Beaver and Sweet Pea finally showed up. They made no effort to fill us in on their little secret, but they were both sporting shit-eating grins, which made Boss and me extremely nervous. Then, as we watched, Beaver very delicately unfolded a swatch of cloth and removed what appeared to be a lightbulb. He slowly rotated the pear-shaped object into a small, threaded orifice that neither Boss nor I had ever noticed before. Suddenly we were basked in a brilliant aura of artificial light that nearly blinded us. For the first time since I had arrived in Vietnam, I was able to see at night without squinting into the flickering glow of a burning candle. So this was electricity! It was breathtaking.

Sweet Pea and The Beaver were overjoyed at the success of their experiment. I doubt if Thomas Edison had been any more excited when he discovered it. Their activities no longer a mystery, the two Lurps couldn't wait to tell us how they had appropriated the spool of commo wire and had secretly spliced into the engineers' generator system.

The light soon attracted a large group of Lurps, who seemed drawn to it like moths to a candle. Finally civilization had come to LRRP Hill.

Five minutes later there was a *tick* at the wall of our hootch nearest the perimeter, and a small round hole appeared in it. No one reacted until a split second later when we heard the distant sound of the shot.

I dove headlong for the floor just a fraction of a second before everyone else in the tent. I learned that it doesn't pay to be the first man in a crowd to hit the deck. The Beaver was the only Lurp still standing, and from the grin on his face it didn't appear he would be joining us very soon. "Get the fuck down, you idiot!" Chad yelled as another shot ricocheted off the rocks below us. Our light had drawn the attention of an enemy sniper.

I looked up through the tangled bodies and saw The Beaver madly trying to unscrew the lightbulb. I screamed at him to forget the damned thing and join us on the floor. When he continued to unscrew the bulb, Boss reached up, grabbed him by the shirt, and pulled him down on the floor with the rest of us. Once we were all safely on the ground, everyone started laughing hysterically at the humor of our situation. There we were, just trying to enjoy the rewards of our labors, and some dumbshit local VC sniper who couldn't hit the broad side of a mountain decided to ruin our party.

Suddenly, Chad decided that he had accrued enough floor time. He reached up and knocked out the precious lightbulb with one swing of his M-16, leaving us to grope on the floor in total darkness. I guess Charlie suspected that the appearance of an electric lightbulb was the sign of a clandestine meeting of high-level officers. Our lonely hootch had become a priority target for a sniper hiding in the abandoned ville down below.

As the excitement died, we continued to party in the dark. Fearful of giving the sniper one last crack at us, no one even dared light a candle.

A half hour later, I slipped out of the tent to empty my over-flowing bladder, and ran into a heavily camouflaged Ernie Winston, who was about to depart on another of his nightly one-man excursions out into Charlie's domain. I hoped that whatever he was looking for out there, he would someday find. Maybe that night he would take care of the neighborhood sniper while he was scouring the bush.

CHAPTER 25

We had just gotten the bad news that Johnson had been evacuated with a severe case of malaria, but it was not the only bad news we would get that day. McKinnon had been moved up to the team leader slot to replace Johnson, and the new man assigned to the team was Twinkle Toes Federov, The Russian. Federov was joining the team as a scout, which didn't make any of us jump for joy. Everyone liked The Russian, but accidents and bad luck seemed to follow him. I hoped that with a little additional training and five teammates who would look out for him, he would be able to cut the mustard.

We had a full day to prepare for a mission we had coming up. As an experiment, we decided to dye our fatigues black. We spent the morning boiling water and soaking our fatigues in the solution until we thought they were ready to take out. After a couple of hours drying in the sun, we were satisfied with the results. Our equipment was packed and ready to go, so we decided to take the rest of the day off.

The following morning I watched as McKinnon returned from the overflight. He was obviously not happy. His usually smiling face was locked in a stony grimace. At the mission briefing, he let us all in on the problems. For one, the insertion LZ was totally devoid of cover and very close to a tree line. Second, it was surrounded on three sides by nothing but brush. All the intel reports on the AO indicated a major enemy presence. It seemed like this was becoming the norm for most of our recent missions.

I wasn't as apprehensive as McKinnon. We had a damn good team. The only question mark was Federov.

To overcome the lack of cover on the LZ, McKinnon decided that we would make a fifty-meter dash for the tree line, where we would lie dog. The insertion went down as planned. We unassed the helicopter and sprinted for the trees. Everything would have gone smoothly if the Russian could have kept ahead of the rest of us. Unfortunately, twenty steps from the chopper, he tripped and fell flat on his face, nearly forcing the rest of us into a major pileup. If Charlie had been in the nearby trees getting ready to fire, he would have been laughing too hard to steady his aim.

I dodged around Federov and ran for the tree line. When I reached it, I spun around to face the LZ to provide security for the rest of the team. The Russian was back on his feet, stumbling and tripping as he tried to keep up. He made more noise than a leg platoon coming through bamboo.

When Federov finally reached the cover of the trees, McKinnon was ready to knife him and leave his body behind. But the team leader didn't say a word. He didn't have to; the snarl on his lips read like a neon sign.

Gino Vendetti made a quick area recon and reported back that he had found no trails or any other signs that anyone had been in the immediate area of the LZ. That was good news and seemed to relieve some of the pressure McKinnon had put himself under.

We moved out a couple hundred meters and checked out the area. We found no signs of the enemy, so we located a suitable spot to settle down for the night. The Russian seemed to have pulled himself together after the fiasco on the LZ. His noise discipline was good, and he had yet to accidentally discharge his weapon.

After we set the claymores out around the NDP, it began to rain. I retrieved my poncho liner from my rucksack and wrapped it around me as McKinnon assigned guard shifts.

Everything was soaked as I took my guard mount at 0300 hours. I listened to the steady rain impacting the trees and pounding hard against the ground. Visibility was down to zero. I looked around, trying to see my teammates, but the driving rain hid them. I was amazed that they were able to sleep so soundly under such miserable conditions.

An hour before first light, the rain slowed to a light drizzle. I was able to wake the rest of the team except for Federov. McKinnon had to smack him on the head to get him to stir. The Russian immediately began rummaging through his rucksack in search of breakfast, making enough noise to alert every VC within a klick. McKinnon grabbed his hand and whispered into his ear. Whatever he said must have been good, because the stocky Lurp lay motionless on the ground.

We waited during the predawn light for nearly an hour before McKinnon signaled it was okay to eat in pairs. I slowly and deliberately dined on cold spaghetti and meatballs as I watched The Russian lying there, staring up at Bob McKinnon. He had not moved since McKinnon had whispered in his ear. There was fear in his eyes. Whatever McKinnon had said must have been life threatening.

Lurch Cornett stood and walked a few feet outside the perimeter to relieve himself. He returned a few minutes later shaking his head. "Check your groins, guys," he whispered. "You're gonna be in for a surprise."

I always liked surprises, but not the one I found when I dropped my pants. A herd—nearly a dozen—of leeches was feeding in the area of my family jewels, and there was no indication they intended to tip the waiter. I ignored the sting and saturated myself with good old U.S. Army insect repellent, a magic formula that would melt the plastic stock on an M-16. The liberal dose caused my hijackers to release their hold and drop off onto the ground writhing in agony. I knew exactly how they felt.

When I checked my armpits, I found a similar collection of hangers-on. The same application produced the same results. With both hands, I probed my backside. I wasn't about to bend over to let any of my teammates check me out. Lurps are close, but not that close. I was lucky; some of my comrades were not.

We hadn't moved two hundred meters after getting rid of our hitchhikers before Vendetti signaled the patrol to halt. The strong stench of *nuoc mam* sauce hung heavy in the rain-soaked air. The VC were somewhere nearby. As the rain let up, the odor became stronger. We eased forward slowly, our senses probing ahead of us. This was hot sign. When you could smell their food, and smell them, you were close—maybe too close. We slowed our pace, stopping often for as long as fifteen to twenty minutes before moving again. Where were they? They had to be somewhere close. We reconned the area for six hours without catching sight of them or finding any trails. It was almost as if the ground had opened up and swallowed them.

Finally, McKinnon halted the patrol for the night. We knew that tomorrow would bring another chance to find them—or for them to find us. That was always a possibility when two predators hunted each other.

Before settling in that night, we taped up every opening in our clothing. No one wanted a repeat of the night before. The hours of darkness passed slowly as the rains returned to soak us again. It was miserable being wet for so long, but miserable was better than dead; wet, you could always dry out.

I woke around 0200 hours and was immediately wide awake. I ran my hand down the front of my pants and could feel the warmth of my own blood. The damned leeches had somehow gotten into my clothing. In the Stygian darkness I could do nothing but let them feed; come morning, it would be my turn.

As soon as it was light enough to see, McKinnon told us to

take care of our leech problem two at a time. I was assassinating mine when The Russian moved just outside the perimeter to relieve himself. I was still wreaking havoc when he returned a few minutes later, holding a C-rat can in his hand. Jesus, I thought to myself, surely he's not that low on water! I watched in silence as he held the can out for McKinnon to see. Shaking his head, McKinnon turned to Sinclair, our RTO, and whispered for him to contact the base camp and inform them that we had a man with blood in his urine. Five minutes later, S-2 replied back telling us that our sick man would be medevacked but the rest of the team would continue the mission.

This was insanity in its finest form. Extracting a team member from a hot AO would pinpoint the patrol's location to every VC in a three-kilometer radius. Without a doubt, we would be compromised, but we had no say in the matter.

But a few minutes later, Eddie Mounts came back from emptying his bladder with the same malady as The Russian. One by one the rest of us found out that whatever vampire had attacked Mounts and Federov had also gotten the rest of us. The upshot of our situation was that S-2 decided to extract the entire team. No one in the rear had a clue as to what new VC weapon was capable of attacking long-range recon teams in such a manner.

On the way back to our base camp, I couldn't help but feel sorry for myself. I had kept the family jewels intact only to endanger the old wonder wand. It was humiliating!

We arrived at the brigade aid station and were subjected to a series of tests, the least embarrassing of which was the standard urine test. As we waited anxiously for our pee to be run through some kind of analyzer, we tried to console ourselves as best we could. The results came back negative. No blood showed up in our urine. We were dumbfounded and shocked. This left everyone believing that maybe we had faked the condition to force our extraction. Any defense on our part was doomed to failure because we had poured our evidence out on the ground back at our last NDP. But then someone theorized that the heavy rain had caused the black dye with which we had colored our fatigues to be absorbed through our pores and that our systems purged it the only way they could. What a double relief that was!

We were still laughing at our own bad luck as we walked toward the LRRP compound. Passing through the gate, we saw Pappy Lynch sitting in a full lotus position, having conversation with a fat, grinning statue of Buddha, three feet tall and slightly damaged. Unaware that we were watching him, Lynch would occasionally take a drag from a cigarette, then say, "Does Buddha want a drag?" He would then take a swig of whiskey and ask, "Does Buddha want a drink?" It was apparent to all of us that Pappy had been out in the sun too long.

When I reached my hootch, I was informed that Pappy's team had been extracted the day I had inserted. They had found the damaged Buddha outside a bombed-out building in the middle of their AO. For some reason, Lynch took it as some kind of omen, sensing that he had been chosen by the gods to guard and protect it. From then on, when Pappy ate or drank, he would offer the same thing to the Buddha. That did it for me! If Pappy didn't think he was losing his marbles, the rest of us sure did.

I cleaned my weapon and equipment before hauling my sore ass off to the shower point to soak away my pain and clean away the filth and grime of the jungle. It had been a relatively short mission, but the continual rains had kept my skin wet. My rucksack had rubbed me raw, and ulcerated sores had developed all over my body.

While I was at the shower point, a curious drama began to unfold in the LRRP compound: Pappy Lynch was up in arms because the S-5 (civil affairs officer) had confiscated his Buddha. The S-5 said they intended to restore it to its previous condition and then make a gift of it to the Vietnamese people to show American goodwill.

Now, this was okay with us as long as they took a patrol down the Tam Ky Corridor and over toward the Song Ve Valley and returned it to its rightful owners. But we knew that it wasn't S-5's intentions to do any such thing. They would restore the valuable icon and give it to some local dignitary.

Since the Buddha had belonged to Pappy for a short time,

we considered the S-5's conduct in very bad taste. We had to develop a plan to reclaim the Buddha and return it to its rightful owners—*us*.

Sergeant Ronnie Weems came up with the right plan. The simplicity of his plan was brilliant. Since REMFs possessed an innate fear of all combat troops, especially Lurps, we would just go down to S-5 and take our property back. If the major didn't like it, that would be tough shit. We couldn't help it if he and his boys were afraid of us.

As darkness settled over the brigade base camp, a dozen Lurps gathered to effect the raid on the S-5 shop. We slipped into the brigade officer's area and searched around until we located the S-5 hootch. We could tell we were there because some fool had painted S-5 on a large wooden sign and had posted it right in front of the S-5 shop. Weems, Pappy Lynch, and I entered the tent with our weapons at sling arms. We stood there for a second to make sure we were in the right place, then Pappy made a simple but direct statement: "We want our fucking Buddha back, sir."

The S-5 major's eyes grew as big as saucers; he was already experiencing the cramping discomfort of shock. Major Morton, our S-2 officer, was sitting in the background. He smiled when he saw what was coming down, but he knew better than to intercede.

"Take it—take it," the REMF major mumbled. None of us could understand how the mere sight of three Lurps, our weapons at sling arms, could elicit such a terrified response. It was a puzzle until we turned around and saw the muzzles of ten weapons pointing in through the flaps. The emphasis suggested by such a display had made our point irrefutable. The major must have honestly believed we would have shot him for a mere graven image. Without a word we picked up our property and withdrew to the compound on Lurp Hill to await the enemy's attempt to retake the Buddha.

Back on friendly turf, we toasted the return of Pappy's chubby pal. I was tired, so I didn't hang around very long. I returned to my tent and slept without stirring for the rest of the night, comforted by the fact that our honor had been restored.

Early the next morning, I got up and went down to Pappy's tent to see how Pappy and the Buddha had come through the night. To my horror, the Buddha was nowhere to be seen. I asked Weems where in the world they had hidden Pappy's Buddha, only to have him tell me it wasn't hidden—it was gone. During the party some of the guys convinced Pappy that S-5 was probably already mounting a sortie to recover the Buddha. After our successful raid, they would come with many warriors to make sure that the Lurps could not gain the upper hand again. Since our numbers were so small, S-5 would surely prevail. This wisdom made much sense, so the majority of the Lurps present voted to destroy the Buddha to keep it out of the hands of the S-5 bandits. They wrapped the idol in C-4 and set it on fire. Within an hour nothing was left of the Buddha but ashes, and even those had blown away in the early-morning breeze.

CHAPTER 26

We didn't have a lot of time to dwell on Pappy's burned Buddha, because we had a heavy-team (twelve-man) mission going into the Tam Ky Corridor. VC forces in the area were being resupplied by mopeds and bicycles. The main road leading into the Song Ve Valley was handling a lot more traffic than usual, and headquarters wanted to know why.

The Tam Ky Corridor was a haven for enemy forces in that part of South Vietnam. Not more than two weeks earlier, there had been one hell of an artillery duel between the Viet Cong and a 1st Brigade firebase. Our artillery had silenced the enemy guns, but not before taking casualties.

It was a bad place to work in the open, but that's exactly

what our commanders wanted us to do. We were ordered to insert into the area and set up along the main road—not much more than a well-used trail—running into the valley. We were to stop and search all traffic we observed heading into the valley. They expected us to take large numbers of detainees for questioning. We were in pretty high spirits because we believed that we would likely see some contact before the mission was over. At least we would take some prisoners, which was just as important as getting a body count. The intelligence secured from interrogating a prisoner could often be invaluable. Brigade must have agreed with us, because the high command offered all kinds of rewards and incentives for capturing a prisoner.

During the early hours of morning, we departed our base camp in two Huey slicks, escorted by a pair of gunships. As we approached the corridor, I was amazed at the number of gutted helicopters that dotted the landscape. We sat down in a dry rice paddy, jumped out, and made our way down a footpath through the brush that paralleled the high-speed trail we were planning to observe.

We ran out of cover five hundred meters from our LZ and decided that it was as good a place as any to set up our OP and start monitoring the "highway." There was a bend in the trail a couple hundred meters away. Anyone coming in our direction from the west would round the bend and still have two hundred meters of open terrain to cover before he reached us, and unless he had real sharp eyes or got extremely lucky, he wouldn't spot us until it was too late.

It wasn't long before we had our first customers, three Vietnamese riding bicycles. The extended handlebars and the large amount of baggage were not indicative of typical South Vietnamese civilians out for a leisurely ride in the country. These three guys were pedaling their asses off, right toward our position. Just before they reached us, Pizza Joe and Dokos jumped into the roadway and stopped them. The look of surprise on their faces bordered on terror. We conducted a quick search of the detainees, then pushed their bikes into the brush. A more thorough search of their baggage produced a large amount of rice and other foodstuffs, along with some medical supplies.

By noon, we had a half dozen detainees along with their supply vehicles and a growing supply of food, clothing, and medical supplies. It was hard to believe that even after our rather noisy insertion into the heavily populated valley, the enemy was still oblivious to our presence.

Early in the afternoon, we spotted our first moped. Unfortunately, the driver must have been one eagle-eyed son of a gun. He hadn't gone twenty meters past the bend in the trail before leaping off the moped while it was still moving. By the time he hit the ground and got his legs back under him again, Pizza Joe Remiro and I were already firing him up. We could see the dust popping off his clothing as our rounds found their mark. The Vietnamese fell to his knees, then got back to his feet and started to move back toward the bend in the trail. I couldn't believe that he was still alive. I dropped the empty magazine at my feet and slammed home a fresh one. I raised my weapon to my shoulder for a head shot, then hesitated, not sure if I was doing the right thing by taking him out. That one-second hesitation was all that he needed. Before I could squeeze the trigger, the VC jumped from the roadway into the jungle. Remiro and I exchanged looks of total disbelief over what we had just witnessed. This guy must have taken at least a half dozen rounds in the chest before running off.

"Limey, Greek, Joe, go check out the area," Weems ordered.

Sprinting across the trail, we ran alongside it until we reached the spot where we had shot the VC. We found a tremendous amount of blood and a dark red trail leading off into the jungle. Pizza Joe and The Greek started off into the bush as I covered them from the road. They hadn't gone more than a dozen meters before they turned around and came back. They had found him, lying dead in the middle of the jungle. His entire back had been blown open by rounds exiting his body. Pure adrenaline must have taken over his body functions.

We recovered his moped with its bundle of supplies and rejoined the rest of the team. We didn't have long before we had more company coming down the road. For once, S-2 knew what it was talking about. The road into the valley was a major enemy supply route. We soon had three more detainees along with their cargo.

By 1500 hours, we had a dozen bicycles, three mopeds, and fourteen detainees, more prisoners and material than we could efficiently handle. At that point, Staff Sergeant Weems got on the radio and requested helicopters to extract the prisoners and equipment. Before long, he was informed that a Chinook helicopter would be at our location in one hour. At gunpoint, we had our detainees push their bikes and mopeds in single file toward the LZ. Claiming it as spoils of war, Pizza Joe took possession of the dead VC's moped. We already had three mopeds, and no one would be satisfied unless we each had our own, so we decided to stick around the area until we got our hands on nine more.

A short time later, the Chinook sat down in the LZ. A squad of MPs exited and quickly took charge of our prisoners and the captured supplies. No longer burdened with the job of guarding our captives, we returned to our position, prepared to liberate nine more mopeds. Alas, the word of our work had finally gotten out, and the traffic dried up completely.

Just before dark, we were informed that another heavy team would join us first thing in the morning. Lieutenant McIsaac was becoming concerned for our safety, and he wasn't the only one. Our success at stopping the local VC logistical effort had probably been noted by the VC area high command, and they would most likely be planning retaliation at that very moment.

Weems set up guard duty in two-man watches. We still felt pretty confident in our ability to fend off any attack. We had over a dozen claymores set out around us, not to mention both artillery and gunship support on standby. Hell, we were ready to kick ass and take names . . . I thought!

Our precarious position didn't keep me from sleeping soundly that night. When I woke during the early-morning hours, I felt fully rested and anxious to see what a new day would bring.

During our morning meal, we were informed that the other heavy team was in the air and would be reinforcing us shortly.

It was still early, and we hadn't seen any traffic on the road as yet. But it would pick up soon. We expected to have a busy day.

At 0800 hours, two Hueys appeared in the distance with the other heavy team. We watched as they set down a few hundred meters away and disgorged their passengers. We expected them to join us within the hour.

I propped myself up against a tree, lit a cigarette, and watched the trail to my immediate front. I was somewhere between alert and daydreaming when I was startled back to reality by the sound of automatic-weapons fire. I jerked my head toward Weems, wanting to know what to do, but he motioned for me to stay in place. He was already on the radio.

"I don't believe that silly fucker," Weems growled as he handed the headset back to his RTO. I waited for him to say something else, but he was silent. Hell, I figured if he wanted to tell us something, he'd do it when he felt like it.

The reinforcing team reached us in short order. For a dozen Lurps, they were making a lot of noise. I could hear Jaybird Magill laughing and chewing out Dufresne. He was telling Dufresne that he'd best get a better weapon if that was as good as he could do with an M-16. When they walked past my position, Jaybird winked. He had this big shit-eating grin on his face. Vendetti was walking right behind Jaybird with his head down like he had just "screwed the pooch" and was ashamed of himself. I knew that something was up, but I didn't say anything. I waited until they had set up in position, then I edged over to Jaybird and Dufresne to get the scoop on the firing we had heard.

After the heavy team had inserted, they decided to move out in a two-team formation. Dufresne was pulling drag for the lead team, and Pappy Lynch, the team leader, had Vendetti run point for the second team. As they moved toward our position, Vendetti chanced across a conical Vietnamese hat that had been dropped by one of our detainees during the previous day's operations. Vendetti thought it would be cool to take off his shirt and put on the Vietnamese headgear. Having done so, Vendetti quickened his pace to catch up to the other team. Vendetti was only fifty meters behind the first team when Dufresne turned around at his rear security position on the lead team and spotted what appeared to be an armed Vietnamese rapidly closing the distance on him. He opened up on Vendetti and fired a full magazine on rock 'n' roll, kicking up dirt at the pint-size Lurp's feet without a single round making connection. Vendetti was one extremely lucky individual, because Dufresne was known as one of the best shots in the company.

Shocked by what he had nearly done, Dufresne watched Vendetti fall to his knees and scream obscenities right there in the middle of the trail. Jaybird sprinted back to give Dufresne a hand and was greeted by the sight of Vendetti sitting in the center of the path screaming his fool head off. As soon as everyone assured themselves that Vendetti had not been hit, the razzing began in earnest. Dufresne, not Vendetti, became the recipient of the good-natured but insensitive razzing over his being unable to hit a barn door at ten paces. But the rest of the day, Vendetti took his share of abuse from the guys, as well. Between detaining prisoners, the Lurps were laying it on unmercifully.

By early afternoon, we realized that the operation had been compromised; no more traffic was coming down the trail, and we had nothing to show for the second day's effort but three detainees and their bicycles. Gone was our dream of a moped for every Lurp. We would have to take turns with the three we had already liberated. The team leader ordered us to take the prisoners and their property to the LZ for extraction. Lieutenant McIsaac didn't want us pushing our luck any more than we already had. He knew that it was just a matter of time before the neighborhood cleanup crew came looking to clean our clocks. After all, we had kept the groceries from getting through for two days!

When the choppers settled onto the LZ, we made the short sprint to the aircraft. I got into too much of a hurry to get to the ship and let my body get ahead of my feet. I fell flat on my face, jamming the barrel of my M-3 into the mud. It was bad enough to pull myself back to my feet to find all the guys laughing at me, but it really hurt when I saw that the detainees were grinning, too. I would really be in a pickle if we suddenly drew enemy fire. With six inches of mud up my barrel, my grease gun had become a poor excuse for a metal cane. Trying to avoid looking anyone in the face, I heaved my sorry ass into the waiting Huey and said a silent prayer that I would fall out on the way back to the base camp.

When we reached the compound, I promptly stripped my weapon and ran a cleaning rod through the barrel to clear it of the cubic acre of muck I'd brought back from the paddy. It was bad enough that I'd fallen on my face in front of everyone, but I didn't want them to know that I'd trashed my weapon in the process.

When I finished cleaning my weapon, I went over for a cold beer, then headed out across the compound to see what the guys were doing with the bikes and mopeds we had confiscated. I didn't see them anywhere, but I did spot Lurch. He had stayed behind during this operation, so I figured if anyone knew what was going on in the camp, he did. I asked him where the bikes were, only to have him mumble something unintelligible and walk away.

Something wasn't right! Lurch never missed an opportunity to fuck with me about the way I spoke. Seeing Wolfman by the TOC drinking a beer, I walked over and asked him if he knew where the mopeds were.

"Sure, Limey, they're over at the brigade motor pool." With that said, he, too, turned and walked away. I now knew for certain that something wasn't kosher. These guys had both stayed behind during our recent mission, and now they were holding something from us.

I went and found Greek and Pizza Joe and told them about Lurch and Wolfman's strange behavior, and with them in tow I headed for the brigade motor pool to recover the scooters so that we could joyride around the brigade area.

When we got there, we were greeted by a couple of MPs who were standing guard over the confiscated property. All our bikes and mopeds were sitting there on the other side of the concertina wire, along with all the brigade's motor vehicles. When we asked the two MPs why our stuff was back there, they responded that they were confiscated property. We told them that we knew that, we were the ones who had confiscated it. One of them smiled and said, "Well, then it's confiscated 'confiscated' property." What he meant was, "Thanks, now your toys are our toys." Somewhat disgruntled, we returned to the detachment area with every intention of raising hell with Lieutenant McIsaac.

Wolfman stopped us as we approached El Tee's hootch and told us what really happened. He also cautioned us about pissing off Lieutenant McIsaac any more than he already was. He said that when the detainees and the bikes had been brought in, the prisoners were immediately taken to the MP detachment's compound and the bikes were hauled off to the brigade motor pool. Lurch and Wolfman had been drinking at the time, and had consumed a few more beers than they should have. When they spotted the mopeds, in their slightly inebriated stupor, they decided to steal them and take them for a joyride. Now, there was nothing wrong with the two Lurps taking the mopeds around the block, but Lurch was so far gone on the beer that he lost control and ran his moped through the brigade sergeant major's tent. Even that wouldn't have been so bad if the sergeant major hadn't been in the tent at the time. He took a rather dim view of a drunken Lurp wrecking his domicile. Not only that, but he had been trying to get some beauty sleep at the time when Lurch decided to give him a wake-up call. Lieutenant McIsaac had to explain to the brigade top sergeant why he couldn't keep his people under control. The only thing that saved Lurch from the gallows was the friendship between our CO and the victim of his DWI.

After Wolfman's explanation, I understood why Lurch had ignored me earlier; the big dummy had screwed up our dream of being the first motorized Lurp detachment in the Vietnam theater. Like all outlaw bikers before us, we were doomed to extinction—in this case before our birth—without anyone's even trying to understand our motives.

CHAPTER 27

It was a glorious morning. A slight breeze was blowing in from the South China Sea, and the temperature was down in the low seventies. I figured that it would be a good day to slum around and forget about missions for a while. I made plans to visit some new friends I had made among the Hawks and Tiger Force. These battalion recon units had seen their share of fighting, and I thought that a change of scenery and some new war stories would do me good.

These thoughts were suddenly dashed when I spotted Lieutenant McIsaac heading my way. It wasn't abnormal for El Tee to visit the troops, since he wasn't your typical standoffish officer. But somehow I knew that this was not going to be a social call. Lieutenant McIsaac was wearing his trademark smirk, the one that always preceded a royal ass-chewing. I braced myself to accept my medicine for whatever escapade he had finally discovered I had participated in. However, to my relief I quickly discovered that it wasn't an ass-chewing I was in for, but a mission.

"Get your shit together, Limey, and report to the briefing tent. You're going out with me" was all that he said before turning back toward the TOC hootch.

I was still trying to figure out what was going on when I reached the briefing tent. A patchwork team was standing around waiting for the briefing that would tell us what we had "volunteered" to do. Wolfman Kraft was the only one present whom I had been out with before, but the rest of the guys were all experienced Lurps with excellent reputations.

Sergeant Rey Martinez had been selected to lead the patrol.

Besides Wolfman and myself, El Tee, Jaybird Magill, and Larry Christian made up the team. I must admit that I felt pretty damned secure in the company of these men. They were some of the finest people in the outfit. There was a lot of experience on the team, and the fact that there were no cherries on the patrol should have warned me that it was no ordinary mission.

El Tee asked me if I had enough ammunition in my rucksack. Since I carried an M-3 grease gun that required .45-caliber ammo, on patrol I made it a point of not carrying less than three hundred extra rounds, in addition to the ten thirty-round magazines I carried on my person. El Tee's concern about my ammo supply was the second hint that this mission was going to be tougher than normal.

We were to insert into an RZ that had captured S-2's attention because of an unusually large number of reports about NVA activity in the area. The intel had come from enemy prisoners, and that kind had usually proven reliable. Our job was to check out the situation and validate the intel.

The usual extra day to prepare for a mission after receiving the warning order was waived for this patrol. We were going in without an overflight or a premission briefing. The brigade Security Platoon was assigned as our reaction force, another sign that the mission was a rush job. None of us wanted to have to rely on the 1st Brigade's "dud detail" to bail us out if the shit hit the fan.

I had less than six hours to adjust my attitude and get my act together. Worrying about where we were going or who would come in to get us was the absolutely worst way to psych oneself up for a mission. My rucksack was already packed and ready to go, but I felt like I was forgetting something. So, to put my mind at rest, I went to see Ernie Winston and begged him to let me bum his 12-gauge pump shotgun and forty rounds of double-0 buckshot for a backup weapon. I had to promise under penalty of death not to get killed or to lose his pride and joy. I was not sure if a backup weapon was what I was having difficulty remembering, but the knowledge that I would have it along made me feel better.

I pulled out my signal mirror and cammo stick and began the tiring but necessary job of turning myself into a piece of jungle. I began the process of convincing myself that I was a tree. I was not satisfied until every part of my face and hands had been converted to splotches and bands of alternating greens and browns. Admiring my work, I realized that I finally felt good about myself. I was mentally, emotionally, and physically ready for the mission.

We boarded the chopper in the reverse order, first in, last out. The team leader and scouts took up positions out on the edge of the cabin, while the RTOs found places to sit in the center. Once we were airborne, I began to experience that inner calm that always came to me when the wind began to rush through the open doors. It gave me the will and determination that only self-confidence can instill. God, did it feel good to be a Lurp!

I glanced over at one of the door gunners and noticed that he was looking at us as if we were all crazy for doing what we did. I smiled to myself, secure in the knowledge that he and his crew were the crazy ones—we weren't the ones who flew around without cover, making ourselves a target for any VC with rifles and the know-how to lead a moving object as big as a hootch. Helicopters flew like rocks when the rotors stopped turning, and a fall of a thousand feet or more was usually enough to ground you for a long, long time.

Our insertion was letter perfect, and we were all out of the chopper and running for cover in record time—everyone, that is, except our illustrious team leader, Sergeant Rey Martinez. He had stumbled unassing the slick and had impaled his ruck-sack on a hardened bamboo stake hidden in the elephant grass. It took us several minutes to pry him from the pointed wooden skewer and get him back on his feet. A few inches either way, and Martinez would have been the meaty part of a VC shish kebab.

We lay dog in the elephant grass until we were convinced that the local guerrilla unit wasn't going to send a scouting party in to see what all the clatter was about. It was fortunate for us that we lay dog right on the LZ, because when we got ready to move out fifteen minutes later, we discovered that the entire area around the LZ had been booby-trapped. I couldn't take five steps in any direction without encountering sharply pointed punji stakes. The enemy had prepared the entire field of elephant grass against a possible air assault.

We worked our way through the punji stakes and held up twenty-five meters from the edge of the jungle to listen again for any sounds of the enemy. Hearing nothing out of the ordinary, we moved silently into the trees. We advanced cautiously, perhaps another twenty-five to thirty meters then stopped again to watch and listen. Luck was still with us; there appeared to be no enemy troops within the immediate vicinity of our insertion.

We moved to the east along the base of a major ridgeline. The triple canopy was choked with thick underbrush and wait-a-minute vines, making us work for every meter we moved forward. The vegetation was so dense that our visibility was limited to less than twenty feet, forcing us to slow to a crawl.

I had just relieved Christian at point when I got an uneasy feeling in the pit of my stomach. I called the patrol to a halt and stood frozen, scoping out the ground to my front. Something just ahead didn't match up. The color of the vegetation was all wrong. The hues weren't quite natural. I inched ahead slowly five or six feet, then peeked through a screen of bushes. Right in front of me was an enemy high-speed trail, less than ten feet away. It didn't take a master's degree in Pioneering to tell that the trail had been heavily used—and very recently. Fresh sneaker prints were liberally scattered around in the damp soil, and the edges had not yet started to harden. I passed the word back to the rest of the team, and we pulled back away from the trail to set up surveillance.

The terrain was in our favor, dense vegetation concealing our presence but still giving us a good view of the trail. I glanced over at Jaybird to see that he was already on the radio, notifying our commo section back at the rear that we had found signs of enemy activity and were setting up surveillance to monitor the trail.

An hour before dark, El Tee and Sergeant Martinez decided that we would not set up in our normal wagon-wheel defense perimeter. Under the circumstances, they thought it wiser to set up in line, facing the trail.

Fifteen minutes later, enemy activity began to take shape out on the trail. I watched an NVA soldier, wearing what appeared to be a brand-new khaki uniform, casually walking down the trail holding his AK-47 by the barrel and balanced over his shoulder. Even the North Vietnamese Army had its cherries, and I was looking at one of them at that moment. There was little doubt in my mind that at least one enemy soldier in our recon zone had absolutely no idea an American long-range patrol was in the neighborhood.

Grinning broadly, I turned and looked back at Martinez. He squinted and gave me one of his don't-you-fucking-dare looks. I got the message. I had no intention of firing up the little bugger. We let him safely pass by.

Lying there in the brush, it occurred to me that we had been beating the enemy at this game consistently for the past couple of months. The reputation of the VC and NVA as being the world's finest jungle fighters was proving to be just another general line of bullshit. With relatively little experience at the deadly game of sneak 'n' peek, we were more than holding our own.

As night overtook us, we heard a tremendous amount of racket coming down the trail. It sounded as if the entire population of North Vietnam was migrating past our position. Mess kits and canteens were banging together, the metallic sounds of uncoiled sling swivels squeaking, and the excited, high-pitched singsong chatter of a large number of enemy soldiers who didn't have a care in the world made up the cacophony. Once again, I found myself wishing that I could understand their language. Something had them so excited that they didn't care about basic noise discipline.

I could catch brief glimpses of shadows as the enemy soldiers passed by my position. I counted twenty-six NVA before I gave up. LRRP SOP was not to fuck with any number of enemy soldiers greater than twelve. It was a good policy that kept us coming back for more. Two-to-one odds and the element of surprise gave us the upper hand. Any more than that, and the odds swung back in the enemy's favor. With the number of enemy soldiers out on the trail, initiating any kind of action would be suicidal. It was one hell of a target-rich opportunity for the air force or the redlegs, but it was too much for us to jump on.

After a while, I discovered that my gut was in a knot, and I was having a difficult time breathing. I guess I had involuntarily shut my system down to avoid having the enemy pick up the sounds of my heart beating. Now I was forced to calm myself down before I lost control. I recalled a childhood game we used to play at the orphanage. Peekaboo, I see you! It worked, and soon I was back in control.

No one dared fall asleep. We all just lay back and enjoyed the parade. Five hours after our first sighting, we saw lights coming down the trail. My heart skipped a beat! Had they become suspicious?

It turned out that they were not flashlights, just lanterns enemy soldiers used to illuminate the trail. But it looked as if the area was being invaded by giant fireflies. There must have been forty or more lanterns out there moving through the darkness. At times, they came too close for comfort, one passing no more than ten feet away from my position.

At 0300 hours, Martinez tapped me on the shoulder and whispered in my ear that we were to start falling back. Slowly, we began to back out of our positions. Our original LZ was only three hundred meters away. The lights began to blink and fade out as we moved farther away.

Suddenly, I bumped into a rigid object behind me. I reached back slowly with my hand and discovered a punji stake just like the ones we had encountered earlier in the day. Lucky for us, the stakes were pointing in the same direction we were traveling. But not so lucky for us, this was not the same batch of punji stakes we had discovered at the LZ. Unknown to us at the time, in the darkness, we had penetrated an enemy command post.

There was no reason to alert the rest of the team of my discovery. They had already made the same discovery for themselves. After what seemed like forever, we made it to the edge of the tree line without further incident.

Lying in the brush, I edged over to Jaybird Magill and whispered that I had stopped counting the enemy soldiers at twenty-six. He hesitated for a second or two, then whispered back, "Limey, I was so scared, I lost count at ninety."

The fear hit me like a ton of bricks. But I loved the rush that came with it. Conquering one's fear is the best feeling there is. Lurps were known to be adrenaline junkies, and I was overdosing just then.

We were far from being safe, yet I felt secure in the knowledge that if things went down hard, I would be in good hands with these guys. Our skill and our nerves had gotten us this far. Luck was the only ingredient missing, and it was often fickle at best. You either got it or you didn't.

We waited in silence for first light. Martinez had gotten on the radio during the night and had requested an emergency extraction as soon as it got light enough to see. It would be counterproductive to remain in the bush any longer. Our mission was to find out if there was enemy activity in our RZ, and we had determined there was a bunch of it. It was up to S-2 and the brigade to take our work to the next level.

Personally, I would like to have reinserted six or seven klicks away on some high ground so that I could watch an Arc Light turn the RZ into salad. Then it would be fun to come back to count the divots and the body parts.

We finally heard the distinct thumping sound of a Huey drawing near. As the noise grew louder, we prepared to run for the LZ. My heart was already pounding. I was praying that the NVA had gone back into hiding during daylight hours. The chopper made its approach as we began to spring for the clearing. The aircraft came in fast and settled into the grass. We dove aboard so fast that I couldn't detect a change in the rotor pitch. We were all aboard and screaming for the pilot to go. The peter pilot turned around, smiled, and gave us a thumbs-up. We forgave the young warrant officer's theatrics. He was just playing a role. But I could have kissed his smiling face anyhow.

As we pulled away from the LZ, I looked back to see clouds of smoke rising from where we had been just seconds before. I glanced over at Lieutenant McIsaac with a look of bewilderment on my face. Grinning, he said, "The fucking dinks are a day late and a dollar short with that mortar fire."

Our mission had lasted less than sixteen hours. It would take me twice that long to come down off the high I was riding.

After our debriefing, Lieutenant McIsaac and Sergeant Martinez reported to brigade S-2. We never called for an emergency extraction unless we were in immediate danger, in contact, or fully compromised. I hoped S-2 would realize this and take appropriate action, which to my mind was a multiplane Arc Light, followed up by a BDA (bomb damage assessment) mission. But our report fell on deaf ears. No Arc Light was assigned to hit the RZ, nor would we ever receive any recognition for a job well done.

Three days after the mission, I went to the brigade bar for some normal conversation and a cold beer. When I arrived at the club, I bumped into Sam "Chief" Ybarra, who, at the time, was far from his normal crazy self. Instead of being half drunk and acting like a madman, he was sitting by himself, talking to no one, quietly nursing a beer. I had never seen him so sullen and morose. Paying for a couple of brews, I walked over to Chief and set one down next to him, then took a seat to his right. I waited for him to say something, but he remained silent.

"You're gonna have to talk to me, Chief. How about 'Thanks for the beer, Limey'?" I said.

Sam lifted his head, and with tears in his eyes he mumbled, "They fucked us, Limey."

I waited patiently for more, but that was all he intended to say for the moment. I pushed him a little harder, and I finally got him to open up. He talked for the next thirty minutes. What he had to say shook me.

Tiger Force had inserted into an LZ that had been heavily booby-trapped with punji stakes strategically placed around in the elephant grass. The paratroopers had taken a few injuries on the insertion, and prepared to evacuate them before they moved off into the jungle. The medevac was successful, and the rest of the platoon started off for the trees. They hadn't progressed two hundred meters when they were greeted by heavy automatic-weapons fire coming from well-camouflaged bunkers just ahead. Pinned down and unable to move, the Tigers were getting systematically picked off, one at a time.

Finally, tired of taking the punishment without inflicting some payback, one of their squad leaders screamed, *"Tiger Force!"* With the battle cry still ringing, the survivors of the recon unit stood up and charged the enemy emplacements. A bloody fire-fight ensued that carried them into the enemy fighting positions, where the combat soon became hand-to-hand. Tiger Force wiped out the NVA in their bunkers, one by one, until it became a complete rout. The remaining enemy fled the battlefield, leaving their dead behind. The victory was complete, but it had cost the courageous paratroopers 80 percent casualties. I asked Chief if the Tigers had taken any prisoners. Silly question.

Sam had been recommended for the Silver Star, but that was not on his mind at the moment. "Limey," he said, "they told us it was a routine sweep of the area. There were not supposed to be any enemy there."

When I quizzed him about the location they had gone into, the area sounded very familiar. It was the same place we had just come out of. We had been extracted from under the very noses of an NVA battalion just three days before Tiger Force walked into a meat grinder in the same AO.

The information we had gathered about large enemy forces in the immediate area had been ignored by someone who saw the opportunity for a chestful of medals. Unfortunately, most of them had been Purple Hearts. I said a silent prayer that the SOB who hadn't passed the word to Tiger Force was among the dead. There was no doubt in my mind that if I was in the Tigers and I knew who was responsible, I would personally inflict some major pain on the incompetent asshole. But all I could do for the moment was to sit and listen to Sam, buy him an occasional beer, and offer my sympathy. He needed someone—anyone—in his time of sorrow, just to ease his pain.

It was a sad day indeed. Brigade had just named another valley after the valiant Tiger Force. How many more Tiger valleys would there be before these damned lifer officers woke up and did their jobs?

CHAPTER 28

Our happy hunting ground was about to be taken away from us: we had received notice that we were moving from Duc Pho to Phan Rang for a stand-down. After that, rumor had it, we would be heading for Chu Lai, farther up the coast on the South China Sea. We wondered why they kept moving us around. We would just get to where we were getting to know an area pretty well, and they would force us to pull up roots and move to a new location. That made it tougher to conduct long-range reconnaissance patrols. Every time they moved us, they brought in a new unit to take our place. Seemed like a poor way to run a war.

We spent the next few days packing all our meager belongings and readying the detachment to move. I watched as the line units came straggling in from the field. It was obvious that Duc Pho had been rough on them. Still, it didn't keep them from grumbling about the move. But we were only soldiers— what did we know?

We decided to drink up our beer supply. It would be one less item for us to haul back to Phan Rang. Of course, it was also a good excuse to have a party and get drunk.

As usual, we soon found ourselves in the hurry-up-and-wait cycle that seemed to dominate any planned army movement. We were in a dilemma of major proportions. Trustingly, we had liquidated our beer supply, but our relocation had been delayed by a full day. We were out of our daily sustenance, and there was no way to get any more. I would be damned if I would hit my personal stash. I had already planned to share it with Eddie Mounts on the long trip south. But instead of grumbling and bitching as Lurps are prone to do, we made our way to the brigade club, hoping that the REMFs had not already closed down one of our regular watering holes.

They had. When we entered the club we were met by a sorry lifer who said that the club had been closed for the duration. That didn't sit too well with the thirsty and thoroughly pissed-off party of Lurps. We gave the unhappy NCO an ultimatum—sell us some beer or we would tear his club down. It wasn't very nice of us, but we were desperate men.

The shaken NCO decided to sell us twenty-four cases of the thirty cases he still had at the club. Taking him up on his generous offer, we launched our final party at Duc Pho. Soon the word got out that the club was still open, and a number of guys began arriving from Tiger Force, Recondos, and Hawk Recon. Many of the recon troopers showed up with bottles of booze that they had hidden away while they were out in the field.

I had never mixed whiskey, gin, and vodka with beer before, but there's a first time for everything. Everyone was soon sampling a bit of everything, and before long, I was feeling no pain. And when Limey is feeling no pain, Limey thinks he is invincible. I was about to make a total ass out of myself.

Off alone minding its own business was a steel helmet. It was sitting on the table next to me where someone had left it. Sitting directly across the table from me was my old Tiger Force buddy, Chief Ybarra, who just happened to have the biggest Bowie knife in the world. Rumor had it that Chief's oversize Bowie had severed the head of more than one VC/NVA. My attention was still focused on the steel helmet, sitting there, waiting for its owner to return, when I asked Chief to lend me his Bowie. I was curious to see if it would penetrate the head armor the army issued its fighting men. Warning me under penalty of death not to damage his knife, Chief handed the weapon to me. In a drunken stupor, I took aim at my target and struck with a vengeance. The helmet jinked to the side, causing me to hit it with a glancing blow that left the knife buried two to three inches in the wooden table.

I got up on the table, straddled the knife, and was trying with all my might to extract it when someone behind me screamed,

"You motherfucker!" And having been called that name before, I knew immediately that he was talking to me.

I looked around and saw this big paratrooper headed right for me. I knew that no explanation was going to suffice. There was blood in his eyes, and his fists were already up. He grabbed me before I could mount a defense. The only thing that saved me from his savage haymaker was the fact that he was just as drunk as I was. We crashed through the wall and landed outside in the dirt. If we hadn't had the club manager's attention before, we sure had it now. Knowing that we would likely finish by destroying his club, he screamed for us to stop. But there was nothing really to stop. We were both so drunk that not one effective blow had been landed as we groveled together in the dirt.

Finally someone pulled us apart. We quickly forgot what we were fighting about and returned to the party. My former enemy had soon become my best friend. Together we sang ballads about the injustices that were inflicted on young soldiers.

But the night would not pass without at least one more Lurp making an ass of himself. The Russian began feeling lonesome and was soon kissing everyone in reach. The Lurps thought this was hilarious. We knew The Russian was straight and didn't mean any harm. Men kissing men was common practice in the Soviet Army. None of the Tigers, Hawks, and Recondos had ever served in the Soviet Army, but enough of them had lived in or around San Francisco to know that men kissing men could have connotations that they didn't want any part of. One trooper from Hawk Recon took particular offense when Federov planted a big one on his lips. He was about to put The Russian in orbit when I stepped in and stopped him. In gratitude, Federov grabbed me in a huge bear hug and flashed his tongue at my throat. I summoned all my strength and managed to break free just in time. Backing away, I told him to go find someone else to play with.

The party was in full swing when we got the word the beer had run out. To make matters worse, there wasn't a drop of the hard stuff left either. Under threat of total destruction, the club's NCOIC produced his private cache of six cases of beer, which he finally agreed to sell us.

Within the hour, the last of the beer was history and the club was loaded with recon troopers drunker than skunks. Out of nowhere, a voice yelled, *"Tear the fucking bar down!"* That's when the demolition started. Within minutes, the club was history, and someone had tossed a few tear-gas grenades into the rubble. It would have been hilarious if the wind had blown the gas toward the MP compound. Alas, the wind was blowing directly toward the brigade staff officers area, which included the brigade commanding general's abode. General Matheson didn't appreciate the wake-up call. Soon the word got out that the MPs were on their way to arrest the perpetrators. It didn't take long for the area to clear out. They were sober, we were drunk. They had big sticks, we were drunk. They had bad attitudes, we were drunk. It would have been no match, so we quietly melted into the night as the MPs arrived. They were smart enough to stay away from our compound. They satisfied themselves with standing among the recently vacated ruins of the brigade club and tossing threats in our direction.

The last thing I remembered was crawling through the brush with Jaybird Magill as we tried to find our way back to Lurp Hill without being discovered by the now marauding NCOs of brigade headquarters.

I woke up the next morning lying next to a thorny bush not more than ten feet from my hootch, pretty good navigating, given the circumstances. Wrapped in the fetal position around the piss tube, Jaybird was nearby. We weren't the only Lurps who had failed to reach our hootches. Several more supine forms were scattered around the detachment area. I crawled into my tent, nearly colliding with the body of Boss Weisberger. He had located the tent, but had given up searching for his bunk in the darkness. Even in a drunken stupor, we highly trained Lurps still realized that it was safer to sleep it off on the ground. Unconsciously, we sensed that you were more likely to fall off your cot than you were to fall off the ground. Call it instinct if you like, but it was something we all had.

As the rest of the detachment began to stir, a few of us drunks managed to regain enough composure to get to our feet. I went through the motions of making coffee, and had it ready when Jaybird came in from his night of bliss with the piss tube.

As we sat mulling over our pounding heads, trying to figure out if a hangover was caused by a swelling of the brain or a shrinking of the skull, I saw Lieutenant McIsaac hang up the field telephone and head in our direction. This was the sign for me to unass the area—pronto. I headed for the shitter to hide out, knowing that someone was about to get a Class Nine ass-chewing. With the hangover I was carrying, I didn't want any part of it.

I waited for about fifteen minutes before returning to the area, keeping a blurred eye out for El Tee. I ran directly into Top Smith. He was looking right at me with a grin on his face, shaking his head slowly from side to side. I envied him his ability to do that. It would have killed me at the moment.

I linked back up with my coffee-drinking comrades and was greeted with a frown from Lurch Cornett. "Did you tie up the S-2 and S-3 sergeants, Limey?" he asked.

"No," I answered. "Who did?" It had suddenly become pretty apparent why Lieutenant McIsaac had stormed over to our little gathering. The new S-2, Major Geecey, was highly per-turbed that person or persons unknown had waited in ambush for two senior NCOs and, after hog-tying them, had left them to the not so tender mercies of the creatures of the night. I thought that hilarious, and would have claimed responsibility in a New York minute if I had thought that I had done it. But I was so damn drunk, I wouldn't have remembered if my life depended on it. What the hell, it sounded like something those crazy bastards from Tiger Force would do anyway!

Finally, word was given to strike our tents and prepare to move out first thing in the afternoon. It didn't take us but a few minutes to disassemble our squalid living quarters. Wait-ing patiently for the big move, we were suddenly hit with the bombshell—we were not going to be choppered down to Phan Rang. We would be taking the scenic route, down Highway 1 in convoy formation.

The trip was boring and uneventful but was made easier by

a liberal dose of whiskey and Coca-Cola that we purchased during the frequent stops.

CHAPTER 29

Arriving at our detachment area, we were greeted by a number of very strange objects that confounded and amazed us. There were regular wooden buildings, cots lining their walls, stacked with clean, neatly folded sheets and blankets. There were even light switches on the walls, and where there were light switches there were usually electric lights. I remembered how they worked from my days as a civilian back in the World. What a wonderful invention! The last time we had experimented with electricity Boss, Beaver, Sweet Pea, Chad, and I had almost got ourselves shot. The recollection made me laugh, and when I turned to say something to Beaver he was laughing, too.

I put my new gear down on my cot and strolled outside to check out our new surroundings. I experienced a sudden pang of unhappiness when I spotted a group of REMFs walking by in pressed fatigues and highly polished boots. I didn't understand how a soldier in Vietnam could remain in the rear away from the war and tell himself that he was doing all he could for God and for Country. Combat units were operating at 50 to 75 percent strength, yet it appeared that many of the units in the rear were at 125 to 150 percent strength—a bloody surplus! I watched with sadness as paratroopers on a punishment detail whitewashed the large rocks that lined the walkway leading up to the brigade headquarters building. Staff officers always amazed me with their penchant for wasted efforts. Next time we have a war, somebody should just keep them home.

I walked around for a while, familiarizing myself with the lay of the land. Then I spotted an unattended marmite can just outside the mess hall. It was calling out to me: "Limey, pick me up and take me back with you. These REMFs don't appreciate me." And that is how I came about liberating the marmite can. It would serve honorable duty as our official detachment mobile cooler. We kept it stocked in our hootch, and sometimes used it for holding cold beer for a team fresh in from the field.

Rudy Lopez and I took the marmite can to the PX, where we stocked it with beer, and then departed for the USO show to let off a little steam while ogling round-eyed women.

We found them set up in a large open area, with a half dozen stages, offering everything from a magic act, to rock 'n' roll, to country. Walking from one act to the next, Rudy and I gulped down enough of the beer that it wasn't long before the brew began to take effect. More than a little inebriated, we watched Connie Francis—or was it Anita Bryant?—belt out some of her latest hits.

After a close call with an air policeman, Rudy and I took the marmite-can cooler and headed back for the LRRP compound, where we were greeted not by a group of brother Lurps but by our beloved first sergeant, Top Smith, who was not in one of his better moods.

"Where have you two orphans been?" Top inquired, standing in front of us with his hands on his hips.

Not wanting Top to see how drunk I was, I just shrugged my shoulders stupidly. Rudy should have done the same, but he decided that he was going to talk his way out of trouble. Unfortunately, as soon as he opened his mouth Top Smith knew that he was plowed. The first sergeant rolled his eyes back in his head, then said, "Okay, you two! Go sleep it off for now, but starting tomorrow morning, you're both on motor-pool detail."

We stumbled to our hootches as Top watched us in disgust. I'm sure that he knew he was going to have a major problem on his hands with his Lurps entering the civilized world of Phan Rang.

When I crawled into my rack, I propped myself up for a moment to ponder the consequences of our night on the town.

I was still not sure if Top's assigning us to the motor-pool detail was punishment or reward. Hell, we only had the Lurpmobile. Since the entire detachment was likely to be assigned one detail or another, working the motor pool would probably be as close to doing nothing as we could get.

The morning came too soon for the two of us, because we were greeted by a great amount of racket and some idiot screaming something about getting up for morning formation. Christ, none of us had seen a formation in nearly four months, and to call one now required a whole new way of thinking.

I started to walk outside my barracks wearing only my underwear, and was promptly screamed at by some authoritative voice that ordered me to return to my barracks and get dressed in the proper military attire. I had no idea who it was who had ruined my day, but I decided to accede to his wishes.

When I finally dragged my butt back outside and found my place in the formation, I looked to the right and the left and saw members of other units also falling in for reveille formation.

Lieutenant McIsaac gave the first inspirational speech of the day to his Lurps, saying, "Men, first we will assign some work details, in which everyone will participate. Second, I have some morning and evening passes for sin city, Chop Ton, and after your details have been completed to my satisfaction, you will have the opportunity to use them." Looking around to make sure he had everyone's attention, he continued, "I'll have no reports on my desk about fighting or any other nonmilitary behavior. And finally, you will all pay your bills at the local establishments or you stay away. No getting laid without the girls getting paid. Is that clear?" A few boos and catcalls greeted this news. El Tee smiled before turning the formation over to Top Smith.

Waiting until Lieutenant McIsaac had cleared the area, Top Smith turned back to us and said, "If you have any sexual encounters be careful, and if you're not, then make certain you see the medics before we move out to our next AO. I don't need a bunch of you lover boys out in the field with the clap. Okay, you're dismissed. Get your details done and go enjoy yourselves."

The formation broke up and we made our way back to the barracks to get organized. Rudy and I were still not sure if the motor pool was a reward or not. We watched as some of the guys started to put out clean clothes and gather up their toiletry items. I figured it was time to find out what details the other guys had drawn. I asked Boss Weisberger what his work detail consisted of. Smiling, he announced, "Oh, we just have to watch the barracks."

I looked over at Beaver, who added, "I'm just supposed to watch Boss watch the barracks." Now I'd heard everything!

I walked over to Lurch and discovered that his detail was to hold a "short-arm inspection," a VD check, for everyone going on a pass. I then looked over at Wolfman, who sheepishly grinned before confirming, "You guessed it, I'm gonna watch Lurch give the VD inspections."

I knew that military discipline had to be maintained, even in a combat zone; however, Rudy and I seemed to have gotten the short end of the stick. Apparently, our detail was the only one that bore any real resemblance to an actual detail. Feeling as if we had been singled out for special punishment, Rudy and I made the three-hundred-meter trek to the motor pool while the rest of our guys made the twenty-five-meter walk to the shower point so they could clean up and smell pretty for the girls of Chop Ton.

When we arrived at the motor pool, we spotted the Lurp-mobile standing off to the side by itself. "Well, there it is, Limey," he said. "What do you think?"

I nodded my head in agreement. "Yep, it appears to be right here, all right," I answered. "Detail's over, let's go get a shower." With that, we called it a day and made our way to the barracks.

By the time we got back, most of the guys were already dressed and heading for the orderly room to pick up their passes.

Finally, after getting spiffed up and sprinkling ourselves with a pint or so of Old Spice, Rudy and I made our way down to the orderly room to pick up our passes, hoping that Top Smith wasn't around. Our luck didn't hold. Sitting at the front desk was a buck sergeant we had never seen before, and behind him Top Smith was leaning against the wall with a big grin on his face. The situation bore all the signs of a linear ambush.

"How's the motor-pool detail coming along, Limey?" Top Smith asked in a tone that smacked of prior knowledge.

"Oh, it's still there, Top," I answered, "and the Lurpmobile is doing just fine, too." I knew I was pushing my luck, but I was driving toward the goal and it was too late to pass off now.

"Okay, troop, A.M. passes are in that box and P.M. passes are in that box," the buck sergeant announced, indicating the appropriate out boxes on his desk.

I reached in and grabbed a stack from each box. By my estimation I had enough passes for every day we were likely to be in Phan Rang.

"Hope you two have plenty of money," Top said as he walked out of the orderly room. Then as soon as he was out of sight he poked his head back around the corner and added, "Make sure that truck is washed tomorrow."

That was it! Our entire punishment was to wash the Lurpmobile. God, were we relieved! Rudy and I could do that with our eyes closed.

We reached Sin City by crossing a bridge and giving the APs (air [force] police) on duty there our passes. When everything checked out, they waved us on, and we passed into the erotic world of the sinners of the flesh. We entered Mai Lai's and found that the party was already in full swing. The place was packed. Lurps, Tigers, Hawks, Recondos, and line doggies had tables piled high with a variety of beer cans and hard liquor bottles. The alcohol was flowing like water, and a large percentage of those present were already in the advanced stages of intoxication. The only sober face in the crowd was that of Eddie Mounts. Unlucky Eddie had been detailed to remain sober to make sure that the Wolfman didn't go off the deep end again.

The only people safe around Wolfman when he was drinking were his fellow Lurps. Everyone else became a target. I had a reputation for getting a little out of control when I was drinking, but the Wolfman had become a legend. He was known to strike out at anyone who displeased him, and after four or five beers, he could find fault with the Pope.

The crowd eventually thinned out, and soon the party was winding down to a Lurp family affair. I knew that all the civilized behavior couldn't last forever. Somebody was bound to strike the first blow for chaos and the fall of mankind.

A young Vietnamese boy came up to our table selling brightly colored parakeets. I was somewhat surprised when Bacek gave the boy twenty piasters and took one of the small birds in his beefy hand.

"Pretty little fucker, ain't it?" the big Lurp team leader said to no one in particular. He then promptly shoved the bird up to his mouth and bit its head off!

That really grossed me out. The little Vietnamese kid started screaming at the top of his lungs, crying and pointing his finger at Bacek. It wasn't long before he had a half dozen bar girls standing at the table looking down at the headless body of the bird lying on the table. Suddenly, all of them were crying and talking all at once.

"Hell, I don't know what they're all so upset about, it was my bird," Walt announced, apparently confused by all the grief. I didn't want to stay around to see how the affair was going to unfold, so I picked up my drink and went elsewhere looking for some female companionship. I figured that it would be a while before the girls at Mai Lai's were in the mood for anyone from brigade LRRPs.

It wasn't hard to find female companionship in Chop Ton. In exchange for a small payment I was soon enjoying all the tantalizing treats of the flesh that five dollars MPC could avail. It was during this short interlude that I made a welcome discovery. I found that I still had feelings for other people besides my fellow Lurps.

I was leaving the back room with the Asian beauty I had spent the last hour with, her arms around my waist as she giggled like a schoolkid. Just when I was beginning to think that she really dug me, in walks the same black AP sergeant who had hassled Rudy and me at the USO show. This time he was pissed off, demanding to know what I was doing with his girlfriend. Since it was my first day on the town, and really not wanting to mix it up with the local cops, I shrugged my shoulders and walked past him. I guess he thought I was shunning him, because he grabbed my arm and brought my forward progress to a stop.

"Hey, if you want that hand, I recommend you get it off my arm," I told him, staring him in the eye but trying to keep my voice as civil as I could. I only wanted to get out of the club, but there was a limit to what I would take.

Thankfully, the eyeball-to-eyeball contact seemed to do the job, and he released my arm. On my way out the door he shouted at me, warning me to stay away from his woman. That was a mistake. Now I made a promise to myself that I would come back to see her again before we left Phan Rang.

Then the incident was forgotten, and I found myself in the middle of another party with Tiger Force and some of my brother Lurps. A platoon sergeant from the Tigers jumped up on the table and yelled, *"Beer on the house!"* at which time everybody in the room cheered him and ordered a beer. Mamma-san was as happy as could be as the drunken paratroopers downed the beer like it was water. Most of us had a beer in each hand, alternating bottles as we sucked them dry. Finally, mamma-san asked for payment of the bar bill. When she was told in sign language what "beer on the house" meant, she came unglued, ran outside, and started screaming for the police.

It wasn't long before the APs arrived and started throwing their authority around. I was trying to maintain my dignity and stay out of trouble, so I retreated to the nearest wall, grabbed a chair, and sat down to watch the fun. It started immediately.

First, one of the recon troopers threw an AP's helmet liner out the front door. This probably wouldn't have started the rumble but for the fact that the AP's head was still in it. By then the fight was on, and it was no match at all. In less than a minute, four APs were lying prone in the street as the Tigers marched away looking for another bar, some more beer, and a little action. I sneaked out the back door and headed just down the street for the Hole in the Wall bar.

Well, the Hole in the Wall was the wrong place to find peace and quiet. Cornett, Martinez, Kraft, and Mounts were already there. Again, the only sober one in the group was Eddie Mounts. Minutes later, we were joined by Jack Flash, a LRRP with a problem I wished I had.

His girlfriend, Moon, was taking him around to meet all her friends, but every time they stopped somewhere, she wanted to get it on with him. Jack had gotten into town at 0900 hours, and he had picked up Moon almost immediately. It was now 1600 hours, and Jack had "ridden the bareback mare" ten times already. This had to be some kind of record, but it was slowly killing Flash. But it was his problem, not mine, so I left him in good company to solve his own dilemma and made my way back to the detachment area still bewildered as to where I had lost Rudy Lopez. Well, Rudy was a big boy!

I was well satisfied with my performance during the day. I had managed somehow to stay out of trouble, and even come away from Chop Ton half sober. That was totally uncharacteristic of me, but it was nice knowing that I would not be waking up the next day with a black eye, busted knuckles, and a killer hangover.

The following day I met up with Rudy and we made our way to the motor pool to give the Lurpmobile its biannual wash. By my calculations, it would take us less than an hour to complete the detail, so we could take the rest of the day off. That all changed when we discovered that the motor pool didn't have a hose. The nearest water point was over a hundred meters away, and what was supposed to be a one-hour job took the entire morning. It was worse on me than Rudy. His stomach wound prevented his carrying the buckets of water from the water point to the vehicle, so I was forced to do all the hauling. I could picture Top Smith over at the NCO club, laughing his ass off at that very minute.

The next three days were a blur of drunken parties and clandestine meetings with the AP's Vietnamese girlfriend. The days and nights ran together, and I soon lost track of who I was or what I was doing. I finally reined myself in long enough to try to get control of myself. My timing couldn't have been better.

It was late afternoon, and I was making another trip to Chop Ton to meet with the AP's girl. I spent a few hours enjoying her favors, then prepared to leave before curfew. She begged me to stay, and against my better judgment I agreed. We spent the night drinking beer and talking about the first thing that came up, and it was late in the morning when I finally fell asleep. My plans were to get up before first light, slip through the wire, and return to my hootch before anyone missed me. Since no one would be out patrolling but the APs, infiltrating the perimeter wire would be a simple task. The only problem was that it was well after daylight before I woke from my alcohol-induced sleep.

It would still be a while before Chop Ton opened for business, and I decided to step outside to recon the situation. It was there I came face-to-face with one very black, very mad AP. He was instantly furious when he saw me, and screamed, "You're under arrest!" Then he made a move for me. I guess he figured he had the drop on me. Well, he figured wrong, and it was he who got dropped.

Now I was in a real sticky situation. I was AWOL, had struck an NCO, and had struck an NCO who just happened to be a military cop. I was looking at at least a firing squad, if not a few months of hard time in Long Binh Jail. My only chance was to infiltrate the Lurp compound, change my identity, and then stay out in the bush for the duration of the war. I was definitely having a bad-hair day.

Exiting the back of the bar as quietly as possible, I tiptoed through the village communal sewer system without being seen, and made haste in the general direction of our rear area. Lady Luck was on my side for once, and the AP jeep that normally patrolled the concertina-wire barricade between the camp and Chop Ton was not on its regular run. I could see the APs bullshitting with some bar girls three hundred meters away. It was a relatively simple chore to slip through the wire and march down the dirt road toward brigade.

Only time would tell if the AP sergeant brought me up on

charges. I hoped that he would be too embarrassed to admit that some young trooper had nailed him *and* his girlfriend. He wouldn't have a difficult time finding me, because I had been wearing the Long Range Recon tab over my Screaming Eagle patch.

For the next two mornings at reveille, I waited for my name to be called out. But my fears were unwarranted. I had not been reported, or someone was doing one hell of a job covering for me. I must have made one hell of an impression on Top Smith and Lieutenant McIsaac when I spent the rest of our stay in Phan Rang in the detachment area, reading a book and drinking an occasional beer.

CHAPTER 30

The "good times" in Phan Rang were drawing to a close. We had just received movement orders that Chu Lai was to be our new base of operations.

After a lot of soul-searching, I came to the conclusion that I no longer desired to be a card-carrying Limey. I had decided that if I was fighting for the good old United States of America then, by God, I ought to have a say in the way things were being run back there. Besides, my British citizenship had some of the guys in the unit accusing me of being a foreign mercenary. I suppose that I could have gotten it done during the recent stand-down, but at the time, partying with the guys seemed more important.

I had a talk with Lieutenant McIsaac and Top Smith. They recommended that I remain behind in Phan Rang for a few more days after the unit moved to Chu Lai so that I could begin filing the necessary paperwork for U.S. citizenship.

Top Smith quickly approved my request but warned me to stay out of any kind of trouble. He said that if I got my tit in a wringer, there would be very little he could do for me up at Chu Lai. Until I rejoined the detachment, I was on my own.

I went over to S-2 and picked up my alien registration card, then reported to the judge advocate's office to fill out the necessary paperwork. I was in no way prepared for the REMF bullshit that greeted me when I entered the JA's building. The specialist sitting behind the desk looked up from the *Daffy Duck* comic book he was reading and threw one of those what-the-fuck-do-you-want? looks at me as I stood waiting to be helped. He wasted little time returning to his comic book.

I stood there patiently for several seconds wondering how he would look with the comic book stapled to his ass while I fed his face through the carriage on his typewriter. Then I decided that I would be a gentleman and give him one last chance.

"Pardon me, stud, but when you finish looking at all the neat pictures in your field manual there, I would really appreciate a few minutes of your valuable time. Hate to take you away from the war and all, but I'd sure like to get some paperwork filled out. Maybe it'll help get you a CIB or something!"

That got his attention. He tossed the comic book facedown on top of his desk and slowly stood and walked over to the counter. With a look obviously meant to intimidate me, he drawled, "Well, what do you need, stud?"

"What I need, *stud,* is to see the judge advocate. You see, I'm a British subject, and I would like to become an American citizen, but after seeing the likes of you I'm not so sure it's a wise move."

The REMF clerk wrinkled his nose and shook his head. "Well, you're out of luck, man. The major is not here at the moment. He's out on . . . er . . . urgent business and won't be back until later in the afternoon."

Urgent business my ass! I thought as I stared at the now somewhat more attentive specialist. The son of a bitch was probably getting stroked into passionate oblivion down at the local massage parlor.

"Okay, dude, then maybe you can help me. Don't really see why I need to bother the major when a clerk can probably do it. I just need to get the necessary paperwork filled out, that's all." The way he was nodding his head, I assumed that I had just picked up an ally, but then, I should have known better.

"Look, man, it's just not that simple. First you got to prove time of residency in the United States, then you're going to have to obtain a whole series of affidavits. Sorry, looks like you're just SOL."

By this time I was more than a little pissed. I half decided to vault over the desk and pound his fucking REMF head into the floor, then tell him to "affidavit this, you cocksucker!" But being the good-natured, mild-mannered Lurp that I was, I just asked him to set up an appointment for me to come back and meet with the major when he returned.

"Oh, no, I can't do that. First you have to have your CO or first sergeant call this office to set up the time of the appointment for you. Then we'd have to check and see what date was open." He was now grinning from ear to ear.

The hair on my back (if I had any hair on my back) was beginning to stand straight up. "Okay, what time do you have open?"

Again with the big shit-eating grin on his face, he said, "I can't tell you that without checking with your CO or first sergeant."

I felt myself losing it. "Look, asshole, my unit has already moved to Chu Lai. I was left behind to get this taken care of."

He almost gloated as he replied, "Well now, you do have a problem, don't you?"

If looks could kill, I was staring at a dead man. I turned on my heel and stormed out of the building, slamming the door behind me on the second of his sarcastic "If I can be of further help . . ." The closed door trapped the rest of his parting shot inside. If I'd remained there any longer he would have become a casualty of friendly fire, and I would have qualified for long-term residency in LBJ.

Dejected, I returned to the LRRP compound. I had been right, most of the guys were already gone, including Top Smith and Lieutenant McIsaac. Only Rudy Lopez was still there. He was waiting for a physical.

We decided that what we needed most was a cold beer, some hot women, and a long massage. We went to Chop Ton, but my heart really wasn't into partying. I returned to the barracks, got my gear, and went looking to bum a ride to Chu Lai.

When I showed up at the chopper pad with my ruck and weapon, a Huey slick was just revving up to depart. The warrant officer in the left-hand seat took one look at me and motioned for me to come over to his side of the ship. He asked if I was a 1st Brigade Lurp. When I nodded in the affirmative, he told me to climb aboard; he was heading to Chu Lai and would be happy to drop me off at the Lurp acid pad.

There was always a special bond between chopper pilots and recon people. We made sure to let them know how much we valued their risking their butts to pull us out of the tight ones, and they always took care of us in return. We were both in high-risk occupations. That common bond between us was simply understood, and words were rarely necessary—or sufficient—to affirm it. We had often aborted missions to go in after downed chopper crews, and they had reciprocated by aborting milk runs to come to our aid, many times flying at night or in bad weather to pull out teams that had been surrounded by overwhelming enemy forces.

The flight to Chu Lai was uneventful, but looking down, I thought about how beautiful the landscape of Vietnam really was. The green and brown checkerboard rice paddies, interrupted by the occasional village and dark patches of dense jungle, provided a panorama of the finest artwork of man or nature. Even the forest-covered mountains in the distance, with their promise of ever-present danger, seemed to beckon one in for a closer look.

The flight to Chu Lai was over too quickly for me. We landed at a rather ugly, unimpressive American base camp. Besides serving as the new home for the 1st Brigade of the 101st Airborne Division, Chu Lai was also the home of the U.S. Marines' Mess Kit Repair regiment (even the rugged Corps had its share of REMFs).

I thanked the chopper pilot, then ducked the spinning rotor blades as I trotted off the penta-prime flight line and headed for the 1st Brigade area and the LRRP compound. I sensed that I was beginning a new adventure.

My first and foremost impression of our new home was "Oh shit!" No longer would Lurps be left alone. We were located in the center of Headquarters & Headquarters Company (H&HC or HHC) of the 1st Brigade. This was no LRRP Hill of the kind we had at Duc Pho. This was true civilization—suburban Vietnam!

Squad-size tents were set out in long, perfect, military rows and already heavily sandbagged for protection against rockets and mortars. A few tents were still without blast walls, but a large pile of white sand and bales of sandbags sat in the center of the compound, promising that the problem would soon be corrected. What made the situation even worse was that a detail of shirtless, sweating Lurps was already at work filling them. Welcome to Chu Lai, Spec Four Limey! Your low-ranking young ass is soon going to be on that very same work detail. Spec Fours and below got all the shitty details in the army. My ghosting days were over!

I reported directly to Top Smith, who seemed somewhat surprised at my early arrival. With my reputation as a party animal, he had fully expected me to show up about twenty minutes before my DEROS date asking after my Freedom Bird.

George "Rommel" Murphy walked me to my new hootch and told me that I had really fucked up this time. "What else was new!" I said as I tossed my ruck onto an empty cot.

The new HHC first shirt, with the Prussian name of Eichelberger, was terrorizing the Lurps. Murphy told me that he was called "Patch Pockets" because of all the medals and military awards he wore. All of them were sewn on his fatigues, one on top of the other, just to let everyone know what a war hero we had on our hands. The first sergeant was proving to be one oversize asshole who was displaying all the traits of a classic Napoleon complex. I was a little surprised by Rommel's analysis of our new ranking NCO, as he seldom said anything negative about anyone. But Rommel swore that he wasn't bull-shitting and promised that I would soon find out for myself.

I put my gear away and walked outside the hootch to find Eichelberger standing there in all his glory, supervising Bob McKinnon, who was, in turn, supervising the sandbag detail. A teammate, Eddie Mounts, waved to me and motioned for me to bug out before one of the lifers spotted me. But it was already too late, as Sergeant McKinnon looked up while I was searching for a place to hide. He sauntered over to tell me to enjoy my day off because I would definitely be on a work detail the next day. I nodded in understanding and slowly walked back to my hootch. I had given up a week of partying in Phan Rang for this!

That night, I prayed that my team would get a mission order before dawn, but wasn't surprised to find McKinnon standing in the doorway of my hootch at 0700 hours, waiting to tell me that Eddie Mounts and I had the shit-burning detail for the rest of the day. It was already apparent that old Patch Pockets didn't miss a lick. I assumed that since I had time-in-grade over Eddie that I was the head shit-burner, and Mounts my assistant.

All the shitters were in line, dress right dress, with the first sergeant's one-holer on the right. It was SOP to burn the first shirt's waste first. Inspired by some force beyond our control, Mounts and I decided that it would be one hell of a neat thing if we somehow managed to burn Eichelberger's shitter down as well. But our ingenious plan failed to materialize, because Patch Pockets showed up personally to supervise the incineration.

Each shitter was built along the order of a traditional rural outhouse. The commanding officer and the first shirt enjoyed the privacy of personal single-holers, but the rest of the NCOs and the enlisted men shared a communal four-holer. One half of a fifty-five-gallon drum was inserted under each hole through a hinged trapdoor in the rear to allow easier access for removal during the incineration process.

Every three or four days, a couple of lucky enlisted men were selected at random to remove the barrels and dispose of the noisome waste products therein by dousing them liberally with a gas-and-diesel-fuel mixture and burning it until nothing was left but black ash. Doesn't sound too bad in the telling except that fully incinerating the waste matter required the disposal crew to frequently stir the burning concoction with a steel fence stake (to bring the unburned material to the surface where it could be reduced by the flames). The black clouds of oily smoke tended to follow us around, seeking out every pore and crevice in the body and filling them with a sooty, noxious, greasy residue. Finishing the detail some eight hours later, we looked very much like Australian aborigines and smelled like the floor of a chicken coop. If Patch Pockets ever swore that his shit didn't stink, Eddie and I could both testify against him.

All day long, the two of us stirred the burning shit until finally nothing was left but a couple of inches of black ash in the bottom of each of the barrels. We had decided to skip lunch at the mess hall, knowing that they wouldn't let us in anyhow. Besides, there really wasn't a hell of a lot of difference between what they were serving and what we were cooking in the barrels.

When we finally had shoved the empty drums back into place, we headed for the showers to scrub off the sooty buildup that covered us from head to toe. It didn't make a lot of sense to either of us to spend an entire day burning shit while just outside the perimeter a war was going on.

Clean once again, we returned to our hootch and went to grab a couple of cold beers out of the large metal cooler. The cooler was empty! I fought back a fit of uncontrolled depression. I was totally demoralized, hurt, and still terribly thirsty. The only place that we could get a beer at that time of the day was from Patch Pockets's personal storage area where he kept the company beer ration. Army regulations authorized each enlisted man in a combat zone a ration of two cans of beer per day, and the first sergeant controlled our ration—from us. He then decided that he would only distribute our ration to us whenever he deemed it appropriate. It was only 1700 hours, and Patch Pockets did not deem it an appropriate time. The appropriate time, in his estimation, was 1800 hours, just before the outdoor movie was to begin. I decided to prop myself up on my bunk and try to pen a letter before our brew was liberated. I looked over at Eddie and saw that he was doing the same thing. The only difference was that he was writing to his wife, while I was writing to an antiwar aunt who was busy working diligently to keep her little Sammy from being drafted. Well, I had to write to somebody!

I was still struggling with the letter when Jaybird Magill, Keener, and The Beaver came into the hootch. I had thought that I was in a foul mood, but I was Mr. Pleasant compared to these guys. Since Eddie and I had skipped chow, we had no idea that Patch Pockets had detailed some of our people to pull kitchen police. But I heard about it now. The three of them never made it clear which of them had been forced to pull KP, but they made it pretty damned clear that somebody was going to pay for a few smart-assed remarks that were thrown their way while they were doing their duty for God and Country!

They were planning some sort of secret mission to retaliate for the injustice done them. I told them that I didn't want any part of anything radical as I had already been in enough trouble recently, and the less I knew about what they were intending to do the better off I was. I said that I would help if they *really* needed me, but I would rather stay out of it.

The magic hour had arrived. The beer was about to flow! A large contingent of Lurps sallied forth to Patch Pockets's area to draw their allotment. This was a low point in my career as a fighting man in the U.S. Army. I was actually forced to thank the first shirt before he would turn over my beer ration. We all sat back like good little Lurps and sipped our beers while the movie played over the hum of the generator. A half hour later, I looked around and counted noses. It seemed that Jaybird, Keener, The Beaver, and a couple of the other Lurps were missing. I knew then that something was up and could hardly wait to find out what it was they were up to. The movie was bad, the beer was too warm, and I was still sober. I decided to go back to my bunk and crash, hoping that tomorrow would be a better day.

We turned out for the morning formation in full fatigue uniform. It was a new experience for us. We weren't used to a real morning formation or to wearing full uniforms. Most of us were wearing old, sun-bleached fatigues and gray, scuffed jungle boots. Vietnam had taken its toll on our clothing, our equipment, and us. Thank God it hadn't broken our spirit.

I couldn't help but notice the HHC Security Platoon and the brigade REMFs. They were definitely strac compared to us. Their clean fatigues and highly shined boots made them look like the top-notch garrison troops that they were. I fought to suppress a laugh when Patch Pockets arrived on the scene. Our fearless war-hero leader stood before us in a new set of starched, razor-creased jungle fatigues set off by the first pair of spit-shined boots any of us had run across since we had arrived in-country. The rest of the REMFs were merely strac; old Patch Pockets was textbook perfect—a career man's poster boy.

In spite of our own somewhat seedy appearance, I felt myself swell with pride as I looked around our platoon formation. We were definitely not pretty, but we possessed a certain noble military bearing that the rear-echelon units could not display on their best day. What soldiers! I felt blessed to be one of them.

Noticing a commotion at the back of the formation, I turned to see Jaybird and The Beaver snickering under their breath in the rear rank. I was a little puzzled at first; then I realized that the two of them were up to no good.

Suddenly, the mess sergeant came storming out of the mess hall, screaming at the top of his lungs. Spotting Patch Pockets, the squatty Puerto Rican made a beeline for our illustrious senior NCO and slid to a halt in front of him. From where we stood, we couldn't make out what he was saying, but the flailing arms and the tears running down his cheeks left little doubt that he was greatly upset about something. I looked back over my shoulder to see Jaybird, Keener, and The Beaver doubled over in laughter.

The HHC first shirt strode over to our formation and drew himself up in his best you-are-about-to-be-addressed-by-God pose. We couldn't help but notice that he was struggling valiantly to maintain his composure.

"Okay, men," he began, somewhat lamely. "Who is responsible for stealing today's meals from the mess hall?"

No fucking way! I thought as Patch Pockets stood there imposingly, actually expecting someone to confess to the crime.

So that's what they were up to! What a coup! The sons of bitches had actually cleaned out the mess hall, and right under the mess sergeant's nose. Beautiful! That was the stuff that legends were made of.

To the rear of the formation someone mumbled, *"Mickey Mouse!"*

That did it! Poor old Patch Pockets's eyes rolled back in his head. "You moldy bunch of foul, undignified bas . . . er . . . troopers!" he screamed. "Who did it?" That was all it took; the entire formation began to snicker.

He came completely unglued. "Okay, you . . . you . . . motherfuckers. Nobody screws with me!" he shouted.

The Lurps began laughing openly, taunting him. He began puffing, his face turned red, he stammered. Finally, he just shook his head, shrugged his shoulders, turned, and walked away in the direction of his tent.

A loud cheer went up from the assembled Lurps. We had challenged his authority and had broken it. Never again would he be able to pull his Mickey Mouse shit on the Lurps. Or so I thought.

Unfortunately, I didn't get to hang around and watch the REMFs enjoy their breakfast of cold C rats. Sergeant McKinnon showed up and ordered Eddie and me to report for trash detail. It could have been worse! Some of the other Lurps had been assigned to burn shit again, and a weeklong epidemic of Montezuma's revenge had guaranteed that all the barrels would be brimming. Funny, I wasn't even upset about being assigned to the trash detail. Our revenge on Patch Pockets had lifted my morale 300 percent.

Twenty minutes later, Eddie and I were hoisting fifty-five-gallon barrels of trash into the bed of a slow-moving deuce-and-a-half. The driver, a cocky Spec Four from headquarters company, kept smiling at us like he was really enjoying seeing us sweating over the barrels. I had had about all of the stupid Ipana demonstrations that I could take. "Fucker's dead meat!" I muttered to Eddie as I headed around toward the driver's side of the truck to drag his ass out into the dust of the road.

His patronizing smile changed to a look of surprise as he

saw me coming. He threw his hands up in front of him and shouted, "Limey, what the fuck's the matter with you? I didn't do anything. You're going to fuck this up, man. This is the best detail in the Nam."

I stopped and looked up at him as if he had lost all of his marbles or something. "Are you crazy? Sitting up there in the cab or that truck might be your idea of the best detail in the Nam, but hoofin' along back here behind you, throwin' these god-damned two-ton trash cans ain't my idea of coasting. Now come on down here, 'cause I'm going to kick your young, blond, California surfin', motherfuckin' ass all over this base camp."

He started laughing and said, "Hey, man, cool it! It's party time." I decided to grant him a temporary reprieve just on the slim chance that he knew what he was talking about. We quickly finished loading the trash barrels, climbed into the cab of the truck, and shot through the main gate with a brief wave to the MPs standing guard.

We drove swiftly through the Marine Corps' Mess Kit Repair area and onto the dirt road that ran down toward the garbage dump. About a klick outside the compound, we came upon an old hootch standing by itself. The driver slid to a stop, jumped out, and disappeared inside the hut. A few minutes later he came back out with a big smile on his face. He climbed up behind the wheel and tossed a slender cellophane envelope containing ten perfectly rolled joints onto my lap. The day was definitely looking up!

We continued on our merry way to the dump, smoking, toking, and joking. This was the first highlight of my stay in Chu Lai. By the time we arrived at the dump, the three of us were totally blitzed. From somewhere beyond the rings of Saturn, the thought reached me that I was in no shape to dispose of those cylindrical repositories of mankind's unwanted waste. Nor did I really give a damn! That was definitely some fine shit we were blowing!

As we stood there contemplating the mysteries of the universe, several Vietnamese suddenly appeared and began to unload the drums of trash. Eddie looked at me as if to say we were witnessing conclusive proof that there really was a God!

The villagers then dumped the barrels onto large sheets of flattened cardboard and began sifting through the trash with such intensity that my first impression was that they were looking for something they had lost.

When they had completed the unloading of all the barrels and had recycled their contents, they cleaned the drums and neatly stacked them back on the truck. I was impressed! The entire operation had taken less than thirty minutes. The driver had been right: this was indeed the best detail in Nam. I decided that I would try to convince McKinnon to keep me on that duty for the duration of the war. It was shitty work all right, but somebody had to do it.

Thirty minutes and two joints later, we were ready to head back to brigade headquarters. We had performed our duties to the best of our abilities. It was high time that we returned to the unit. If the VC came along now and captured us, I was pretty sure that they wouldn't have a very difficult time getting us to talk. Matter of fact, I doubted if they would be able to shut us up. If Patch Pockets ever found out about our activity, he would hang us high from the headquarters flagpole by our scrotums.

On the way back, the driver looked at us through glazed eyes and asked if we were hungry. We were not only starving, but we were also dying of thirst. Funny we hadn't noticed it before!

Not waiting for our answer, he grinned. "Great! Next stop— the Korean compound." I was beginning to like this guy, even if he was an REMF. Maybe he even knew where to find some women! If you find yourself in heaven, you might as well check out all the rooms!

We pulled to a stop in front of a quaint little Korean café. A middle-aged Korean appeared from out of nowhere and asked us in English if we were ready to order. We started out with some canned squid and a round of chilled bottles of Crown beer. I had never cared for Oriental beer before, but it tasted great that day. As a matter of fact, it was the best food and beer I had ever had. Man, was I fucked up!

A couple of ROK NCOs came over to our table and stood

looking us over as if they were trying to figure out how many pieces they were going to chop us into. Then they spotted our LRRP scrolls and it was Katie bar the door. ROKs ordered beers for us as quickly as we could down them.

An hour later, distant rumblings from deep in the pit of my stomach warned me that it was about time to call it quits. The three of us stumbled back to the truck for the short journey home. We were only about two miles from camp, but it seemed more like two hundred. When we drove through the main gate, an acrid, somewhat evil-smelling smoke greeted us. Trying to focus our bloodshot eyes through the free-running tears streaking our cheeks, we realized that some idiot on the shit-burning detail had evidently burned more than the shit—all of the crappers were aflame!

Obviously, there had to be a reasonable explanation for the burning shitters, but it would have to wait for a better time. I was in no mood to discuss anything intelligent—or intelligibly—with anyone. I climbed awkwardly down from the cab of the truck and staggered off in the general direction of my hootch. I had to get inside and wrap my pillow around my head before it exploded and killed somebody. The last thing I remembered was promising God that if he let me live through the hangover that was pounding my skull apart, I would never smo—never drin—well, I'd never eat squid again.

CHAPTER 31

We finally got a mission, but it was not what we were really looking for. Brigade was unable to furnish us with helicopters, so we were forced to run a short recon patrol outside the base camp; without adequate air support, it was impossible to operate in a long-range patrol capacity. For that reason, Lieutenant McIsaac requested a walk-off patrol so that we could get our feet wet in the new AO. He knew that morale was starting to sag a little because we were being used to do jobs that should have been going to the brigade's battalion recon units, such as Tiger Force, the Hawks, and Recondos. All any of us wanted was a legitimate long-range patrol. But that was not to be, so like a number of other Lurps, I volunteered for a heavy team that was being put together to run a patrol out of a firebase manned by units of the 2/327th.

We were flown out to the firebase early in the morning, and immediately discovered that the patrol had all the ingredients of a lousy mission. The firebase commander reported that they had been seeing lights down in the valley below their hill. He was becoming concerned about the safety of his camp and wanted someone to go down there and check it out. Since the battalion CO had already assigned the Hawk recon platoon to pull firebase security, the commander had no choice but to call in a recon unit from outside his own command. The Hawks, on the other hand, were really upset that we had shown up to do their job. The aggressive recon troopers were already bored with the role of security forces, and they were chomping at the bit to get down off the hill to find something to kill. Since we had been brought in to do just that, some of them were looking at us as if we were the enemy.

I was standing around shooting the bull with some of the Hawks when one of them warned me to watch my ass out there. When I asked him to be more specific, he told me that on the day before we arrived, the Hawks had pulled a close-in patrol a couple hundred meters into the jungle and had surprised and killed two trail watchers in the same area that we were going to pass through. The only time Charlie used trail watchers was when he had something to protect. This could mean a cache, a rally point, a hospital, or a base camp. We would soon find out.

We sat around waiting for our briefing. Two hours later found us still waiting. Finally, late in the morning, our team leader, Walt Bacek, was ordered to report to the FDC area.

Fifteen minutes later, he was back with the news. It was just as we had been told earlier—lights had been spotted down in the valley, and we would be going out to scout the area and set up an overnight ambush. So this was all about some stupid lights! It was okay that Charlie was out there, as long as he was in the dark. Hell, we were in a free-fire zone; why didn't the firebase commander give his redlegs some target practice, or call in an air strike? I would have guaranteed him that either response would have gotten the bad guys to turn off their lights.

We moved out early in the afternoon. We traveled at a forced-march pace the first five hundred meters across the open terrain, then slowed to a crawl after we entered the safety of the jungle. But Bacek soon whispered for our point man to pick up the pace. Our late departure from the firebase meant that we had to violate our own SOP if we were to get to the floor of the valley before dark. A short time later, we discovered a high-speed trail heading in the direction we wanted to move. We did the unpardonable and followed it.

I was pulling drag at the time, and following the rest of the team down that open trail soon had me sweating bullets. Even though I was being extremely cautious, I was getting some bad feelings about using the trail. I stopped every one hundred meters or so and let the rest of the team continue on without me. While they moved out, I would squat behind a tree or in some heavy vegetation to wait and watch for a few minutes. I would then hurry down the trail to catch up to the rest of the team, then turn around and do the same thing again. It was stressful and exhausting, but it would keep the patrol from getting surprised from behind. I continued the maneuver until the patrol suddenly stopped. When no explanation was passed down to us, I told Dave Walford to watch the rear while I went up to the front of the column to talk with Bacek. It didn't take long to find out why we had stopped. Directly ahead, the terrain opened up. We had come as far as we could without running the risk of being observed.

Bacek and McKinnon moved to the edge of the jungle to scope out the floor of the valley with their field glasses. Bacek signaled me to move up and handed me his binoculars, pointing at a specific area. He turned to talk with his ATL. After adjusting the focus, I plainly saw two Vietnamese bending over along a paddy dike, not ten meters away from a hootch. As I was watching, I suddenly saw a gigantic puff of smoke and witnessed the two Vietnamese being blown to bits, parts of their bodies flying in all directions.

When the smoke finally cleared, I could see that even the near side of the hootch had disappeared. I had either just witnessed the most accurate one-round artillery barrage ever, or two VC had been shredded in the premature detonation of a booby trap they were burying.

As the noise of the explosion reached us, it immediately got Bacek's attention. He retrieved his binos from me and stood up to scan the area below us. Two minutes later, he turned to me and said, "Where the fuck are those two dinks, Limey? Where in the hell did they go?"

I couldn't tell him a lie, so I whispered, "All over the fucking place, Walt—here, there, and everywhere." He shook his head and went back to eyeballing the area some more. I quietly told him that I was going to take Walford and move a couple hundred meters up our back trail to make sure we hadn't been followed. He nodded without taking his eyes from the field glasses.

Walford and I found good concealment a hundred meters from the team's location and set up surveillance on the trail. We remained motionless for over an hour, until we were satisfied that we had not been followed. Just before dark, we made our way back to the team, satisfied that our NDP was secure. When we reached the patrol, we found that they were already set up in a wagon-wheel perimeter. My position had already been designated between McKinnon and Lurch, and my rucksack was there waiting for me. Lurch told me that I had watch from 0300 to 0400. It was the easy watch because, at the end of it, I was supposed to wake up the rest of the team so we could observe the lights if they came on at their usual time. I pulled my poncho liner out and prepared to sack out for the night.

Just as I was about to doze off, I was startled by the most ungodly racket coming from Hines. I sat up to see him noisily pulling a section of canvas tarp out of his rucksack. I couldn't believe it!

"What's your fucking problem, Hines? You know better than that shit," I growled.

"Sorry, Limey, I didn't realize it was so noisy" was all that Hines could say. But instead of putting it away, he wrapped himself up in it and went directly to sleep. John was a cherry; I guess he didn't fully realize what a mistake he had made. I promised myself that I would burn that damn tarp at the first opportunity.

Suddenly, I was startled awake by the sound of gunfire coming into our perimeter. As green tracers crossed my chest and face, not more than a few inches away, I tried to screw myself into the ground. My only thought was, Please, God, let me get a shot off before I go. Begging God to help me kill someone before I died may not have been the wisest prayer I could have offered, but in the heat of battle He must have understood. He answered my prayer.

The gunfire stopped as suddenly as it had begun. I took advantage of the lull and grabbed for my grease gun. But instead of my trusty M-3, my hand closed on someone's ass. Yelling for whoever it was to get his ass off my fucking weapon, I heard Lurch mumble a hasty apology. As I grabbed my weapon, I heard McKinnon yell out that Hines had been hit. Seconds later, Wolfman added, "He's dead!"

I was stunned. "He can't be," I said. "Check again." But there was no mistake. Wolfman hesitated for a moment before shouting back, "Limey, he's dead."

I was trying to gather my thoughts when I heard the spoon fly off a fragmentation grenade. Oh no, I thought, don't do it. But it was already too late. Somebody was throwing grenades out from the perimeter, but we were sitting in the middle of double-canopy jungle! I grabbed my groin and curled into a ball as I heard the grenade ricochet off the trees. It exploded not more than twenty meters out from our position.

I heard another spoon fly and another grenade bounce off a tree. This one exploded a lot closer than the first, spraying shrapnel back over us. But cooler heads took over, and the excitement soon began to die down. Bacek ordered everyone to get ready for a "mad minute" on his command, and seconds later the night erupted as eleven weapons tore the living hell out of the jungle around our perimeter. Finally, screaming for a cease-fire, Bacek yelled for me to secure Hines's radio. I crawled over to his pack and attempted to pull his quick-release straps, but they wouldn't break loose. Taking out my knife, I dropped to my knees and sliced off the top flap on his rucksack. I passed Hines's radio over to Bacek, then crawled back to my position.

A short time later, lying on the ground facing out, I looked up and spotted movement to my front. I held my fire and whispered to Lurch that I could see them directly to our front. "Yeah, and they stink like shit, too" was Lurch's only reply. He was right, I could smell them, too.

I lay there waiting . . . no . . . hoping they would attack. Anything was better than just waiting. Anticipation was always worse than the actual battle. We knew that they probably had us surrounded.

I pulled extra ammunition from my pack and began reloading the two magazines I had fired during the mad minute. As I finished reloading the first, I began to wonder why they had not yet attacked. Could our mad minute have wiped them out or killed all their officers?

My thoughts were interrupted when Bacek yelled for us to keep our heads down. I was wondering what he knew that I didn't, when all of a sudden I heard the whistling of artillery rounds passing overhead. They impacted two hundred meters away. I knew what was coming next. Bacek began to walk the rounds back toward our perimeter. When he had them hitting about seventy-five meters away he called, "Cease fire, and mark." During the entire fire mission, I prayed that we wouldn't catch a short round. It was always a distinct possibility when you were sitting directly between the firing battery and the target (on the gun-target line). Then I realized what Bacek was doing: the redlegs had our position marked in case we needed another fire mission. This made me feel a hell of a lot better. Now, if Charlie had any intentions of overrunning us, he was going to pay dearly for it.

Trying to keep my mind off our predicament, I found myself bullshitting with Lurch about french fries and the land of the twenty-four-hour generator. I had resigned myself to the fact that we were going to be in for one hell of a firefight sometime before morning. All we had to do was to wait until Charlie got his shit together, and he would be coming.

About half an hour after Hines had been killed, Bacek whispered the command to prepare for another mad minute. It didn't take me long to burn up the two thirty-round magazines I had just loaded. I hoped a few of our rounds connected out there in the dark. Once again, I stared into the night as I thumbed rounds into the two empty magazines.

An hour and a half after our initial contact we were given the word that Hawk Recon was on its way to relieve us. That got me feeling better, until the Hawks radioed to request that we fire tracer ammunition into the air so they could locate our position. The problem with that idea was that we had already expended all of our tracers during the two mad minutes. Bacek told the Hawks to wait for daylight before coming down to us.

A short time later, we heard noises around our positions, then we noticed that the strong, rotten fish smell around us seemed to be dissipating. Soon the jungle was again quiet. The VC had pulled out of their positions.

At first light, the point element of the Hawk Recon Platoon reached our position. They had not seen or heard any enemy soldiers on their way down to us. Because of our artillery support and the Hawks' approaching, the VC decided that the odds were no longer in their favor.

As I stood up, I observed just how powerful my M-3 grease gun really was. Not a bush or limb had been left standing in front of my position. I had cleared away a perfect firing lane. Walford drew my attention to his rucksack. The top of the metal frame had nearly been cut away by small-arms fire. But he had been luckier than Hines. One round had hit John Hines in the upper left quadrant of his chest and had killed him instantly. There was no blood on his clothing or on the ground where he lay.

We wrapped Hines's body in the same tarp he had pulled out of his rucksack, and carried him out of the jungle to the nearest LZ. Ten minutes later, the helicopters arrived, and we were extracted. We were a somber group of Lurps on our way back to the compound. We had lost another brother on a humbug mission.

A CBS camera crew was waiting for us when we arrived back at Chu Lai. They were ready to use us as the latest dose of bullshit to force-feed the American public on the six o'clock news. Some longhaired asshole asked me where Hines's body was. *Big mistake!* I was furious. To him, John Hines was only a piece of dead meat to exploit for his own selfish motives. To me, he was a brother Lurp.

I didn't want to spend the rest of my days in Leavenworth for killing a civilian, so I swallowed hard and directed him to graves registration, telling him he could photograph all the dead bodies he needed there. Then I turned on my heel and went to my hootch to wait for Lurch to get back from delivering Hines's body to the morgue.

Lurch returned a short time later. I asked him for Hines's tarp. He told me that he had left it at graves registration. Hitching a ride over to the morgue, I recovered the tarp and burned it. While I watched the black smoke curl up toward the heavens, I whispered a silent prayer to Hines telling him I was sorry for being so rough on him over the tarp. It had been only his second mission.

CHAPTER 32

I was beginning to think the bullshit would never end. On two occasions, we had been given mission briefings, had cammied up, and were waiting at the helipad when we got word that the operation had been canceled. Each time, we returned to our compound to find that arrogant asshole, Patch Pockets, waiting to get some cheap shots in. Patch Pockets was becoming a bigger pain in the ass each day that passed. He had a bad attitude, and he didn't like Lurps. He was intent on making our lives miserable.

The benevolent headquarters first sergeant wanted nothing more than to give his pets from the brigade Security Platoon a break from their normally mundane rear-echelon duties. I guess life is pretty tough when all you've got to do is make formation, shine your boots, and kiss the first shirt's ass once a day.

Patch Pockets had decided that a dozen Lurps were to be volunteered for perimeter guard duty. Once again the fickle finger of fate sneaked up and smacked me right across the side of my head. Along with Cecena, Beiber, Magill, and Weisberger, I was directed to report to a perimeter bunker that would serve as our home for the night. It was worse than garrison duty. Here we were in a shitty sandbagged bunker, watching the perimeter, when we could have been in the bush or at the outside movie drinking a beer alongside our fellow Lurps. The pukes and rejects from the Security Platoon were at the movies. I was really pissed, and by the looks on the faces of the rest of the guys, I wasn't alone.

We were not the kind of people who stayed down for long,

and it didn't take too much imagination for us to come up with a plan to make our life a little more tolerable. Since we were on the perimeter, we decided to extend our area of responsibility to a ville approximately eight hundred meters to our front. We had decided that what we needed was beer.

It was pitch-dark by 2200 hours. There were no moon or stars out to give away our movements. Silently, we slipped through the perimeter wire, destination the nearby village. Outside the small village were no neon signs inviting conquering heroes in for drink and making merry. It was just pitch-darkness, along with an eerie silence. Creeping forward, we found the hootch that looked the most promising—it was the only one showing any signs of life. Candlelight could be seen from our vantage point. It seemed to almost beckon us forward. Beaver, Magill, and I entered the thatched hut but found only an old mamma-san sitting in the corner, cuddling a couple of scared kids and whispering quietly to them.

"Okay, Beaver, where's the bar?" I asked.

"Hell, I don't know," he replied. "How about you, Jaybird?"

We looked at Jaybird, who shrugged. We were eight hundred meters outside the perimeter in no-man's-land, and no one knew where we were going. To make things worse, we had not found any beer. The better part of valor was to withdraw to our guard post before we managed to get our asses shot off, or worse, by marauding dinks. Maybe an American ambush was out there, ready to waste anyone or anything that entered their kill zone. We realized we had really pulled a boner this time.

Gathering up the rest of our group, we started moving back toward the perimeter. But we soon became disoriented. We were not sure we were heading in the right direction when we suddenly spotted lights from inside the brigade perimeter. That solved one problem, but we didn't know what part of the perimeter we were moving up on.

Twenty-five meters ahead, the outline of a bunker could be seen. We didn't have any idea whose bunker it was, but we had to take a chance it was the one we were supposed to be manning. Moving forward, we were greeted by exploding hand flares. We yelled at the top of our lungs, *"Don't shoot. We're Americans!"*

Luck was with us. The guys manning that part of the perimeter were not trigger happy, nor were they overly surprised by movement outside their wire. We entered the position to find that the paratroopers from the 326th Engineer Battalion weren't too happy with us showing up in their wire. They directed a number of insults at our sanity. I ignored their remarks. I was just glad to be back on the inside of the wire. Our escapade could have gotten all of us shot. Thank God none of our team leaders had been around to see us acting like a bunch of amateur hikers.

Returning to our bunker, we tried to put together a good excuse for abandoning our position and leaving the perimeter unprotected in case the engineers ran off their mouths to the officer of the guard. We'd always had a good relationship with them, so the chances were slim that some loose lip would cause our demise. Nevertheless, we still had to come up with some kind of excuse, just in case. The best we could do on short notice was that we had all gone out looking for a lost comrade who had become disoriented while out taking a piss. We knew that it would never satisfy Patch Pockets, or anyone else for that matter.

With great apprehension, we slunk back to our area when daylight arrived and our guard mount came to an end. We really worried that our night sortie would result in our courts-martial, but to our great relief no one seemed the wiser. The engineers kept their mouths shut. You got to love them for their discretion! Thank God that their bunker had not been occupied by those rejects from the Security Platoon. I could hear them now: "First Sergeant! First Sergeant! I saw Lurps outside the wire last night." He would smile and say, "Thank you, troops. You're all good little boys, here's your candy bars." Eichelberger would then scream for the Lurps to report for another dose of ass-chewing and extra duty. It was a hell of a way to fight a war!

Relieved that we had escaped a just punishment, I stowed my gear and sat down to chat with Eddie Cecena. Our bullshit session was cut short minutes later when McKinnon came in and told me to report to Lieutenant McIsaac and Top Smith. Jesus, I thought, they must have found out about our trip to the ville.

I took my time walking down to the TOC tent. I was trying to come up with some excuse that would save me from the firing squad. I was one of the few Lurps who had not yet been caught committing some minor infraction. My record was clean. Much of that was due to my uncanny ability to sense trouble coming, giving me time to disappear before the shit hit the fan—unlike poor Rudy Lopez, who was always left holding the bag, even when he was totally innocent.

When I reported to Lieutenant McIsaac, Top Smith was standing off to the side. Neither man was smiling. I braced myself for the worst. But I was shocked when I discovered that El Tee and Top had called me down to inform me that they had submitted my name for promotion to E-5.

There were other Lurps more qualified for the stripes than I, but I figured that they had turned my name in because I had a better chance to receive the promotion with a full year and a half time in grade as an E-4. Transferring from the MPs to the Lurps had killed my chance at an early promotion, but my patience had caught up with me. The LRRP Detachment got only cast-off slots as they became available. The REMFs got all the promotions as they came down through headquarters to us. It was a shitty system, but it didn't do any good to complain.

Smugly satisfied with my good fortune, I unthinkingly broke one of my own cardinal rules: Thou shall not walk around the area during daylight hours. I was promptly nailed by the first sergeant, who informed me that I had just volunteered for trash detail and would drive the company deuce-and-a-half. When I asked him if he had contacted my team leader, McKinnon, he immediately read me the riot act, telling me that he didn't have to contact anyone to assign me to a work detail. When I tried to point out that I didn't have a military driver's license, he ordered me to shut up. In fact, the only vehicles I had ever driven had been a car and a jeep.

I had no trouble getting a couple of volunteers to join me on the work party. Trash detail was a puss job, and Wolfman Kraft and Eddie Cecena were only too happy to find an excuse to get out of the company area and go down to the Korean compound for some serious drinking.

Within an hour we—and our Vietnamese helpmates—had dumped the trash, cleaned out the cans, and were well into our first six-pack of beer at the ROK bar. The suds were flowing freely, and we were soon mellowed out enough to return to the company area. Since I had been appointed the designated driver by none other than Master Eichelberger himself, it was my job to get us back to the compound. I put the truck in gear, and leaving three or four pounds of gear in the roadway, I started back for the company area. In any state in America, I could have been convicted of driving under the influence.

Attempting to keep the truck centered somewhere between the ditches that bordered the sides of the road, I tried to content myself with the fact that if I wasn't killed on the way back, it would probably be my last detail. The promotion to E-5 would put me in the group that supervised only those shitty details.

As I approached the main gate, I saw the MP at the guard shack waving at me. Friendly cuss, I thought. I don't even know him! I thought it strange when, seconds later, I saw him dive to the side of the road and into the ditch. It was stranger still when splinters of white planking came flying over the cab of the truck. I think it was at that moment that I first realized I had just run over the guard shack. Thank God it was nighttime!

I drove on until I thought it was safe to stop, then woke Wolfman and Eddie and told them to get out of the truck so I could get it over to the motor pool. When I got there, I spent several precious moments trying to park it, then left it sitting in the roadway. I climbed down, and as I walked past the front of the truck I ripped my pants. Looking down at the front of the truck, I was shocked to see that large pieces of splintered wood and concertina wire had somehow entangled themselves around the bumper and in the grille. For the first time, I realized that my contact with the guard shack had been dead center.

I was in no mood to be apprehended, and in my physical

condition I couldn't be held responsible for my mouth or my actions. The best thing I could do would be to go crash somewhere and hope that things would look up in the morning. So that's exactly what I did. Sticking to the shadows, I made it back to our area without getting caught. As I infiltrated our area, I made sure that none of Patch Pockets's REMF lifer buddies saw me. When I finally stumbled across an empty cot in somebody's tent, I immediately passed out.

The morning found me once again nursing a one-thousand-pound headache, and my mouth tasted like it had been used as the litter box for the Vietnamese National Water Buffalo Foundation. I was one sick and sore Lurp. I would have welcomed Death with open arms, if only I could have lifted them.

I went in search of Wolfman Kraft, my friend and medic. I knew that he could help me. After a couple of Darvon and a cold beer, I began to feel better. I told Wolfman that we needed an excuse for the previous night's incident, only to draw a blank stare in return. He shook his head and told me that he didn't have any idea what I was talking about.

I gave up on Wolfman and returned to my tent to locate Eddie Cecena, but he was still sleeping off his own drunk. Somewhat depressed, I realized that I was going to have to face Patch Pockets alone.

My mind didn't seem to be functioning properly, and I couldn't seem to come up with any excuse that sounded remotely plausible. Claiming that the truck had been stolen wouldn't cut the mustard, because whoever had taken it would never have returned it to the motor pool after driving over the MP shack at the main gate. Besides, there was a witness. The MP had managed to jump out of the way before I took out his shack, and I was sure that he was still around and willing to tell his story.

I had no idea what I was going to say, except that being British I wasn't used to driving on the right side of the road. So resigning myself to the fact that I was screwed and tattooed any way I looked at it, I decided to go ahead down to the first sergeant's lair and turn myself in before he came looking for me—sort of throw myself on the mercy of the court kinda thing.

But at the last minute, I decided that if there was a will, there was a way. Thank God for American clichés! As I passed near the MP tents, I stopped to look up my old friend, Sweet Pea. I spotted him standing in a doorway smiling at me. He didn't say a word, just winked and ducked back inside his hootch. Was it a sign that the MPs were covering for me? After all, they didn't like Eichelberger either. And without a witness, Patch Pockets had no proof it had been me behind the wheel of the truck.

The first sergeant had a smug look on his face when I entered his hootch. Apparently he had been waiting for me to show up. My mind was racing a mile a minute, trying to formulate a last-minute plan of attack. A good Lurp always took the initiative.

"Okay, Specialist Walker, what do you have to say for yourself?" the first sergeant demanded, his nostrils flaring in contempt.

"What do you mean, First Sergeant?" I responded. "I thought you sent for me."

"The truck, Walker, the fucking truck! You were driving the truck, weren't you?" he bellowed.

"Why no, First Sergeant, don't you remember? I told you yesterday I didn't have a driver's license," I stated simply, acting surprised that he didn't recall.

He hesitated, taking his eyes off me as he searched his memory for a replay of our encounter the previous day. When he began to speak again, all the bluster was gone as he stammered and stuttered, a little lost for words. At that moment I knew I had him. He couldn't remember.

Glaring at me in anger and confusion, he asked, "Well, who was driving the truck during the trash detail?"

"Hell, I don't know, First Sergeant," I mumbled. "I was so drunk I don't remember nothing."

By now he was furious, and he ordered me out of his tent. To throw a little fuel on the fire, I asked, "Oh, First Sergeant, do you know if my promotion came through?"

"Get the fuck out of my quarters, Walker!" Patch Pockets screamed at the top of his lungs.

I backed out of his hootch and headed back to the LRRP compound, ignoring the crowd of headquarters types who had gathered around in anticipation of my execution.

Totally exhausted by my ordeal, I downed a quick beer and went to my hootch to get some sleep. This time it came easily, and I slept like a baby.

Sometime in the early afternoon, I was shaken awake and told to report to the first sergeant. God, would this shit never end? I told myself not to antagonize Patch Pockets more than I already had. I would just take whatever ranting and raving he threw at me, and then quietly leave when he was finished. I found him outside his hootch with a smile on his face. The hair on the back of my neck stiffened immediately. He had to be up to something—the crusty old son of a bitch never smiled.

I was disarmed by his friendly bearing as I approached him, and was totally surprised when he apologized for being somewhat rude during our morning meeting. He then said that he would be unable to promote me because of a clerical error— my MOS was still listed as 95B, Military Police. It had not yet been changed to 11F2P, Infantry Intelligence (Airborne). Well, that was okay with me. It was only money!

"Look, Walker," he said. "I like your spunk. If you volunteer for the Security Platoon, I'll make sure you get your promotion."

I was stunned by this attempt to get me in his grasp. "First Sergeant, I'd rather be a fucking private E-1 in LRRPs than a sergeant E-5 in Security Platoon," I responded without taking time to weigh the impact of my words. He gave me a look that promised he would try to see that I got my wish.

That was the end of the conversation. He didn't say another word, and I didn't hang around long enough to give him the chance to. There was little doubt that I had made an enemy at brigade headquarters.

CHAPTER 33

Beer was getting pretty scarce around the LRRP compound, and the first sergeant was really enjoying his role as the local bartender. Since he had taken control of our stash of booze, it forced us to treat him with more civility than he deserved. Even I was forced to greet him with a smile and a cheery "hello" when I passed him. He loved it. I hated it. Of course, under my breath I still had the personal satisfaction of telling him exactly what a wonderful person he really was—for a low-down rotten prick.

Anyway, after a few days of suffering through this degrading treatment at the hands of our Headquarters & Headquarters Company ranking NCO, some of the team leaders held a secret strategy meeting to decide how this problem could be remedied. After all, the consumption of beer was a right that we as grown men and courageous warriors had earned. None of us needed an overweight, balding, REMF first sergeant treating us like a troop of Boy Scouts.

I watched with great interest as Weems and Bacek left the meeting, only to return a little later with a starlight scope and a pair of field glasses. Then they all piled into the Lurpmobile and drove out of the brigade area.

Upset at not being invited along, I got in line at the supply tent and drew my two-beer allotment for the day. I then headed over to where the REMFs showed movies each evening. I watched ten minutes of a movie I had already seen twice in Chu Lai, once in Duc Pho, once in Phan Rang, and God knows how many times in Cam Ranh, then gave up and returned to my tent, hoping to find a book to read. I finally fell asleep, reading a rat-eared Zane Grey novel I had finished two months before.

To this day, I'm not sure if it was some subconscious sixth sense or Bacek's bad breath in my face that woke me out of a sound sleep, but I sprang awake to find Walt standing over me. "Come on, Limey," he whispered, "help us unload the truck."

Putting on my boots, I quickly joined Bacek and some other guys outside next to the tarp-covered Lurpmobile. Pulling the cover back over the bed of the three-quarter-ton truck, we were all overjoyed to see the gifts that Weems and Bacek had returned with. The vehicle was loaded to the brim with beer and soda.

"How much shit did you get, Ronnie?" I asked Sergeant Weems.

"Hell, I don't know. Just start unloading the truck before Patch Pockets sees us."

For over an hour, we quietly unloaded the truck as we alternated turns watching for anyone coming from the HHC area. The final count was over 150 cases of Budweiser and Miller, and about 60 cases of assorted sodas. Our trusty team leaders had found a new supplier. For the past few days, some of us had noticed that they had not been around much. No one had really given that much thought; we assumed that they were just goofing off somewhere. In reality, they had been pulling a reconnaissance of the Marine Corps supply dump.

When they had left earlier in the evening with the starlight scope and the field glasses, they had gone back to the supply dump and timed the routes of the armed Marine sentries as they walked their posts. Satisfied that they had the jarhead routine down pat, they then cut a path through the wire and removed the beverages to the Lurpmobile, one case at a time. The entire operation had taken less than four hours.

The giant cooler in the detachment area was now well stocked with a generous supply of beer and soda, thanks to our enterprising team leaders. Soon it would be full of fresh ice, and we would be back in business.

Early the next morning, we were awakened with the news that three teams would be receiving a warning order for a mission. Since my team leader, Sergeant Bob McKinnon, was away at MACV Recondo School in Nha Trang, I knew that the only way I would get back out in the field was for one of the selected teams to come up short a man. But I was even more disappointed when I found out later that the three-team mission had been scrubbed, and a single team would be going out with Lieutenant McIsaac filling in for its missing team member. Even El Tee was getting tired of all the bullshit in the rear.

With Lieutenant McIsaac going out on patrol and Top Smith in Nha Trang doing whatever senior NCOs do in the rear, it seemed as if the rest of us were now at the mercy of Patch Pockets. I particularly felt as if someone had painted a bull's-eye on my back and Eichelberger was about to use it for target practice.

The remainder of the day proved uneventful as we watched our comrades depart for a five-day mission into the bush. Patch Pockets had managed to make himself scarce for the day, lulling us into a false sense of security and leading me to commit another boner.

Magill and I had loaded our personal red-and-white cooler to the brim with cold beer from our private stash. But not being satisfied, we decided to get into the first sergeant's beer line to claim our daily allotment. We had plenty already, but it didn't seem right to let those four extra cans of brew go unclaimed. Everything probably would have been all right except that after we picked up our allotment we sort of hammered it up a little and made a big show out of trying to get those four extra cans of beer into our already-full cooler. Unable to find enough room in the cooler, we finally put the four cans in the cargo pockets of our pants and started to walk off. I could feel the first sergeant's eyes boring holes in my back as we left the beer garden. I *was* feeling pretty smug, but at the same time, I realized that I had probably gone a little too far. After all, Eichelberger had the army on his side; I had only my fellow Lurps.

Later, at the movies, I wasn't paying much attention to the film but was busy trying to down my share of the beer while trying to participate in the general bullshit session. Pizza Joe Remiro got up and headed in the direction of the shitters. Before too long he returned, got another beer, and sat down to join in the small talk. A few minutes later, Patch Pockets materialized in the middle of our group. Suddenly he was just there. He didn't say anything; he didn't have to. His eyes were shouting at us. Grinding and gnashing his teeth, his eyes darted from one Lurp to the next, as if he were searching for someone to vent his pent-up rage upon. Almost as if it was planned, everyone present returned to their beer and conversation as if the sudden appearance of Patch Pockets in our midst was nothing more than an unwelcome but unimportant apparition. Eichelberger stood fuming for ten or fifteen *lonnnnnng* seconds, just to show us that he was still in authority, then he turned and stomped off to lifer land. Uttering a silent prayer that I wouldn't turn into a pillar of salt, I cast a furtive glance over my shoulder and saw a large, red, smoking stain on the back of Patch Pockets's jungle shirt—I swear to God.

Hoping he could provide an answer, my questioning look at Pizza Joe was quickly returned by a big, shit-eating grin. The culprit was at hand!

After the movie, we strolled nonchalantly back to the detachment area, but not before stopping off at the latrines to deposit recycled pilsner in the piss tubes. It was then that I discovered why Patch Pockets had nearly gone into convulsions when he had joined us at the Bijou. Off to the side of the common-soldiers community drain field, the Headquarters & Headquarters Company first sergeant's private personal one-holer sat covered with bright scarlet dust, the remnants of one well-placed MIA "Smoke Grenade, Red." Eichelberger had been given *the* message by someone (don't ask me who!). The "dye" had been cast. He could do only one of two things now—either back off or get tougher on us. Personally, I expected him to choose the latter, because the dumb bastard didn't have enough sense to take a hint.

It didn't take him long to prove me right. The next morning I was selected for sandbag detail, a longtime favorite among us Lurps. I guess I realized that someone had to do it, but why did I have to qualify as somebody? There just wasn't anyone else left to perform this demeaning chore. I knew the guys in the

Security Platoon couldn't do it since they were on some kind of alert. Alert to do "what" I didn't have a clue, but if it was to go into combat, then the war was lost!

Anyway, I did my duty, filling a mountain of sandbags while maintaining a pretty good attitude about the whole detail. I filled and stacked sandbags all day, not realizing that the eyes of old Patch Pockets followed my every move. Finally, something penetrated my self-induced euphoria, and I sensed that someone had me in a radar-lock. I turned around to find Eichelberger squint-raping me.

"Walker, take off your floppy hat and put on a baseball cap," he roared.

I didn't say anything, I just looked at him and ignored his command.

"Walker, I just gave you an order," he screamed, loud enough for everyone in the entire province to hear.

"The only way I'll take off my floppy hat is if Top Smith or Lieutenant McIsaac says it's no longer part of our uniform," I countered.

The first sergeant's response floored me. "You're no longer in LRRPs, Walker. Sergeant Smith no longer wants you in his unit."

I didn't believe it. I knew the big asshole was lying, but I had no choice but to obey his order, since El Tee was out on patrol, and Top Smith and McKinnon were both at Nha Trang. I went back to my tent and donned the hated OD baseball cap, the head covering made famous by three million leg REMFs.

I spent the remainder of the day totally dejected as I continued filling and stacking sandbags. On occasion, some of my buddies would come by and offer their condolences, usually punctuated with degrading comments about how "REMFy" I looked with the cute cap on my head. But not even their encouragement could help me. I was stuck in this hole I had dug for myself until Top Smith returned to the detachment and bailed me out.

I was unofficially detached from the Lurps for a little over twenty-four hours before my rescue occurred. I was on my second day of sandbag duty when Top Smith returned to the

LRRP compound. It didn't take him long to find me and ask why I had "quit" the Lurps. When I told him that I hadn't quit, that I was told that he had thrown me out, I was given the best order I was ever to receive in my entire military career.

"Limey, you're a Lurp until I personally say you're not or you just plain quit. Now, get rid of that ridiculous baseball cap and put your floppy back on."

Suddenly elated, I wasted no time in transitioning from REMF to LRRP, and reported back to my detail. I probably could have avoided returning to the sandbagging detail, but I couldn't pass up the opportunity to get a final dig at Patch Pockets. It didn't take long.

"Walker, you're disobeying a lawful order by wearing that unauthorized hat. You're no longer a Lurp. I can have you shot!" (Well, maybe he didn't actually threaten to have me shot!)

Casually ignoring him once again, I cast a glance toward the LRRP compound and spotted Top Smith standing there with his arms folded across his chest, watching.

"Go tell that to Top Smith, First Sergeant," I answered, grinning from ear to ear and pointing toward my boss.

Glancing back over his shoulder, Eichelberger spotted Top Smith. With a snarl, he spun around with a look of disgust on his face (or was it . . . "a look on his disgusting face"?), then turned around and left.

Top Smith came over and dismissed me from the detail, then followed after First Sergeant Eichelberger. I had the feeling that Patch Pockets had pushed his luck too far, especially by using Top Smith to promote a lie. Top Smith was not the type of man to create a disturbance, but even a man with a kindly disposition cannot be trifled with too far.

An hour later, Top Smith returned and asked me if I had tossed the smoke grenade into Eichelberger's shitter. I was quick to respond, "Why no, Top, I didn't even think about it."

"Too bad," he replied as he turned and walked away.

That night, we listened with pleasure as our S-2, Major Geecey, screamed and hollered at someone over at the head shed. There was a general feeling of ecstasy all around, knowing that the recipient of this royal ass-chewing was First Sergeant Eichelberger. I had never realized that majors in the United States Army were capable of such profane and vulgar language.

CHAPTER 34

We were still laughing and joking about the royal ass-chewing old Patch Pockets had received from Major Geecey when Top Smith stepped into the hootch and told me to get my ruck packed for a mission. My first thought was that Top was trying to find a way to get me out of Dodge until the dust settled. Patch Pockets was undoubtedly mad, and it was no great secret that he would give two-thirds of his chevrons to see me spread-eagled high over the camp's main gate.

Two of our teams had been scheduled to go in on a 2/502d Infantry Battalion firebase, then do some walk-off missions outside the wire. This wasn't our favorite type of operation, but almost anything was better than playing brain tag with a company full of headquarters personnel.

My team inserted early that afternoon and spent the next couple of hours visiting and shooting the bull with the redlegs manning the big guns on the tiny firebase. None of us really knew for sure exactly what we were supposed to be doing. Apparently, no one in the position to know had bothered to pass us "the word."

As we were preparing to slip out through the wire, some half-cocked artillery officer, I think he was a major, walked up and asked us what we were doing on his firebase. As usual, I let my mouth overload my brain and responded with a "Fuck if I know, sir. We're still waiting for an operations briefing."

The major gave me an incredulous look that bordered somewhere between shock and constipation, then turned on his heel and stomped away. I saw him stop, just before entering the FDC bunker, and turn and look back at me like he was trying to remember my face from some previous encounter.

A short time later, when an E-4 cannoneer walked over, I discovered that it wasn't my face the major thought he recognized, it was my accent. The E-4 grinned when he told me that the major was the same officer whom I had popped off to over the air during a recent fire mission. At that time, the good major had attempted to remove a rather large portion of my posterior for using improper radio procedure. He had been unsuccessful in locating the source of his irritation at the time, but hearing my voice again had gotten him thinking. My newfound friend warned me that the disgruntled officer still wasn't sure about me, but the incident had gotten him back on track. All in all, I sensed that it was a good time to make myself scarce until we got off the firebase.

Finally, after waiting in the hot sun for two hours, the firebase commander called our team leaders, Sergeants Bacek and Weems, in for the mission briefing and told them why we were needed by the 2/502d Infantry. The Recondos, the "Oh-deuce's" reconnaissance platoon, were already outside the wire running short-range patrols in the jungles east of the firebase. Their battalion commander wanted us to recon the bush west of the camp to ascertain whether the NVA were out there somewhere massing for a surprise attack on the perimeter. There had been no indication that such an event was about to occur, but the firebase commander's advanced case of terminal paranoia demanded the assurance that only continuous patrolling would provide.

Under Bacek, our team would move out first, to be followed an hour later by Weems and his LRRPs. The plan was for us to do a hasty reconnaissance of the selected patrol area and then move on while the other team moved in behind us to fine-tooth-comb the area we had just scouted. Or to look at it in another way, we were the bait and Weems and company were to be the cavalry in case we ran into Indians. Sounded like a wonderful plan—especially if you were in the cavalry.

None of us was overly enthused. Brigade Lurps had an enviable record for *not* walking into ambushes while out on patrol, and there was little chance now that we were going to blunder down a wide trail into a waiting VC/NVA ambush just so Charlie could get in a little target practice before our reaction force arrived on the scene to claim a big body count. Each of us was aware of the scuttlebutt coming down from S-2 that PAVN HQ had recently put a healthy bounty on the heads of Lurps killed or captured. We had already decided that no VC/NVA was going to get his rice farm and retirement pension at our expense.

The team leaders moved us off by ourselves and designated a couple of guys to keep their eyes open while the rest of us kicked back and relaxed a little. The infantry company stationed at the firebase was tasked with perimeter security, but our team leaders thought it wise to have a couple of our people keeping an alert eye out too. We were well rested and fresh, but the poor grunts had been busting their asses digging defensive positions, filling sandbags, and stacking ammo, and all of this after a night of standing 50 percent alert. There was no way the line doggies could pull additional guard duty without dozing off. It never ceased to amaze us how the officers who commanded them never realized how insane it was to push the troops until they dropped during the day, and then expect them to be alert and ready to do combat at night.

I had just dozed off in the comfortable warmth of the afternoon sun when the big guns in the center of the firebase opened up. Shocked out of my stupor and a year's growth, I grabbed for my weapon and leaped to my feet, expecting to be met by hordes of NVA pouring through the wire. Seeing no tracers flying my way and that no one around me was jumping into action, I realized that we were not under attack. As I rubbed the sleep from my eyes, a few of my comrades were bitching and moaning about the noise the big guns were making. I countered that the noise was probably a hell of a lot noisier on the receiving end of those outgoing rounds.

After fifteen or twenty minutes, the guns grew silent. By then fully awake, I was unable to go back to sleep, so I went over to the nearest gun pit to find out what the redlegs were blasting away at. They told me that they were shooting H & I (harassment and interdiction fire). H & I was designed to keep the enemy on his toes and to let him know that we were still thinking about him. To me, it seemed that we were wasting a lot of taxpayers' dollars, blowing holes in the jungle and wasting ammunition that could be better used helping some line unit up to its ass in screaming gooks. It was especially irritating when we were on a mission and found out that our fire support was restricted because of a shortage of artillery rounds.

We ended up spending the night inside the firebase; the major decided that it would be better for us to go out in the morning after a hearty breakfast and a good night's sleep.

We arose at first light, downed hot C-rat coffee and a LRRP ration, then quickly cammoed up and moved off the hill into the surrounding jungle. We were elated to escape the redlegs' rustic "civilization" and get back out into an environment we were more comfortable in.

Out in the bush, we had little problem finding signs of the enemy's presence in the area. Numerous trails everywhere showed recent use. Intersecting paths and secondary trails criss-crossed through the dense vegetation west of the firebase. They fed into an elaborate system of well-camouflaged high-speed trails.

This was not the heavy triple-canopy jungle that we had patrolled in the Song Ve Valley, but it was a very close second. It was impossible to parallel a trail without quickly running into another one running perpendicular to the first. None of us had seen anything like that before.

Bacek decided to take a westerly track along a narrow path that veered away from a major high-speed trail. It wasn't long before we began to find the devastation wrought by artillery and air strikes. Each time we ran into one of those areas, we had to stop and cover each other until we cleared the brush-littered openings and reached the cover of the jungle on the other side.

We encountered our first VC just before noon. We were moving cautiously along a well-worn footpath when the point man spotted a dead enemy soldier lying on the high side of the trail. Bacek moved past the point man to check the corpse for booby traps. When he was finished, he moved back to where the rest of the team knelt waiting. He dropped to one knee beside me and whispered in my ear, "Limey, give me one of your smoke grenades." I pulled a yellow one from my web gear and handed it to him, then watched as he unscrewed the fuse and placed it on the ground at his feet. He then repeated the process with a frag grenade and interchanged the two fuses: he now had a smoke grenade with a five-second-delay fuse and a frag that would detonate the second after the spoon was released.

Pointing at the dead VC, Bacek grinned and whispered, "Look under the fucker's right leg." I craned my neck to see around him, then noticed the stick handle of a ChiCom grenade showing from just beneath the dead man's knee. The bastards had booby-trapped their own dead.

Bacek told me to lift up the corpse's shoulder while he cautiously pulled the pin on the altered frag and wedged it under his back. When this was done, I slowly lowered the dead man's shoulder onto the spoon as Bacek slid his hand out. I fully expected the grenade to go off and kill both of us, but Bacek had done this too many times before. Now when the enemy finally decided that their little booby trap hadn't caught any unwary GIs, and they returned to bury their dead comrade, they would discover that two could play their little game. A classic example of "you fuck with us, we'll fuck with you."

Bacek pulled the team thirty feet from the trail and set up an OP so that we could observe the body. We wanted to be there when the fun started.

An hour later, the body smelled a little too ripe, so we quietly withdrew another thirty feet to where the odor wasn't quite as strong.

Two more hours passed and the gooks still hadn't shown. Our sister team radioed that they were approaching our location. After we linked up, Bacek told Weems to remain there and watch the body while we moved on ahead. The looks on the faces of the other Lurps, especially Jaybird Magill, were an indication that Bacek hadn't given them an assignment they relished. The nearly visible aroma of the rotting corpse had permeated our little perimeter.

We moved out for another couple of hours before deciding to call it a day. So far, except for the dead dink, the mission had been nothing but a lazy walk in the woods. We hadn't seen any fresh sign of the enemy, but we knew that the dead VC had to have some buddies out there somewhere. He hadn't booby-trapped his own body. I spent my first watch thinking about the sorry-assed place we had been assigned to. It hadn't made a lot of sense to any of us as to why the brigade had been pulled out of its old AO and then dumped into the TAOs (tactical areas of operations) of the Americal Division and the First Marine Division. What could an Airborne brigade accomplish that two infantry divisions couldn't handle?

The next morning, I skipped breakfast. I could still smell the sickening aroma of the dead VC. I wasn't sure if the odor had permeated my clothing or if it had just left a lasting impression on my senses. I just knew that a beef and rice LRRP ration didn't have a snowball's chance in hell of finding a welcome home in my stomach.

Before we could move out on patrol, somebody from the 502d radioed and told us to remain in position. After a few minutes, he radioed back and ordered us to move to an LZ for extraction. A line company was preparing to sweep through the area we had covered the day before in hopes of flushing out some of the resident VC. The news created a bit of a dilemma for us, since we couldn't very well warn them about our doubly booby-trapped friend back there on the trail without informing any VC/NVA radio operator who might be eavesdropping.

Our sister team had already reached the LZ and was waiting to be extracted. As luck would have it, only one slick was available to extract both teams. Since the other team was already at the LZ, they would be picked up first.

Hoping that our haste would not lead us into an ambush, we gathered our gear and began a forced march back to where we had left the booby-trapped gook. When we arrived less than an hour later, sweating and gasping for air, we took a break in the middle of the trail before moving up to remove the booby traps. The sickening odor was everywhere and smelled worse than Patch Pockets's personal latrine. The dead soldier's corpse was blackened and grotesquely bloated. If it were a banana, it would have been six days too overripe to eat. The aroma of the gasses of decomposition had been trapped under the overhead vegetation and saturated the entire area. Rodents had discovered the body and dropped in for lunch. I was glad that I hadn't forced down breakfast that morning, because I was quite certain that if I had, it would have been spraying the jungle claymore-fashion right about then.

Bacek looked back over his shoulder and whispered to me, "Limey, we're going to blow the booby traps. Get your rope and tie it to the dink's arm. When I tell you to give it a yank, you pull, okay?"

The look on my face surely must have read go fuck yourself, Sarge, but Bacek didn't seem to notice. He pointed down the trail and whispered a little louder this time, "Do it." It was the closest I ever came to hearing him issue a direct order to anyone, so I knew for certain that he was dead serious.

I slowly removed the coiled fifty-foot section of green nylon rope from my ruck and carefully approached the body. Holding my breath to keep from gagging, I tied the trailing end of the rope to the dead VC's left arm. I couldn't help but notice the maggots that had set up residence in the dead man's eye sockets. My stomach was doing cartwheels as I retreated back to where the rest of the team sat waiting alongside the trail. They were all grinning! I wasn't. I dropped to one knee next to Bacek and handed him the end of the rope. He solemnly shook his head and whispered, "No way, Limey! It's your rope, so he's your dink." With that he turned and moved the rest of the team back up the trail in the direction whence we had come, and left me standing there like a dummy with the rope in my hand.

I turned and backed about forty feet down the trail, as far from the body as I could get and still hold on to the rope, then squatted behind the biggest tree I could reach and gave a mighty pull. The next thing I knew, I was falling backward down a steep incline, with the rope still clutched in my hand. I finally stopped rolling when the base of a large tree got in my way.

I lay there momentarily stunned, wondering what the hell had happened and why I had not heard the double explosions of the two grenades going off. I looked up and spotted Bacek standing out on the trail, his hands over his mouth suppressing his laughter. Real fucking funny! I quickly worked up one real bad case of the ass as I scrambled back up the slope to where he stood. I had every intention of freaking out on him when I spotted the detached arm suspended in the bushes at the edge of the trail. Tied to the grisly appendage was the other end of my rope.

Bacek looked at me and whispered, "Limey, I think you must have pulled a little too hard!" He clutched his stomach and doubled over in uncontrolled laughter.

My anger escaped me as the humor of the whole damned scenario suddenly became apparent. I held up my end of the rope and grinned like an idiot.

We had less than thirty minutes to go before the chopper returned to extract our team, and we still had to get rid of the booby traps. Bacek moved up beside me and whispered, "Fuck it, Limey, shoot the damned body with your blooper. What's another explosion more or less?" With that he turned and walked back down the trail away from the body.

I picked up my ruck and lugged it about forty meters down the trail to where the rest of the team had set up security. I set it down and pulled the sawed-off M-79 from its scabbard on the side of my ruck, dropped an HE (high explosive) round into the chamber, and turned to take aim. Since I had removed the sights on the M-79, "taking aim" meant pointing the weapon in the general direction of the target. I must have been blessed by the gods, because I had never before hit anything I had aimed at on the first shot. The round hit the dink dead center and exploded as I dove for cover behind a cluster of trees lining the trail. As I scurried on my hands and knees through the under-brush, I heard two more distinct detonations.

The adventure, I thought, was finally over. I started to crawl back to the trail to grab my rucksack and haul ass with the rest of the team, when I heard Bacek order the others to move back into the brush along the trail in case the dead VC's comrades showed up to investigate the source of the explosions. After all, it's basic human nature to return to your trapline to see if you've been successful. Dinks are no less curious than we.

A short time later, Bacek was on the radio talking with our slick pilot when a single VC showed up, bobbing and weaving as he checked each side of the trail. Walt had been right when he'd assumed the enemy would probably send someone to check on the explosions.

When I spotted the enemy soldier moving toward us, I silently slipped the safety cover from over the bolt on the receiver of my weapon, pressed the trigger, and slowly moved the bolt back-ward to the cocked position. When I let the trigger go, the bolt stayed in position. My grease gun was now ready to fire on the still-unsuspecting VC.

I watched through squinted eyes as the enemy soldier swung his SKS carbine from side to side as he checked out everything in sight. He was being overly cautious, but his problem was that the six of us were not quite in his line of sight. Bacek slowly pointed at me and motioned that I was to take him out. I made a mental note to remember to talk with Walt about his finger-pointing after we got back to the base camp.

When the VC was within twenty feet, I let go with a slow burst of five rounds from the grease gun. The heavy .45-caliber slugs hit the man across the upper chest. He staggered back and collapsed to the ground.

I know that the whole thing took only a couple of seconds, but it seemed like several minutes as it slowly replayed on the monitor of my brain. I broke from cover and snatched up the SKS as Bacek yelled for us to move out. The chopper was already airborne and less than five minutes away.

We sprinted down the trail for about fifty meters, then turned sharply into one of the bombed-out areas we had crossed the day before. Somebody tossed a smoke grenade into the clearing, just as the Huey cleared the top of the trees. As we sprinted for the hovering slick, both door gunners began to yell at us and waved for us to hurry up.

We dove through the open doors of the cabin as the door gunners began firing into the jungle. No one bothered to ask what they were firing at because none of us really cared to know. I still had the captured SKS carbine that I had taken from the VC I had killed, and that was all that mattered to me at the moment.

When the chopper set down in the center of the firebase, we were greeted by the same redleg major who had eye-fucked me the day before. He promptly took the SKS from me with the explanation that he would see to it that it went directly to the division museum back at Fort Campbell, Kentucky.

Yeah, you bet, Major! Mine and about fifteen hundred others that you fucking REMF officers stole from the poor line doggies who risked their lives capturing them. There was no doubt in my mind that this damned officer would hang my souvenir SKS over his mantel back in the World and spend his retirement telling both of his friends how he, in mortal combat, had wrestled the weapon from the hands of some drug-crazed Commie colonel who was about to take the life of some famous American general. Well, fuck him! There were more souvenir SKSs where that one came from. I would just have to get another one and make sure that I hid it from the admiring eyes of the lifer pigs in the rear.

In addition to my losing the SKS, the guys on my team began razzing me about the body count I had gotten. They felt that I should also count body parts in my final tally.

After several more days of trudging around the firebase in search of the elusive VC, our mission was scrubbed by the commanding officer of the 2/502d, who decided that he would rather have his own infantrymen pulling platoon sweeps in the jungle surrounding the firebase. He just couldn't quite understand how a couple of six-man LRRP teams could cover enough ground to locate the hordes of enemy soldiers he knew were waiting out there to attack his troops. It was fine by us, except we knew that we would have to go back to HHC and into the clutches of Patch Pockets.

As the choppers arrived to ferry us back to the base camp, Jaybird yelled, "Okay, guys, let's shake a leg. Everyone except you, Limey! You can shake an arm." Everyone got a good laugh at my expense. It was a sick remark, but those were sick times.

When we landed back at Chu Lai, it was already late in the day. Everyone was too damned tired and disgusted to make the trip to the showers before evening mess. So we did the unpardonable and got into the chow line smelling like the sclf-dcprccating assholes that we were. Wc had viewed some strange sights during our Vietnam experiences, but never before had any of us witnessed an entire company of headquarters personnel step back to permit a couple of LRRP teams to move ahead of them in the chow line. That was indeed a "first"!

Just when we were beginning to appreciate the newfound respect that the REMFs had suddenly developed for us recon men, good old Patch Pockets walked up and screamed, *"You stinking goddamned people get out of my mess hall, right fucking now. Clean up, take a shower, change your clothes, and . . . and . . . shine your boots! Now, move out!"*

We backed out and left the mess hall, mumbling under our breath. Sure, we probably did stink a little! So goddamned what! Shit, you can't spend an entire week fucking around in the steaming jungle, playing with dead bodies, and living like a wild animal without smelling like Mother Nature. That's what they paid us for! We didn't smell that much worse than the mess sergeant's cooking. It didn't mean nothin'! Besides, LRRP rations were a helluva lot better than old army chow anyhow. It was obvious that good old Eichelberger was heading for a complete nervous breakdown and seemed hell-bent on taking a few of us along for the ride.

CHAPTER 35

I was sitting on my bunk, engrossed in James Bond's latest effort to extricate himself from another sticky situation, when Doc Neihuser stepped in and interrupted my train of thought. "Hey, Limey, I needed to talk to you about Sully."

"This had better be important, Danny. Double-oh-seven's got his ass hangin' out to dry, and I want to see how he gets himself out of this one," I said as I bent down a corner of the page to mark my place, then tossed the book on my cot.

Doc spent the next five minutes telling me about the Dear John letter that Sully had just received from his girl. He felt that the brokenhearted Lurp was pretty freaked out over it and might do something stupid.

I was having a difficult time relating to how anyone could get that upset over a love breakup. But then, my only personal romances had always been of the wham-bam, thank you, ma'am type, which hardly qualified me to judge. After realizing that Sully's emotional trauma could be dangerous to both himself and the rest of the team, I decided that I would talk to him and see if I could offer any help. If a shoulder to cry on was what he needed, then I would make mine available.

A short time later, I entered Sully's tent and found him sitting on the side of his cot. His head was bowed, and the Dear John was crumpled in his hand. He didn't bother to look up as I stood waiting at the end of his bunk.

"Feel like talking, Sully?" I asked, hoping that he would get up and throw me out of his tent. I really didn't have any idea what I was going to say next.

It seemed like minutes passed before he looked up and started talking about his girl. Once he began, I thought he would never stop. It just kept pouring out. By the time he had run out of things to say, I knew everything about every date the two of them had gone out on from grade school through high school. The guy was really in bad shape, trying to make sense of the end of so many great memories.

It took all my self-restraint to keep from calling his former girlfriend a bitch or something worse, but I knew that if I did, I would find myself in some deep shit with Sully long before I cleared the door of his hootch. The loss was too recent, the pain was too great. So I just stood there like some great mute toad, inflating my cheeks to say something intelligent, but I accomplished nothing more than a series of halfhearted tongue thrusts. Then Sully told me about his recent premonition of death. I had never before heard anyone forecast his own demise with such intense conviction. There was little doubt in my mind that he would survive his tour.

When the shock of his revelation wore off, I finally rediscovered my voice. "Sully, you stupid son of a bitch, you're just screwy because your fuckin' girl dumped you. Man, you're better off without her. All they do is give you something else to worry about. You asshole, you and I have only got six weeks left in-country. We just need to play it safe, and we'll be ridin' that old Freedom Bird back to the World."

Now, it wasn't very often that old Limey put that many sentences together without stopping to let the other person take over the conversation, and I had just about talked myself into believing that I was doing some good, when Sully stood up and said, "Limey, the more bullshit you throw at me, the more convinced I am that I'm going to die. No amount of talking is going to change my mind." The premonition was just too real. By then, I was getting a little frustrated over where the conversation was going, so I told Sully to stay put and that I would be right back.

As I double-timed across the detachment area, I mulled over a plan that was coming together somewhere in the unused portion of my brain. I knew that Sully had a bad case of jungle rot on his feet. I reasoned that if it was bad enough, maybe Lurch could bench him for the rest of the game. With less than two months left in his tour, it wouldn't take more than a two- or three-week profile to keep him from ever going out on another mission. I was determined to keep Sully out of the field until his DEROS, and I was beginning to feel pretty damned proud of myself. My good buddy was no longer an asset to his team. He had just become a liability. He was a risk to himself and to those around him. Besides, the last thing in the world I wanted now was to lose a friend so close to going home.

Finding Lurch was never a problem; I had only to locate the beer supply, and the oversize, blond Lurp was sure to be in the area. Sure enough, he was next to the cooler. "Limey, sit down and take a load off your mind. Have a brew!" he said, offering me a cold beer from the chilled box.

Nodding my gratitude as I opened the can, I asked, "Hey, Lurch, how's Sully's jungle rot coming along? Ya think he'll be able to go out again?"

He took a deep swallow, belched loudly, and answered, "Hell, Limey, he'll be lucky to pass a DEROS physical with his fucked-up feet! Why do you ask?"

I faked disinterest and said, "Oh nothing! I was just wondering. Thanks for the beer." I made a quick exit. His response had put me at ease. It was not necessary for him to know my reason.

Full of good cheer, I returned to Sully's tent to tell him the good news. He was sitting where I had left him. Sully now had a big smile plastered across his face. I was mystified! He looked up and said, "Look, Limey, just forget what I said. I was just feeling sorry for myself. You were right, I'm probably better off without her."

I'd made a lot of stupid purchases in my life, but I wasn't buying any of what Sully was trying to sell. There were only two people in the brigade Lurps that you could make book on—Top Smith and Sully. I knew a con job when I heard one, and I was listening to one then. "Okay, man, but you know I'm gonna have to tell El Tee about this shit, don't you?"

I knew when I said it that it was the wrong thing to say, but diplomacy had never been a real strong point with me. Sully stood up and stepped toward me, fists clenched at his sides. I could do little more than brace for the clash. He stopped two feet away, jabbed his index finger through my breastbone, and yelled, "Look, you bastard, you ain't tellin' El Tee or anybody else about any premonition. I was just pullin' your leg. It don't mean nothin', Limey!"

I took a step back to get out of killing distance of his finger and started to calm him down when none other than Lieutenant McIsaac walked in and joined our little war party. It was obvious that he had overheard the shouting, because he immediately asked, "What's the problem here?"

I knew that I was now fully spread-eagled between the rock and the hard place. I wanted to help a friend who didn't want my help. Now I had to avoid giving the wrong explanation to a commanding officer who wanted the right story.

"No problem, Lieutenant, I just don't understand how you guys can get so emotional over a silly-assed game called baseball. Cricket or rugby I can understand, but fucking baseball!" With that, I turned around and shagged ass, leaving El Tee and Sully looking at each other in total astonishment. In my heart, I knew that I should have told Lieutenant McIsaac about Sully's problem, but there was no damn way that I could abandon the trust that Sully had always shown me.

I didn't have much time to cry in my beer as the word got out that we had a mission coming up. We would be going out in detachment strength, so we knew it wasn't a recon mission. They told us not to be concerned with our rucks but to make sure that we drew extra ammo and frags. It sounded like another raid. Of course, it could just as easily have been another well-thought-out humbug assignment from the brigade S-2 think tank. Either way, I was looking forward to getting into some type of contact. The recent walk-off missions had been real drags, so if we kicked a little ass, there might be a chance that brigade would cut loose with some of its choppers and assign us a few real LRRP missions.

A short while later, a bunch of us were piling on the Lurp-mobile for the trip down to the helipad when El Tee walked over and told me that I was to stay in the rear to pick up a batch of cherries who were scheduled to arrive the next afternoon. He wanted me to bring them out to 1/327, the firebase where the rest of the detachment would be waiting. I wasn't really happy with the assignment, but I realized that if I could duck old Patch Pockets for the remainder of the day, I would have a cooler full of beer to share with Rudy Lopez and the commo section that evening.

Early the next afternoon, two newbies reported with orders assigning them to the detachment. I wasted little time squaring them away before getting Rudy to drive the three of us out to the helipad. During the short trip, I discovered that it was getting a helluva lot tougher to find replacements for the Lurps. "What unit are you guys from?" I asked.

They looked at each other a little confused. The taller of the two answered, "B Company, 3d of the 325th, 82d Airborne."

Holy fuck! These guys were FNGs (fucking new guys) right off the plane. It looked like we were going back to square one, the way things had been when I had joined the unit, with one minor exception—back then most of the newbies had at least three months in-country and had seen a little action before coming to the Lurps. They probably meant well by volunteering, but undoubtedly they didn't know their ass from a bomb crater. I asked them if they had zeroed their weapons yet and was met with a couple of blank stares. It was going to be a long day!

I took them over to the ammo bunker and made sure that their magazines had rounds in them. Lieutenant McIsaac would have my balls if I brought these two former all-Americans out to Indian country with no real bullets in their guns.

A short time later, the three of us were climbing onto a Huey for the thirty-minute ride out to the 1/327th firebase. I watched with a certain amount of detachment as the two new recruits prodded each other and pointed out the aircraft at various sights of interest to their innocent curiosity. I muttered a silent prayer that they would be around long enough for those sights to become commonplace.

The chopper reached the firebase and circled once before spiraling down to land on the PSP helipad. I motioned for the two cherries to follow me as I unassed the chopper and headed across the perimeter to join the Lurps I had spotted milling around outside the wire on the north side of the firebase.

I ran into Eddie halfway between the chopper pad and the perimeter wire. He moved in alongside and began filling me in on what I had missed while I was slopping suds with Rudy back in Chu Lai.

"Limey, did you ever fuck up this time!" he announced as we neared the edge of the firebase. "You should have stayed back in the rear. Charlie mortars this fucking place every afternoon. So far they haven't hit the perimeter, but we expect a visit at any time, maybe tonight!"

Great, I thought as I looked around for Sully. All I needed was a chance to get my young ass blown away defending somebody else's base camp.

"Where's Sullens?" I asked as we reached the exit through the perimeter wire. Eddie pointed toward a sandbagged position a few meters away. With the cherries in tow, I went over to where my friend sat lounging in his fighting hole. I had every intention of chewing his ass out for not staying back in the rear where he belonged, but my heart wasn't in it when he looked up and grinned at me.

"What the fuck are you doing here, Sully?" I asked halfheartedly as I dropped into the hole next to him.

"I'm here to kill dinks. The same as you, Limey. Say a word to El Tee, and we're through, you hear me?" he said, the grin still spread across his face.

I nodded. "Sure, man, I understand. I won't say a thing. Just keep your fucking head down." I patted Sully on the side of the face and climbed out of the hole to lead the newbies over to where Lieutenant McIsaac stood talking on the radio.

"What was that all about?" one of the cherries asked as he sped up to walk alongside me.

"None of your fucking business," I snapped. I had a bad feeling, a feeling like I hadn't had since Jeep had gotten hit back at Duc Pho.

I dropped the recruits off at El Tee's position, but I didn't stay around to shoot the breeze, fearing that I would drop a dime on Sully. Instead, I went over to Eddie's position to get the scoop on the mortar fire that he had told me about earlier. When he saw me coming, he got out of his bunker and grabbed my arm. "C'mon, Limey, it's beer time! Follow me."

We walked across the perimeter to where a line of soldiers was already beginning to form. It was obvious that the 1/327th had a battalion commander who cared about his troops enough to make sure that they caught their two-daily beer ration—even in the bush. We stood in line, making sure to stay five meters apart, while we waited to get our two cans of beer apiece. Eddie kept glancing nervously at his watch as if they were going to stop issuing the brew at a certain time. After we picked up our ration, we made our way back to his bunker. I sat down on top of the fighting position and started to open my first can when I noticed that Eddie had dropped down between the sandbags and was motioning for me to join him. I was just about to ask him why when I heard someone across the perimeter yell *"Incoming!"* Like a moron I just stood there, looking out to the front to see if I could spot the flash of the rounds leaving the tube. The loud *karoomf!* of the first round impacting behind me at the crest of the hill convinced me that mortar barrages were not meant to be a spectator sport; I dove headlong into the protective cover of Eddie's bunker.

The rounds were going overhead and impacting across the high ground in the center of the firebase. It was obvious that they were after the 105s and the ammo bunkers. With my rear end at max pucker, I closed my eyes and prayed silently for the barrage to stop.

The chatter of an M-60 opening up on my right and the distant *ploomf* of an M-79 going off to my left brought me back to reality. Holy shit, we're under ground attack! I thought as I rose up to deal with the massed red hordes coming through the wire. It was only our guys shooting at the unseen enemy out of frustration—sort of an unofficial mad minute.

I took a deep breath as the last of the mortar rounds exploded behind me. Looking back toward the center of the firebase, I could see a lot of activity near the artillery positions. I heard the screams of several wounded men and could hear someone yelling for a medic. Smoke and dust were saturating the area.

I directed my attention back to the front, expecting the VC to follow up their mortar barrage with a ground attack at any minute, but it appeared that they were only maintaining their regularly scheduled shelling. It was a full thirty minutes before the first of the dust-off choppers landed.

I found out later that the FDC had taken a direct hit—there were no survivors.

My mouth was dry as I lit a cigarette and sipped my now warm beer in silence. A few minutes later, Eddie announced, "Just like yesterday, they hit us at 1600 hours."

I thought they were kidding before. "You mean this is SOP? They hit at the same time before?"

Eddie nodded and replied, "According to the redlegs, this shit is a daily occurrence."

At first, I was amazed at how lucky we had been, then I realized how fucking stupid it was for a battalion commanding officer to issue the beer ration in the middle of the afternoon each day when he knew Charlie was dropping in for drinks at about the same time. If Chuck decided to show up fifteen minutes early, he would blow the hell out of half the firebase defenders. Combat was no place for creatures of habit!

We spent that night on 50 percent alert. I doubt seriously if any of the brigade Lurps slept at all. We were too used to being out in the bush, where it was safe. Mortars were too impersonal for recon men. They had a way of making us sleep with our eyes and ears open. We had at least one thing in common with the VC—they didn't want us up on that hill, and we didn't want to be there. Surely, there had to be some way we could reach an agreement!

All night long, the ground beneath us shook from the outgoing rounds of our own artillery. They were firing H & I (harassment and interdiction) to keep Charlie from moving about freely through the jungle. I'm sure that we killed more animals than enemy soldiers, and I'd bet that we lost more sleep than Charlie did.

When the sun finally popped up, the H & I fire ceased, and a contingent of bleary-eyed Lurps surfaced from their holes to boil water for early-morning coffee.

All we wanted was to get on with our mission so we could get off the firebase. None of us liked the idea of spending another day dead-centered in the middle of a VC firing range. We had never received a mission briefing, and to my knowledge, none of us had the vaguest idea what we were doing out there. As usual, we were the last to find out.

Lieutenant McIsaac finally gathered the detachment together to tell us what was coming down the pike. The first thing out of his mouth was "Limey, you and the two new men will stay here on the firebase as radio relay." I was stunned at the thought of having to remain behind in the relative safety (ha!) of the firebase with two greenhorns while my buddies were out visiting death and destruction on our enemies. It just wasn't fair! Rather than make an issue out of it in front of my fellow Lurps, I just turned and walked away while El Tee briefed the rest of the unit.

The briefing took less than five minutes. As the guys broke up and returned to their positions to get ready, I went back to Lieutenant McIsaac for an explanation of why I had been singled out to baby-sit the newbies while he and the rest of the detachment got to go out and play with our neighbors. I had been on every detachment-size operation we had been on to date, and I was curious as to what I had done to piss him off.

"Well, Limey, I've got two good reasons for assigning you to radio delay. First, you're one of the best RTOs I've got. Second, we're going in as a blocking force for a line company, and our position is going to be nearly two hundred meters across an open area from a wood line. If we make contact, it will come from there. With that grease gun you're carrying, you couldn't hit the Russian embassy at that distance."

He made a lot of sense, but I was already prepared to be flexible. "Look, El Tee, I'm not the best RTO in the unit. As far as the grease gun goes, I can trade it for one of the 16s the new guys are carrying." But argument was useless! No amount of talking on my part was going to change the CO's decisions.

I felt the anger rising in me as my fellow Lurps loaded into choppers and flew off to set up a blocking position. I could do little more than watch and pray that everything would turn out okay.

As the noise of the chopper faded in the distance, I sat down on the sandbags lining the edge of the bunker and lit up a cigarette. I turned on the radio and set the proper frequency. The two FNGs walked up and asked me what I wanted them to do. I looked up at them, blamed them silently for my present situation, and told them to go fuck off and leave me alone. It was not my finest hour! The two confused young soldiers sulked off, wondering what they had done to incur the wrath of that crazy motherfucker in the commo bunker, but at that particular instant, I really didn't give a shit what anyone thought.

Fifty minutes later, my radio began crackling with traffic. I could hear our Lurps in contact. A short time passed, then they radioed in to request a medevac. Two minutes later, I was called to relay a message to Chu Lai. I took out my pen and pad and radioed back that I was prepared to copy. I nearly went into shock when the message read that the unit had taken a Dogwood 5 (WIA) and a Dogwood 6 (KIA). I waited impatiently as Lieutenant McIsaac gave me the phonetic spelling of the Dogwood 5. "The Dogwood 5, I spell B-I-N-G-S-T-O-N. The Dogwood 6, I spell S-U-L-L-E-N-S. How copy, over!"

I asked him for verification, hoping that if he gave it again, the name would change. It didn't. I repeated the message back to him, then fought back the tears as I relayed it on to Chu Lai. Fighting to control my voice, I radioed Lieutenant McIsaac, requesting permission to be inserted with the new men as I saw a chopper revving up over at the FDC. He quickly radioed back that permission was denied, and all that I could do was to sit back and listen as the detachment continued its mission. A sense of helplessness tore at my soul.

It seemed like forever before the VC broke contact and the detachment was extracted and we were picked up for the long ride back to Chu Lai. Everyone on the chopper was in a foul mood over the casualties we had suffered. I felt guilty that I had somehow let the unit down by not being there when the fighting was going on, and I was especially upset with Lieutenant

McIsaac for not allowing me to go out on the operation in the first place. But just before we landed, I realized that I was most upset with myself for not informing El Tee of Sully's premonition two days before when there was still time to do something about it.

When we landed at Chu Lai, I found a few Lurps still hanging around the chopper pad and asked them to fill me in on what had happened out there in the bush. They told me that the unit had moved into its blocking zone while the line company was making its sweep. Within the hour, there was heavy enemy movement in the clearing in front of the Lurps' position. The detachment put down a heavy volume of fire, which devastated the enemy ranks.

Lieutenant McIsaac ordered the Lurps to advance as the surviving enemy soldiers withdrew toward the wood line. The detachment moved out on line in pursuit of the fleeing VC and were met by a volley of automatic-weapons fire from the wood line two hundred meters away. Sullens and Bingston were hit in the initial burst of fire and fell to the ground. The remainder of the Lurps put out a tremendous volume of suppressive fire as Sergeant Rey Martinez and Wolfman Kraft went to Sully's assistance. The two Lurps dragged him over to the protection of the paddy dike in order to give him first aid, but it was futile! Sully had been struck numerous times in the chest and had evidently been killed instantly. There was little either one of them could do to save him.

Bingston had been struck in the throat and had been lucky to have fallen near Lurch. The big medic and Boss Weisberger dragged him to cover, where Lurch was able to open his airway with a tracheotomy and get him quickly plugged into a can of serum albumin. A medevac chopper arrived on the scene in a matter of minutes to carry Bingston to a surgical hospital in Chu Lai. Lurch said that he was sure the wounded Lurp would make it.

It was a sad day indeed as the Lurps took their fifth KIA since arriving in-country. The worst thing about the loss of Sully was that it was on another goddamned humbug. We were recon soldiers! Every time they sent us out to do someone else's job, we ended up losing someone. This time it was a good friend. But who was I trying to fool? It wasn't anyone else's fault that Sully was dead. It was mine!

For the first time in my life, I knew what it was to feel the heavy burden of guilt. I felt it crushing me to the ground. I was hurt, bitter, angry, but worst of all, I was to blame for Sully's death. If I had only let El Tee know about the damned premonition, Sully would still be alive today. Stupid, Limey, stupid, stupid! If there was any way I could've turned back time, I would have gladly traded places with him. Oh God, how I wished I could do it all over again! Sully, wherever you are, forgive me, buddy!

CHAPTER 36

Our team integrity had gone to hell after our arrival in Chu Lai. Some of the guys were off at Recondo School in Nha Trang, others were away on R & R, and a number were injured or sick, so we had to put together teams from scratch on a daily basis. I wasn't too happy with MACV for canceling all Recondo classes for the month of October and blowing my chance to go. Now here it was November, and I still hadn't gotten the opportunity to attend. With the number of guys ahead of me, it was beginning to look like I would never get a slot.

I was lucky to have Bob McKinnon as my team leader again, but the rest of the makeshift patrol were guys borrowed from other teams. This mix 'n' match patrol consisted of Mc-Kinnon, TL; me and Gene Ackerson, RTOs; Frank Shanley and Eddie Cecena, scouts; Lurch Cornett, the team medic.

McKinnon came by my hootch and told me to follow him to

the premission briefing. When I asked him why he wanted me there, he informed me that I was to be his ATL on this patrol. That was okay with me, but I doubted I was the best man for the job. I loved being a Lurp, but I didn't want the full responsibility for the entire team's safety. I could only hope that McKinnon would not get greased.

When we walked into the TOC, I followed McKinnon's lead and took out a notebook and a pencil to jot down notes. Before long, McKinnon was the only one taking down the information. I was so totally wound up in the information we were getting that I forgot to write it down.

We were told that an entire NVA regiment was hiding somewhere in our RZ. Our mission was to locate it and keep tabs on its activities, i.e., we were to find the dudes, then follow them around to see what they were up to.

McKinnon was taking all this in stride, but I was trying real hard not to swallow my tongue. I don't know if S-2 was intentionally trying to put the fear of the Lord in us, but as far as I was concerned, I was going to find a chaplain as soon as the briefing was over. With a month to go on my tour, and the recent losses of Hines and Sullens, baby-sitting an eight-hundred-man NVA regiment was not high on my list of last-minute things to do. Hell, the entire LRRP detachment wouldn't stack up in a fight with an NVA regiment. We would just have to make damn sure that we didn't get spotted. But I kept thinking about something a wise old deer hunter from Indiana used to tell me—sometimes you eat the bear, and sometimes the bear eats you. For the first time in my life, I knew exactly what he meant.

After the briefing, we went back to the team. Neither of us said a word, until I suddenly began to laugh.

"What the fuck is your problem, Limey? This mission ain't funny. It's already scaring the living shit outta me," McKinnon complained as he scratched his head.

I looked him straight in the eyes and answered, "Yeah, me too. You wanna quit?" McKinnon smiled. Hell, everybody took the same chances.

We turned to the team and gave them the lowdown on the

briefing. They took it with a grain of salt. After spending fifteen minutes going over everything, we broke up to get our gear ready for the patrol. I made a beeline to Winston's hootch to bum his shotgun one more time. I was hoping he had picked up a couple hundred rounds of double-0 buckshot, but he said that he had only a dozen rounds left. He tried to explain how he had used up a couple dozen shells in a recent firefight. Sounded like a great war story, but I didn't have the time or the mind-set to listen. So I passed on the shotgun and returned to my hootch for my sawed-off M-79 and a bunch of canister rounds. I had to dump some weight, so I got rid of all the cans of C rations in my ruck and replaced them with dehydrated LRRP rations. The thought of leaving behind my cans of fruit cocktail, peaches, and other goodies brought tears to my eyes, but firing canister rounds would protect my ass better than throwing cans of fruit.

I was in the middle of rearranging my ruck when McKinnon gave me some more good news. He told me that he had to go down to brigade to take care of some business, so I would have to do the overflight. Well, if I was ever going to get my NCO stripes, I would have to get some of this stuff under my belt.

I reported to the flight line with my weapon and a couple of bandoliers of ammo. The only chopper was a Huey slick sitting there with a 1st Cavalry insignia emblazoned on the nose. Unaware that the 1st Cav was in our AO, I waited around the helipad, hoping that someone would notice me. It wasn't too long before a PFC crewman came up to me and asked if I was a 101st Lurp. When I nodded, he told me to follow him.

A short while later, I was looking down from one thousand feet up, courtesy of the 1st Air Cav. I was wearing a set of headphones so I could converse with the pilot to explain exactly what kind of LZ I was looking for. Scanning back and forth between the map on my lap and the ground below, I explained over the intercom that I didn't want any LZ that looked man-made. Nor did I want any clearing large enough to handle more than one Huey at a time. We soon located one covered with elephant grass, about a hundred meters from the trees. It would serve our needs perfectly. We would have concealment while we lay dog immediately after the insertion, and we'd only be a short hump from the protection afforded by the jungle.

I returned from the overflight, convinced that the mission was off to a good start. McKinnon seemed satisfied with my selection of LZ, which gave me some much-needed self-confidence. I decided to retire to my hootch to get some sleep before the big day.

Sleep came hard that night, but I managed to get three or four hours before the sun came up. I dressed and went down to the mess hall for a cup of coffee. A big mistake; I had to dump the strong-tasting mess hall joe, and went back to my hootch to brew up some good C-rat coffee.

Soon, the rest of the team arrived and moved in to form a circle. We drank coffee for an hour and shot shit about things in general. We seldom talked about an upcoming patrol. It was almost as if we feared that if we talked about it, we would jinx the whole mission. Even Ackerson, who was going out on his cherry mission, soon got into the mood. He didn't ask any of the cherry questions that we all knew he was dying to ask—and we were dying to avoid.

I didn't eat anything at all that day for fear that a nervous stomach would have me wanting to scrape a cat hole minutes after the insertion—when I couldn't. The thought of humping the boonies for five days with my pants full of shit didn't appeal to me at all.

We finally broke up to get our gear and put on our cammo, after which we would meet at the flight line. It was time for the last-minute rituals, private affairs that enabled us to leave our fears and anxieties in our footlockers. And allowed us to psych ourselves up to do what had to be done.

When we reassembled at the helipad, the chopper was waiting, its engines warmed up and ready to go. Within seconds, we were airborne for a tiny clearing in the jungle, forty miles from Chu Lai, near the Laotian border.

I cringed involuntarily as the Huey made the final approach over the AO. The aircraft flared over the LZ as the pilot slowed to a hover ten feet above the elephant grass. When the door gunner gave us the signal to unass the ship, I thought he must have been nuts. We were ten feet above elephant grass that was probably fifteen feet high, and he wanted us to dive out with seventy-pound rucksacks on our backs. When the door gunner yelled for us to either get out or abort the mission, McKinnon made the choice to go. As Lurps are taught to do, we followed him down.

I hit the ground with enough force that I was temporarily knocked unconscious. When I came to, I felt like my ankles were rubbing my armpits. If the enemy had picked that very moment to attack, we would all have been in some very deep doo-doo.

I looked around for the rest of the team and saw that they were in no better shape than I was. It took nearly ten minutes to triage our injuries and get ourselves put back together. Ten minutes later, we formed a ragged perimeter and lay dog listening for sounds of the enemy. Somewhere back in the jungle, I thought I heard laughter.

Just before we moved out on patrol, Ackerson turned to me and whispered, "Limey, if this is a normal insertion, you can all kiss my ass good-bye, 'cause I'm outta here when and if we ever get back."

Ackerson's remark caused me to grin in spite of the pain from my compressed spine. The helicopter crew was probably making its first Lurp insertion. I couldn't help but confirm the new guy's irrational fears. "No, Gene, this ain't a normal insert. We usually do it from about forty feet. SOP is thirty knots for the drop-off," I whispered back. I think he thought I was serious.

We waited fifteen minutes longer, then moved out. Within an hour, we were deep in the jungle, where we stopped for another break. We checked in with the relay site to confirm that we still had commo, then slowly moved out again.

Shanley took point, with Cecena at slack, as we patrolled through the area at a cautious pace, looking for anything that would pinpoint the NVA regiment. Shanley finally called a halt and signaled for McKinnon to move up to the point. The rest of us automatically took up a 360-degree security posture. Cornett, at drag, covered the rear as Ackerson and I took the flanks and Cecena the front.

McKinnon finally moved down to where I was watching the jungle on the left and whispered, "Okay, Limey, we got a problem." He hesitated to let that sink in, then added, "We're either in or on the outskirts of a dink base camp. You stay here with Cecena and Lurch and be ready to call in a fire mission to cover our withdrawal if the shit hits the fan; got it?"

I tried to keep the anxiety out of my voice as I replied with a smile, "Sure, Bob. Do you have our coordinates, by any chance? Be careful, I don't want to get to be a team leader by default."

McKinnon, Shanley, and Ackerson cautiously patrolled ahead into the enemy base camp. It seemed like an eternity before they all returned in one piece. They said that the base camp was old and had been abandoned. Much relieved, we moved carefully through the enemy camp, being careful not to leave any sign of our passage. The interior of the camp was surrounded by a ring of defensive bunkers facing out, and a large number of spider holes were located next to trees in the next defensive ring. It would have been suicide for an infantry unit to attempt an assault on the camp. Every bunker and spider hole had interconnecting fields of fire.

We passed through the encampment and continued on for perhaps another three hundred meters before finding a suitable place to take a break. We had covered nearly eight hundred meters in less than three hours. We took turns putting out claymores, then ate our evening meal before settling in for the night. I was given last watch, so I wasted no time wrapping up in my poncho liner and going to sleep.

It seemed like only minutes had passed before I was shaken gently awake. I stuck my head under my poncho liner and eyeballed my watch, only to discover it had indeed been just a few minutes since I had gone to sleep. Then I felt McKinnon's breath in my ear. "Limey," he whispered, "we're in deep trouble. Brigade just called and said an air force surveillance plane just reported that a large enemy concentration is heading right for us."

McKinnon put the team on a 50 percent alert, i.e., three men were awake at all times. But the rest of the night proved uneventful until about 0500 hours, when the entire team was awake. It was right after that that we heard the enemy troops entering the valley below us. I noticed two things about them immediately. Number one, they were practicing absolutely *no* noise discipline; number two, there was one hell of a bunch of them.

We were just below the summit of the mountain. The enemy soldiers were down in the valley below us. We could easily hear their equipment banging and incessant yakking.

McKinnon was arguing with someone on Ackerson's radio. Even though McKinnon never raised his voice once, the grimace on his face made an explanation unnecessary. S-2 wanted some visible proof. Listening to a couple hundred enemy soldiers passing us just wasn't enough.

"Well, here's the scoop," McKinnon finally offered. "S-2 has ordered us to saddle up and move down into the valley to see if we can put a unit ID on those dinks below. They also want an accurate body count and some information on the type of equipment they're carrying."

I started repacking my rucksack, hoping that any minute McKinnon was going to announce that his message had been a big joke. No such luck. Within fifteen minutes, we were making our way down the mountain toward the enemy soldiers massed in the valley below. The closer we got, the more tense we got. Finally, Shanley called a halt to our march and sent for McKinnon to move up to the front of the patrol.

When McKinnon returned to his place in the patrol, he was immediately on the horn reporting that we had beaucoup NVA regulars just thirty meters away. I half expected McKinnon to get off the radio and tell us that S-2 had just ordered us to attack the enemy and keep them pinned down until S-2 could get a squad of CIDGs in to pile on! But the next words out of McKinnon's mouth were music to my ears. He said, "Back up slowly, we're getting the fuck out of here, pronto. We have thirty minutes to get to an LZ on top of the mountain to get extracted."

Now, I don't mean to bitch and sound ungrateful, but we had just taken an hour coming down the mountain to the spot where we were standing. How in the hell did they expect us to go back up that steep mountain to our original NDP in only thirty minutes? Well, it wasn't going to happen with us standing around bitching.

We backed cautiously uphill until we thought we were outside of the enemy's hearing, then we pulled a Jesse Owens and sprinted all the way to the top. I had no idea I could run nearly a full klick up the side of a cliff with half the weight of a full-grown man on my back. But like the rest of my teammates, I was inspired. We didn't quite reach the top, but we came damned close. We were still two hundred meters from an LZ when McKinnon got on the radio and told the pilot to make his final approach. If it was the same pilot who had flunked our insertion three days before, he had sure learned some valuable pointers about flying Lurps. This guy got a big A+ on the extraction.

The chopper touched down just as we were coming out of the bush. There was less than ten feet of open space between its blade tips and the edge of the jungle. We piled on, and within seconds, were on our way back to Chu Lai and a cold beer.

When we were dismounting at Chu Lai after our deliverance, I overheard Ackerson asking McKinnon if all LRRP missions were as hairy as this one. McKinnon laughed and said, "No, normally they're a lot worse than this."

We'd had a lot of newbies quit the LRRPs in the past during their first briefing. Some waited until after their very first mission. But Gene Ackerson stayed on with the unit, and before long, he was just as nuts as the rest of us. The old-timers used to say that one mission doesn't make a Lurp. It's having the intestinal fortitude to keep coming back for more that makes a soldier a true long-range recon patroller. Some people have it, some don't. Gene Ackerson had it.

We were debriefed by a sullen bunch of S-2 officers, including our brigade commander, Brig. Gen. Salvatore Matheson. I don't know if they were upset because we came out without a body count or because we didn't lay our eyes on them at all. We came out of the debriefing believing that we had somehow failed in our mission. It wasn't until later that I discovered that our brother paratroopers of the 173d Airborne Brigade were in a battle for their lives at a place called Dak To in Kontum Province. From the map overlay it appeared that the direction of march of the NVA that we had discovered was on a direct route to that particular area. I could only hope that our intelligence report had been of some help to the guys in the Herd.

CHAPTER 37

We knew our time in Chu Lai would soon be coming to an end when Top Smith sent two teams back to Phan Rang to run recon patrols for the 3/506 Infantry—the spearhead battalion for the rest of the division. The rest of us "lucky" souls continued to run missions around Chu Lai, operating mostly from firebases.

During a short formation, Lieutenant McIsaac was awarded the Bronze Star for valor, and within two days, he was gone. Without our beloved commander, we were now under the total control of Top Smith! For some unknown reason it felt a little strange not being able to gripe about the old El Tee. Things would never be the same again.

I had already made up my mind to extend my tour for another six months, but decided to wait until I reached Phan Rang before submitting the paperwork.

It was the second week in December when we arrived in Phan Rang. Chu Lai was already nothing more than a bad memory. We seemed to have accumulated a lot of those lately. Thank God for all the good ones we had salted away!

It was after we had stored our equipment that we discovered that the two teams that had preceded us had in fact had one hell of a lot of fun in the bush during our absence. One of the teams had uncovered an enemy field hospital and had played hell with the medical staff. Wolfman was running point for his team and had bumped into an enemy nurse, firing her up without a second's hesitation. No one knew why she had been running point for her group, but she would never run point again. Maybe her commander had hoped that the Americans would hesitate for a moment if they spotted a woman. Unfortunately, no one had told him that Lurps don't hesitate for anyone. Naturally, her companions took offense at her being killed, and before the LRRP team knew it, they were being greeted by bugles and whistles. That told them that they were facing a lot more unfriendlies than a local VC platoon. They were heavily outnumbered, so they beat a hasty retreat. Luckily, they were extracted, under fire, before they were chopped to bits.

The commander of the 3/506th was so impressed by the LRRP teams he had on loan that he extended an open invitation for any 1st Brigade LRRP to join his recon unit. This would have been the perfect time to get a promotion, but I decided it was not for me. Only Pizza Joe Remiro took him up on his offer.

I was lying on my bunk reading a book when an unknown individual came into our barracks and began going through a stack of books we had piled on an unoccupied bunk. I watched him for a while, then asked him what he was doing in our hootch. At first he ignored me, but when I sat up and asked him again, he wanted to know if I knew Sullens. When I told him I did, he said a few things about Sully that I took exception to. I approached him at normal speed and, without another word, struck him squarely between the eyes. When he fell to his knees, I hit him again and began to shove him out of the barracks. This all happened just as Jaybird Magill and Rey Martinez started to come into the hootch. They quickly moved to stop the fight. When Martinez asked the stranger what the hell was going on, he smarted off and again popped off with something about Sullens. This time Jaybird took exception and tattooed the dazed idiot with a right to the jaw. As this was going on, S. Sgt. Ronnie Weems showed up and wanted to know what was going on. I said something unmilitary, and Weems gave me a pop to the side of the head and told me to go to sleep. With a splitting headache, I made it to my bunk, wondering why Ronnie had decided to pull the plug on me.

The following morning I was greeted by Lieutenant McIsaac's replacement. This tall, blond-haired West Pointer, by the name of Kinane, had come to LRRP after having served as a platoon leader with a line company. I am sure he was well versed on how a line company was run, but he definitely was not aware of how a LRRP unit was managed. Someone had told him that S. Sgt. Weems had struck me and that a fight had ensued. He wanted to know the details as he was not going to have an NCO fighting with the men in his unit. Basically, I did not lie to the lieutenant when I told him that there had not been a fight between myself and Weems; after all, he had hit me, and I had hit the bunk. It could all be verified by Sergeant Weems himself. This was the last I ever heard of the matter.

A few days later, I reported to the orderly room for another "friendly" encounter with Patch Pockets. I cannot recall a time when I ever saw the first sergeant laugh, but I sure did when I asked for the necessary paperwork for an extension. He grinned and told me that God Himself would have to personally come down and order him to let me extend before he would do so.

I couldn't believe it! Here I was willing to do another six months in-country, while draft dodgers were pouring into Canada in droves, and he was telling me no way. I was more than a little disheartened and totally fed up with the system by the time I left Patch Pockets's orderly room. The only thing left was to go drown my sorrows in a beer.

On 21 December I was told to report to the orderly room with bags and baggage. The army, in its wisdom, had decided to let me go home three days early so I could spend the Christmas holidays in the good old United States of America. On the way there, I ran into a trooper I knew from the Recondos. He wished me good luck and gave me a Christmas card he had picked up somewhere. When I opened it up and read the caption, I had to laugh: "Jingle Bells, Mortar Shells, VC in the grass. Take your Merry Christmas and stick it up your ass." How appropriate!

On 23 December, I boarded the military transport plane at Cam Ranh Bay airport. I took my seat with a deep sense of regret, feeling that I was deserting my family. I sat dejectedly as the plane took off toward Manila, the first leg on our long journey home. Without warning, one of the GIs on board yelled, "We made it home safe!" Many of the passengers roared their approval. I looked around and spotted a couple of guys wearing CIBs. We looked at each other and just shook our heads. They just didn't understand.

EPILOGUE

After I left Vietnam and returned to the States I was assigned to the 82d Military Police Company at Fort Bragg, North Carolina. After attending the Third Army Noncommissioned Officers Academy at Fort McClellan, Alabama, I was promoted to sergeant (E-5) and given a waiver in time and grade for staff sergeant (E-6), but things were not the same.

Racial unrest in the military was starting to increase, and the slogan "This is a white man's war!" was showing up everywhere. Military personnel were being treated with contempt, and I was just plain tired of being a second-class citizen. I had finally taken the oath of allegiance in November 1968, and I was proud to be an American citizen. Unfortunately, even though I'd fought for my new country, it seemed no one was proud of me.

Burdened by all the mixed feelings I was having, I decided to leave the army and return to society. Nearly thirty years later, I find myself still trying to fit in. For years, whenever I was asked if I was a Vietnam veteran, I would mumble something unintelligible, then turn and walk away. I was proud of what I had done, but I just didn't want the extra baggage that came along with talking about it. The overwhelming majority of civilians I encountered just weren't willing to understand.

Like many veterans, I agonized over the television war and what the media and the politicians had done to demean our efforts, but I refused to talk out against it. That would have been a betrayal of myself and of comrades who had fought and died. When the writing was on the wall that we weren't going to win in Vietnam, even the politicians who had started the war began degrading those of us who had fought it.

There were very few days that the headlines did not scream out about some crazed Vietnam veteran killing someone. Society was out of control and had found someone to hang all its sins on. We veterans had become the whipping boys, the poster children responsible for all the evil in the country.

As all these things were going on around me I knew—we all knew—that the war had not been started by warriors; it had been forced upon us by the politicians who sought money and power. We were the means to an end. While we were bleeding in the jungles, forests, and rice paddies of Southeast Asia for twenty-five cents an hour, the sons of those well-off enough to keep them in college completely avoided military service and ended up with well-paying jobs and the perks that went with them.

All wars come to an end, and so did Vietnam. I was disgusted when Nixon announced that we had reached a peace agreement with dignity. I bought into that statement just as I did the one about pigs being able to fly. A few years later, I watched as Saigon fell to the North Vietnamese. Even after seeing that, I did not believe our sacrifices were for nothing. America had asked its youth to fight another war, and as always America's youth had come through. Only this time they did it without the support of their Country.

GLOSSARY

AA Antiaircraft.

AC Aircraft copilot.

acid pad Helicopter landing pad.

aerial recon Reconning a specific area by helicopter prior to the insertion of a recon patrol.

AFB Air force base.

airburst Explosive device that detonates above ground.

air strike Surface attack by fixed-wing fighter-bomber aircraft.

AIT In the U.S. Army, Advanced Individual Training that follows Basic Combat Training.

AK A Soviet bloc assault rifle, 7.62 caliber, also known as the Kalashnikov AK-47.

AO Area of operations, specified location established for planned military operations.

ao dai Traditional Vietnamese female dress, split up the sides and worn over pants.

ARA Aerial rocket artillery.

Arc Light A B-52 air strike.

artillery or **arty fan** An area of operations that can be covered by existing artillery support.

ARTO Assistant radiotelephone operator.

arty Artillery.

ARVN Army of the Republic of (South) Vietnam.

A Team Special Forces operational detachment that normally consists of a single twelve-man team composed of ten enlisted men and two officers.

ATL   Assistant team leader.

A Troop or **Alpha Troop**   Letter designation for one of the aero-rifle companies of an air cavalry squadron.

baseball   Baseball-shaped hand grenade with a five-meter kill range.

BCT   In the U.S. Army, Basic Combat Training every trainee must complete upon entering service.

BDA   Bomb Damage Assessment.

beat feet   To run from danger.

beaucoup or **boo koo**   French for "many."

beehive   Artillery round filled with hundreds of small metal darts, designed to be used against massed infantry.

berm   Built-up earthen wall used for defensive purposes.

Big Pond   Pacific Ocean.

Bird Dog   A small fixed-wing observation plane.

black box   Sensor device that detects body heat or movement. They were buried along routes used by the enemy to record their activity in the area.

black PJs   A type of local garb of Vietnamese farmers also worn extensively by Viet Cong guerrillas.

blasting cap   A small device inserted into an explosive substance that can be triggered to cause the detonation of the main charge.

blood trail   Spoor sign left by the passage or removal of enemy wounded or dead.

Blues   Another name for the aero-rifle platoons or troops of an air cavalry squadron.

body bag   A thick black plastic bag used to transport American and allied dead to graves registration points.

break contact   Disengaging from battle with an enemy unit.

bring smoke   Placing intensive fire upon the enemy. Killing the enemy with a vengeance.

B Troop or **Bravo Troop**   Letter designation for one of the aero-rifle companies of an air cavalry squadron.

bush   The jungle.

buy the farm   To die.

C-4   A very stable, pliable plastique explosive.

CA Combat assault.

cammies Jungle-patterned clothing worn by U.S. troops in the field.

cammo stick Two-colored camouflage applicator.

C & C Command and Control.

Capt. Captain.

CAR-15 Carbine version of the M-16 rifle.

Cav Cavalry.

CCN Command and Control (North), MACV-SOG.

Charlie, Charles, Chuck GI slang for VC/NVA.

cherry New arrival in-country.

ChiCom Chinese Communist.

chieu hoi Government program that encouraged enemy soldiers to come over to the South Vietnam side.

Chinook CH-47 helicopter used for transporting equipment and troops.

chopper GI slang for helicopter.

chopper pad Helicopter landing pad.

CIDG Civilian Irregular Defense Group. South Vietnamese or Montagnard civilians trained and armed to defend themselves against enemy attack.

clacker Firing device used to manually detonate a claymore mine.

CO Commanding officer.

Cobra AH-1G attack helicopter.

cockadau GI slang for the Vietnamese word meaning kill.

Col. Colonel.

cold An area of operations or a recon zone is cold if it is unoccupied by the enemy.

commo Communication by radio or field telephone.

commo check A radiotelephone operator requesting confirmation of his transmission.

compromised Discovered by the enemy.

contact Engaged by the enemy.

CP Command post.

Cs Combat field rations for American troops.

CS Riot gas.

daisy chain Wiring a number of claymore mines together with det cord to achieve a simultaneous detonation.

debrief The gleaning of information and intelligence after a military operation.

DEROS The date of return from an overseas tour of duty.

det cord Timed burn fuse used to detonate an explosive charge.

diddy boppin' Moving foolishly, without caution.

di di Vietnamese for to run or move quickly.

DMZ Demilitarized zone.

Doc A medic or doctor.

double canopy Jungle or forest with two layers of overhead vegetation.

Doughnut Dollies Red Cross hostesses.

drag The last man on a long-range reconnaissance patrol.

D Troop or **Delta Troop** Letter designation for one of the aero-rifle companies of an air cavalry squadron.

dung lai Vietnamese for don't move.

dust-off Medical evacuation by helicopter.

DZ Drop zone for Airborne parachute operation.

E-1 or **E-2** Military pay grades of private.

E-3 Military pay grade of private first class.

E-4 Military pay grade of specialist fourth class or corporal.

E-5 Military pay grade of specialist fifth class or sergeant.

E-6 Military pay grade of specialist sixth class or staff sergeant.

E-7 Military pay grade of sergeant first class or platoon sergeant.

E-8 Military pay grade of master sergeant or first sergeant.

E-9 Military pay grade of sergeant major.

E & E Escape and evasion, on the run to evade pursuit and capture.

ER Enlisted Reserve.

ETS Estimated termination of service.

exfil Extraction from a mission or operation.

extension leave A thirty-day furlough given at the end of a full tour of duty after which the recipient must return for an extended tour of duty.

FAC Forward air controller. Air force spotter plane that coordinated air strikes and artillery for ground units.

fast mover Jet fighter-bomber.

field Anywhere outside friendly control.

finger A secondary ridge running out from a primary ridgeline, hill, or mountain.

firebase or **fire support base** Forward artillery position usually located on a prominent terrain feature, used to support ground units during operations.

firefight A battle with an enemy force.

Firefly An LOH observation helicopter fitted with a high-intensity searchlight.

fire mission A request for artillery support.

fix The specific coordinates pertaining to a unit's position or to a target.

flare ship Aircraft used to drop illumination flares in support of ground troops in contact at night.

flash panel A fluorescent orange or yellow cloth used to mark a unit's position for supporting or inbound aircraft.

FNG Fucking New Guy. Slang term for a recent arrival in Vietnam.

FO Forward observer. A specially trained soldier, usually an officer, attached to an infantry unit for the purpose of coordinating close artillery support.

"foo gas" or **fougasse** A jellied gasoline explosive that is buried in a fifty-five-gallon drum along defensive perimeters and when command-detonated sends out a wall of highly flammable fuel similar to napalm.

freak or **freq** Slang term meaning a radio frequency.

G-2 Division or larger intelligence section.

G-3 Division or larger operations section.

ghost or **ghost time** Taking time off, free time, goofing off.

gook Derogatory slang for VC/NVA.

grazing fire Keeping the trajectory of bullets between normal knee-to-waist height.

grease Slang term meaning to kill.

Green Beret A member of the U.S. Army Special Forces.

ground pounder Infantryman.

grunt Infantryman.

gunship An armed attack helicopter.

H & I Harassment and interdiction. Artillery fire upon certain areas of suspected enemy travel or rally points, designed to prevent uncontested use.

HE High explosive.

heavy team In a long-range patrol unit, two five- or six-man teams operating together.

helipad A hardened helicopter landing pad.

Ho Chi Minh trail An extensive road and trail network running from North Vietnam, down through Laos and Cambodia into South Vietnam, which enabled the North Vietnamese to supply equipment and personnel to their units in South Vietnam.

hootch Slang for barracks or living quarters.

horn Radio or telephone handset.

hot A landing zone or drop zone under enemy fire.

HQ Headquarters.

Huey The Bell UH helicopter series.

hug To close with the enemy in order to prevent his use of supporting fire.

hump Patrolling or moving during a combat operation.

I Corps The northernmost of the four separate military zones in South Vietnam. The other divisions were II, III, and IV Corps.

immersion foot A skin condition of the feet caused by prolonged exposure to moisture that results in cracking, bleeding, and sloughing of skin.

incoming Receiving enemy indirect fire.

Indian country Territory under enemy control.

indigenous Native peoples.

infil Insertion of a recon team or military unit into a recon zone or area of operation.

intel Information on the enemy gathered by human, electronic, or other means.

jungle penetrator A metal cylinder lowered by cable from a helicopter used to extract personnel from inaccessible terrain.

KCS Kit Carson Scout. Repatriated enemy soldiers working with U.S. combat units.

Khmer Cambodian.

Khmer Rouge Cambodian Communist.

Khmer Serei Free Cambodian.

KIA Killed in action.

killer team A small Lurp/Ranger team with the mission of seeking out and destroying the enemy.

LAW Light antitank weapon.

LBJ Long Benh jail. The in-country military stockade for U.S. Army personnel convicted of violations of the U.S. Code of Military Justice.

lie dog Slang meaning to go to cover and remain motionless while listening for the enemy. This is SOP for a recon team immediately after being inserted or infilled.

lifer Slang for career soldier.

LMG Light machine gun.

LOH or **Loach** OH-6A light observation helicopter.

LP Listening post. An outpost established beyond the perimeter wire, manned by one or more personnel with the mission of detecting approaching enemy forces before they can launch an assault.

LRP Long-range patrol.

LRRP Long-range reconnaissance patrol.

LSA Government-issue lubricating oil for individual weapons.

Lt. Lieutenant.

Lt. Col. Lieutenant colonel.

LZ Landing zone. A cleared area large enough to accommodate the landing of one or more helicopters.

M-14 The standard-issue 7.62mm semiautomatic/automatic rifle used by U.S. military personnel prior to the M-16.

M-16 The standard-issue 5.56mm semiautomatic/automatic rifle that became the mainstay of U.S. ground forces in 1967.

M-60 A light 7.62mm machine gun that has been the primary infantry automatic weapon of U.S. forces since the Korean War.

M-79 An individually operated, single-shot, 40mm grenade launcher.

MAAG Military Assistance Advisory Group. The senior U.S. military headquarters during the early American involvement in Vietnam.

MACV Military Assistance Command Vietnam. The senior U.S. military headquarters after full American involvement in the war.

MACV Recondo School A three-week school conducted at Nha Trang, South Vietnam, by cadre from the 5th Special Forces Group to train U.S. and allied reconnaissance personnel in the art of conducting long-range patrols.

MACV-SOG Studies and Observations Group under command of MACV that ran long-range reconnaissance and other classified missions over the borders of South Vietnam into NVA sanctuaries in Laos and Cambodia.

mag Short for magazine.

Maguire rig A single rope with loops at the end that could be dropped from a helicopter to extract friendly personnel from inaccessible terrain.

main force Full-time Viet Cong military units, as opposed to local, part-time guerrilla units.

Maj. Major.

Marine Force Recon U.S. Marine Corps divisional long-range reconnaissance units, similar in formation and function to U.S. Army LRP/Ranger companies.

MARS Military/civilian radiotelephone system that enabled U.S. personnel in Vietnam to place calls to friends and family back in the United States.

medevac or **dust-off** Medical evacuation by helicopter.

MG Machine gun.

MIA Missing in action.

Mike Force Special Forces mobile strike force used to reinforce or support other Special Forces units or camps under attack.

Montagnard   The tribal hill people of Vietnam.

MOS   Military occupation skill.

MP   Military police.

MPC   Military payment certificates. Paper money issued to U.S. military personnel serving overseas in lieu of local or U.S. currency.

NCO   Noncommissioned officer.

NDP   Night defensive position.

net   Radio network.

NG   National Guard.

no sweat   With little effort or with no trouble.

Number One   The best or highest possible.

Number Ten   The worst or lowest possible.

Nungs   Vietnamese troops of Chinese extraction hired by U.S. Special Forces to serve as personal bodyguards and to man special strike units and recon teams. Arguably the finest indigenous forces in Vietnam.

nuoc mam   Strong, evil-smelling fish sauce used to add flavor to the standard Vietnamese food staple—rice.

NVA   North Vietnamese Army.

ONH   Overnight halt.

OP   Observation post. An outpost established on a prominent terrain feature for the purpose of visually observing enemy activity.

op   Operation.

op order   Operations order. A plan for a mission or operation to be conducted against enemy forces, covering all facets of such mission or operation.

overflight   An aerial reconnaissance of an intended recon zone or area of operation prior to the mission or operation for the purpose of selecting access and egress points, routes of travel, likely enemy concentrations, water, and prominent terrain features.

P-38   Standard manual can opener that comes with government-issued C rations.

pen flare   A small spring-loaded, cartridge-fed signal flare device that fired a variety of small colored flares used to signal one's position.

peter pilot Military slang for the assistant or copilot on a helicopter.

PFC Private first class.

Pink Team An aviation combat patrol package composed of an LOH scout helicopter and a Charlie model Huey gunship or an AH-1G Cobra. The LOH would fly low to draw enemy fire and mark its location for an immediate strike from the gunship circling high overhead.

pith helmet A light tropical helmet worn by some NVA units.

point The point man or lead soldier in a patrol.

POW Prisoner of war.

PRC-10 or **Prick Ten** Standard-issue platoon/company radio used early in the Vietnam War.

PRC-25 or **Prick Twenty-five** Standard-issue platoon/company radio that replaced the PRC-10.

PRC-74 Heavier, longer-range radio capable of voice or code communication.

Project Delta Special Forces special unit tasked to conduct long-range patrols in Southeast Asia.

Project Gamma Special Forces special unit tasked to conduct long-range patrols in Southeast Asia.

Project Sigma Special Forces special unit tasked to conduct long-range patrols in Southeast Asia.

PRU Provincial Reconnaissance Units. Mercenary soldiers who performed special military tasks throughout South Vietnam. Known for their effective participation in the Phoenix Program, where they used prisoner snatches and assassinations to destroy the VC infrastructure.

Ps or **piasters** South Vietnamese monetary system. During the height of the Vietnam War, 100P was equal to about $0.85 U.S.

PSP Perforated steel panels used to build airstrips, landing pads, bridge surfaces, and a number of other functions.

P-training Preparatory training. A one-week course required for each new U.S. Army soldier arriving in South Vietnam, designed to acclimatize new arrivals to weather conditions and give them a basic introduction to the enemy and his tactics.

Puff the Magic Dragon AC-47 or AC-119 aircraft armed with computer-controlled miniguns that rendered massive support to fixed friendly camps and infantry units under enemy attack.

pulled Extracted or exfilled.

punji stakes Sharpened bamboo stakes, embedded in the ground at an angle designed to penetrate into the foot or leg of anyone walking into one. Often poisoned with human excrement to cause infection.

Purple Heart A U.S. medal awarded for receiving a wound in combat.

PX Post exchange.

radio relay A communications team located in a position to relay radio traffic between two points.

R & R Rest and Recreation. A short furlough given U.S. forces while serving in a combat zone.

Rangers Designation for U.S. long-range reconnaissance patrollers after January 31, 1969.

rappel Descent from a stationary platform or a hovering helicopter by sliding down a harness-secured rope.

reaction force Special units designated to relieve a small unit in heavy contact.

rear security The last man on a long-range reconnaissance patrol.

redleg Military slang for artillery.

REMF Rear-echelon motherfucker. Military slang for rear-echelon personnel.

rock 'n' roll Slang for firing one's weapon on full automatic.

round-eye Slang for a non-Asian female.

RPD/RPK Soviet bloc light machine gun.

RPG Soviet bloc front-loaded antitank rocket launcher used effectively against U.S. bunkers, armor, and infantry during the Vietnam War.

RT Recon team.

RTO Radiotelephone operator.

ruck   Rucksack or backpack.

Ruff-Puff or **RF**   South Vietnamese regional and popular forces recruited to provide security in hamlets, villages, and within districts throughout South Vietnam. A militia-type force that was usually ineffective.

saddle up   To prepare to move out on patrol.

same-same   The same as.

sapper   VC/NVA soldiers trained to penetrate enemy defense perimeters and to destroy fighting positions, fuel and ammo dumps, and command and communication centers with demolition charges, usually prior to a ground assault by infantry.

satchel charge   Explosive charge usually carried in a canvas bag across the chest and activated by a pull cord. The weapon of the sapper.

Screaming Chickens or **Puking Buzzards**   Slang for members of the 101st Airborne Division.

SEALs   Small U.S. Navy special operations units trained in reconnaissance, ambush, prisoner snatch, and counterguerrilla techniques.

search and destroy   Offensive military operation designed to seek out and eradicate the enemy.

SERTS   Screaming Eagle Replacement Training School. Rear-area indoctrination course that introduced newly arrived 101st Airborne Division replacements to the rigors of combat in Vietnam.

SF   U.S. Special Forces or Green Berets.

SFC   Sergeant First Class (E-7).

Sgt.   Sergeant.

shake 'n' bake   A graduate of a stateside noncommissioned or commissioned officer's course.

short rounds   Artillery rounds that impact short of their target.

short-timer   Anyone with less than thirty days left in his combat tour.

single canopy   Jungle or forest with a single layer of trees.

sit rep   Situation report. A radio or telephone transmission usually to a unit's tactical operations center to provide information on that unit's current status.

Six Designated call sign for a commander, such as Alpha-Six.

SKS Communist bloc semiautomatic rifle.

sky To run or flee because of enemy contact.

sky pilot Chaplain.

slack Slang for the second man in a patrol formation. The point man's backup.

slick Slang for a lightly armed Huey helicopter primarily used to transport troops.

smoke A canister-shaped grenade that dispenses smoke, used to conceal a unit from the enemy or to mark a unit's location for aircraft. The smoke comes in a variety of colors.

Snake Cobra helicopter gunship.

snatch To capture a prisoner.

Sneaky Pete A member of an elite military unit who operates behind enemy lines.

snoop and poop A slang term meaning to gather intelligence in enemy territory and get out again without being detected.

socked in Unable to be resupplied or extracted due to inclement weather.

SOI Signal operations instructions. The classified codebook that contains radio frequencies and call signs.

Sp4. or **Spec Four** Specialist fourth class (E-4).

Spectre An AC-130 aircraft gunship armed with miniguns, Vulcans, and sometimes a 105mm howitzer, with the mission of providing close ground support for friendly ground troops.

spider hole A camouflaged, one-man fighting position frequently used by the VC/NVA.

Spooky AC-47 or AC-119 aircraft armed with Gatling guns and capable of flying support over friendly positions for extended periods. Besides serving as an aerial weapons platform, Spooky was capable of dropping illumination flares.

spotter round An artillery smoke or white phosphorus round that was fired to mark a position.

S. Sgt. Staff sergeant (E-6).

staging area   An area in the rear where final last-minute preparations for an impending operation or mission are conducted.

stand-down   A period of rest after completion of a mission or operation in the field.

star cluster   An aerial signal device that produces three individual flares. Comes in red, green, or white.

starlight scope   A night-vision device that utilizes any outside light source for illumination.

Stars and Stripes   U.S. military newspaper.

stay behind   A technique involving a small unit dropping out or remaining behind when its larger parent unit moves out on an operation. A method of inserting a recon team.

strobe light   A small device employing a highly visible, bright flashing light used to identify one's position at night. Normally used only in emergency situations.

TA   Target area. Another designation for AO or area of operations.

TAC air   Tactical air support.

tail gunner   Rear security or the last man in a patrol.

TAOR   Tactical area of responsibility. Another designation for a unit's area of operations.

TDY   Temporary duty.

tee tee or *ti ti*   Very small.

ten forty-nine or **1049**   Military Form 1049, used to request a transfer to another unit.

thumper or **thump gun**   Slang terms for the M-79 grenade launcher.

Tiger Force   The battalion reconnaissance platoon of the 2/327, 101st Airborne Division.

tigers or **tiger fatigues**   Camouflage pattern of black and green stripes usually worn by reconnaissance teams or elite units.

time pencil   A delayed-fuse detonating device attached to an explosive charge or a claymore antipersonnel mine.

TL   Team leader.

TM   Team.

TOC Tactical operations center or command center of a military unit.

toe popper Small pressure-detonated antipersonnel mine intended to maim, not kill.

Top Slang term for a first sergeant, meaning top NCO.

tracker Soldiers specializing in trailing or tracking the enemy.

tri-border The area in Indochina where Laos, Cambodia, and South Vietnam come together.

triple canopy Jungle or forest that has three distinct layers of trees.

troop Slang term for a soldier, or a unit in a cavalry squadron equal to an infantry company in size.

tunnel rat A small-statured U.S. soldier who is sent into underground enemy tunnel complexes armed only with a flashlight, knife, and pistol.

URC-10 A pocket-size, short-range emergency radio capable of transmitting only.

VC Viet Cong. South Vietnamese Communist guerrillas.

Viet Minh Short for Viet Nam Doc Lap Dong Minh, or League for the Independence of Vietnam. Organized by Communist sympathizers who fought against the Japanese and later the French.

VNSF South Vietnamese Special Forces.

warning order The notification, prior to an op order, given to a recon team to begin preparation for a mission.

waste To kill the enemy by any means available.

White Mice Derogatory slang for South Vietnamese Army MPs; originally referred only to Saigon police.

WIA Wounded in action.

World Slang term for the United States of America or home.

WP or **willy pete** White phosphorus grenade.

XF Exfil. Extraction from the field, usually by helicopter.

xin loi/sin loi Vietnamese for sorry or too bad.

XO Executive officer.

X-ray team A communication team established at a site between a remote recon patrol and its TOC. Its function is to assist in relaying messages between the two stations.

Yards   Short for Montagnards.

zap   To kill or wound.

zipperhead   Derogatory name for an Oriental.